GUIDING YOUR CHILD
TO A MORE
CREATIVE LIFE

GUIDING YOUR CHILD
TO A MORE
CREATIVE LIFE

Fredelle Maynard, Ph.D.

DOUBLEDAY & COMPANY, INC.

GARDEN CITY, NEW YORK

ISBN: 0-385-08619-9
Library of Congress Catalog Card Number 72–92230
Copyright © 1973 by Fredelle Maynard
All Rights Reserved
Printed in the United States of America

Portions of Chapters I and II contain material originally published in *Woman's Day* (January 1970) as "How to Raise a More Creative Child."

Portions of Chapter II were first published in *Woman's Day* (September 1970) as "I Can Do It Myself!"

Portions of Chapters III and VI contain material published in *Family Circle* (June 1973) as "Ninety-nine Balloons."

Chapter VII contains material originally published in *Canadian Weekly* (February 17, 1965, and September 25, 1966) as "The Wonderful World Inside a Children's Book," and "How to Help a Child Who Won't Read."

For permission to reprint copyrighted material, grateful acknowledgment is made to the following sources:
Agathon Press, Inc., excerpts from CHILDREN IN NURSERY SCHOOL by Harriet M. Johnson; Atlantic-Little, Brown and Co., excerpts from LIFE OF DYLAN THOMAS by Constantine Fitzgibbon, copyright © 1965 by Constantine Fitzgibbon; The John Day Company, Inc., excerpts from CHILDREN'S ARTS FROM DEEP DOWN INSIDE, copyright © 1966 by Natalie Robinson Cole; E. P. Dutton & Co., Inc. and McClelland and Stewart Limited, Toronto, excerpts from WHEN WE WERE VERY YOUNG by A. A. Milne, decorations by E. H. Shepard, copyright 1924 by E. P. Dutton & Co., Inc. Renewal, 1952 by A. A. Milne; E. P. Dutton & Co., Inc. and McClelland and Stewart Limited, Toronto, excerpts from THE WORLD OF CHRISTOPHER ROBIN by A. A. Milne, Compilation and new color illustrations copyright © 1958 by E. P. Dutton & Co., Inc.; Follett Publishing Company, excerpt from THE EGG by Dick Bruna, copyright © 1968 by Follett Publishing Company; Harper & Row Publishers, Inc., excerpts from GOODNIGHT MOON by Margaret Wise Brown, copyright 1947 by Harper & Row Publishers, Inc.; Harper & Row Publishers, Inc., excerpts

Dedication

To my daughters, Rona and Joyce,
who with their father taught me the most important things
I know about the creative life.

Contents

Acknowledgments

Many friends have contributed, over the years, to the information and attitudes presented here. I am particularly grateful to Dr. Marion Mainwaring, who has greatly influenced my thinking about education and the arts; Dr. Annette Silbert, who during our joint tenure at the Radcliffe Institute became an invaluable guide to current child development research; Marilyn Hapgood, who has generously shared her experience with the innovative British primary schools. The section on music owes much to Professor Mary Rasmussen; on dance, to Johanna Hatch and Judith L. Jacobs; on photography, to Don Brown; on children's reading, to my daughter Rona; on the arts and crafts, to my daughter Joyce. Others helpful in the book's early stages include Til Thiele (pantomime), Principal Laura Schissler and the staff of the Huron Street School, Principal James Donnelly and the staff of the Ossington Street School—all of Toronto. I should also mention Charlotte Chase, of the University of New Hampshire Bookstore, for directing me to material I might otherwise have missed. My special thanks go to three members of the University of New Hampshire Library: Carolyn Jenks (Children's Room) for bibliographical assistance, Hugh Pritchard (Reference) for suggesting provocative questions and helping me find answers, and Lillian Deichert (Loan Desk) for her infinite patience.

The "Indispensable Books" annotations at the end of Chapter VIII are the work of Miranda Hapgood, who at fifteen is just close enough to remember and detached enough to judge.

Preface

To the parent of young children, any day's newspaper suggests cause for alarm. Problems once regarded as adult now make their appearance among twelve-year-olds. In New York City, according to recent report, half the high school students and one-fifth of those in junior high take some kind of drugs. New York may not be typical, but all across the country, the signs are ominous. Vandalism, a peculiarly juvenile crime, has increased dramatically; so has shoplifting. Sexual activity often begins at what used to be the age for slumber parties and sandlot baseball; illegitimate births, abortions and venereal disease are all on the rise among American teen-agers. Satanism and the occult flourish. School authorities don't talk about playing hooky anymore. They worry about dropping out—of school, and of organized society.

These troubling, immensely complicated social phenomena don't lend themselves to simple explanation. But they have, I think, a quality in common: in one way or another, they are responses to boredom and emptiness. The fifteen-year-old who gulps an LSD tab or tampers with a railway signaling device may say he's thumbing his nose at the establishment. What he's trying to do is feel more *alive*. The kid not tempted by meaningless or destructive excitement, on the other hand, is generally the one who has found something real he can do, something that matters. He plays basketball, sings with a rock group, acts or paints or builds radio sets or grows orchids.

Here is where the parent comes in. He can't reverse the overwhelming pressures toward mechanization and impersonality. He can't protect his child from exposure to distracting or dangerous temptations. What he can do is help a child develop inner resources and a sense of self. "A child's mind," Sylvia Ashton Warner observes, "is a twin fountain of creativeness and destructiveness, and the more open we keep the creative fountain, the more we help to close the destructive one."

This book is about keeping open the creative fountain. Though professional educators, quick to adopt fashionable terms, now ask earnestly, "What turns kids on?" the real question is, "How do we avoid turning them *off?*" How do we keep alive what Rachel Carson calls "the sense of wonder"?

> A child's world is fresh and new and beautiful, full of wonder and excitement. It is our misfortune that for most of us that clear-eyed vision, that true instinct for what is beautiful and awe-inspiring, is dimmed and even lost before we reach adulthood. If I had influence with the good fairy who is supposed to preside over the christening of all children I should ask that her gift to each child in the world be a sense of wonder so indestructible that it would last throughout life, as an unfailing antidote against the boredom and disenchantments of later years, the sterile preoccupations with things that are artificial, the alienation from the sources of our strength.

So this is not a book about converting orange juice cans into pencil holders, a how-to-use-junk-for-fun-and-profit guide. Nor is it about making every child a genius. The creativity I'm concerned with is not the power to produce masterpieces—the creativity of Shakespeare, Mozart, Picasso, Dostoievski—but creativity with a small "c," the kind possible to every person alive because every person is unique, seeing things in his own way and speaking in his own individual voice. Creativity, in short, as originality. You don't have to be startling to be original—or novel, or strange. You have only to be yourself.

When I was very young my father said something that has reverberated for me all through the years. I had gone to him with a small defeat that looked enormous (lost a spelling bee, probably). He tried, first, assuring me I'd done very well, but I was inconsolable. "I don't want to do *very well*. I want to be *special*." And my father said, "You *are* special. Always remember: never, since the beginning of time, has there been anybody just like you." That sense of specialness, I think, is the most priceless gift any parent can give his child. NEVER SINCE THE BEGINNING OF TIME HAS THERE BEEN ANYBODY JUST LIKE YOU. You have something unique to offer.

How does the child find his voice, discover his own best self? By early induction into all those areas of human life which promote joyous self-expression and self-development: literature, the visual arts, dance, music, handicrafts, family activities and creative play. The chapters here on music, say, or dance, are not aimed at producing musicians and dancers. They are concerned with what music and dance can contribute to the growth of complete human beings, sensitive and alive.

I have tried to write the kind of book I wished for when my own children were small, a volume combining general guidelines and goals with specific suggestions. *Guiding Your Child to a More Creative Life* deals with large problems ("How do I evaluate a children's book?" "Which toys stimulate imaginative play?") and with small practical matters ("How can I make fingerpaint or paste for a three-year-old?"). To answer these questions, I have drawn on a lifetime's reading about child development and the arts in general, on my many years as a teacher, on the help of friends more knowledgeable than I in specialized areas— and above all on my happy, richly educational experience as a mother.

For simplicity's sake, I refer throughout to the child as "he"; obviously I am as interested in girls as in boys. And since a limit must be set somewhere, I have focused on the first ten years of life. The principles outlined here, however, seem to me valid for any age.

1

What Is Creativity?
Can It Be Cultivated?

Almost any child, at four, can paint what he feels—a happy flower, maybe, or a big sheltering house. Almost any four-year-old can make up a story, dance spontaneously to music, build with blocks. He sees fresh possibilities in junk: a coffee can is a drum, an old roller skate the base for a covered wagon. He studies seeds and tadpoles. He wonders, "What makes waves?" "Why is a rainbow?" Endlessly he explores, taking things apart to see how they work, or putting them together in new combinations. The nursery school playground buzzes with painters and architects, poets and musicians and botanists and engineers.

Five years later, most of these eager spirits are strangely changed. The boys work with model airplane kits, are scornful of "girl stuff" like dancing and poetry. The girls draw stilted imitations of cartoon characters; they shy away from activities that are "dirty" or "messy," have decided that machines are for boys. A common question now is, "How do you want me to do this?" The odd child who retains his creative independence is regarded as just that—*odd*. Teachers find him a nuisance in the classroom ("He dreams too much," "Doesn't follow instructions") and his classmates prefer the company of tamer spirits. The average fourth grade, in short, is full of children who have learned to do approved things in conventional ways.

The melancholy decline of creative powers between the ages of four and ten has been verified by many researchers. Paul Torrance, after studying over fifteen thousand children, concluded that creative thinking skills generally reach one peak of development at about four and a half. There's a drop at five, when a child enters kindergarten, followed by a steady gain over the next three years. Then, near the end of third grade or the beginning of fourth, at age nine, youthful creativity drops sharply —almost to prekindergarten level. Some educators accept this pattern as inevitable, part of the growing-up (and civilizing) process. Experts in the field of creativity, however, take a different view. Children lose spontaneous curiosity, excitement and originality, they feel, because the message beamed from the world around them is, *Do what you're told. Follow the leader.* "Society in general," Torrance claims, "is downright savage toward creative thinkers, especially when they are young."

Often the chief extinguisher of creativity is the very agent one would expect to encourage it: the school. A six-year-old sets off, one momentous autumn morning, eager for the great adventure; he's starting first grade. Probably he knows the alphabet already and, thanks to television and much question asking ("What does that word say?") can even read a little. He can hardly wait to tackle *real books*. If he's lucky, if he finds himself in an "open" school modeled on the British system or in one of the many experimental "free" schools, he may indeed plunge into real books, guided by a teacher who takes her cue from him. But systems change slowly—and some individuals, some teachers, cannot change whatever the system. The standard schoolroom situation in the United States is still an authority figure at the front desk with pupils (probably too many pupils) lined up in rows. Now this arrangement works very well in some respects. It's one perfectly good way to communicate information. But in the interests of order, it frequently does violence to a child's deepest impulses and needs. So the six-year-old who at home has been going through Dr. Seuss on his own now finds himself in a reading readiness group, sounding out letters. The youngster whose parents have encouraged him to do things *his* way discovers that in the brave new world of school there's *one* way, the teacher's.

An educator, prominent in creativity research, describes a visit to a kindergarten group making May baskets. All materials had been "prepared" in advance: pieces of paper just the right shape with dotted lines showing where to fold, strips for the handle and diamond-shaped pieces of contrast color to decorate the finished product. Having explained exactly how the baskets were to be constructed, the teacher moved up and down the aisles, checking. Most children diligently followed instructions. One little sinner, however, had pasted on his diamond decorations vertically, not horizontally as directed. Teacher pointed out the error. When the child insisted, "I want to do mine *this* way," she briskly peeled off his "mistake" and pasted on a horizontal diamond. He wasn't even allowed to leave a fourth side plain. Further checking revealed a still bolder heretic—a girl who, observing that other children's paper handles didn't stick properly, had chopped hers up and used the bits for ornamental touches. "Oh, you've spoiled your basket!" the teacher moaned. "It's all messy and it doesn't have a handle."

Such discouraging of initiative is not unusual. Most parents of school-age children could provide examples of their own. I think of the first-grade teacher who put a rubber band on a little girl's book at reading time, to prevent any turning of pages. (An early reader, the child was bored with "See Spot, See Spot run" and impatient for stories.) I remember the friend who was summoned one morning by an irate teacher. Frantic, she rushed to the school—to be confronted with the horrifying evidence. Her nine-year-old daughter had written a story with *dirty words* in it. "It was a marvelous little story," my friend reported. "Funny and true to life. But Peggy'd been made to feel she was a wicked, unnatural child." I remember a sixth-grader who came home in tears with her composition paper. The trouble? For the assignment, "Give three reasons why spring is your favorite season," she'd written a poem telling why she loved summer best of all. *F*, the teacher had printed. "*Not what I asked for.*"

As children move through the grades they learn, usually, to do what's asked, to follow directions, not rock the boat. Education becomes a matter of outguessing the teacher—giving a wrong answer, if necessary, when that's what's *wanted*. And in the process, often, the creative spark that is every child's natural heritage flickers and dies.

Obviously there are exceptions. Many children—particularly those with a strong, supportive home atmosphere—refuse to surrender their private vision for the public view. Many teachers welcome and encourage creative independence. But most find creative children "difficult"—as indeed they are. They are often unruly, stubborn, irreverent, domineering. They daydream, ask troublesome questions, work only at what interests them. In a revealing study of teacher attitudes, J. P. Getzels tested high school students both for intelligence as conventionally defined and for creative originality. He then asked teachers to compare two groups: one scoring in the upper 20 percent on IQ but not on creativity, the other scoring in the upper 20 percent on creativity but not on IQ. Overwhelmingly, the teachers preferred the high IQ group—a preference, incidentally, usually shared by the general student body at any school.

What happens in school, then, is what psychologist Harold Anderson calls a "polite cultural brainwashing" made up of small incidents, small obstructions, small deflections. "Like lead poisoning in the blood stream, [it] is not sudden, dramatic, or easily detected. But after months and years, if the child has not revolted, the spirit becomes heavy, the motivation is sluggish, and activity lacks direction, meaning or purpose." The free spirit becomes self-conscious, self-protecting, conforming, *uncreative*.

What exactly do we mean by "creative"? Laymen apply the word indiscriminately to a range of activities extending from composing symphonies at one end to do-it-yourself hobby kits at the other. Scholars disagree. Alfred Adler sees creativity as a response to impediment or sickness (Beethoven wrote music because he was losing his hearing); Rollo May regards it as evidence of emotional health. Some writers focus on the nature of the person who creates, others on the process of creating, still others on the product created. Some reserve the term for original contributions to art or knowledge. By this standard, Pythagoras demonstrated creativity when he announced that the square of the hypotenuse of a right-angled triangle equaled the sum of the squares of the other two sides—but a child who discovered this principle for himself would not be creative. Psychologists discuss creativity in terms of thought patterns. J. P. Guilford contrasts it with analytical or "divergent" thinking, I. A. Taylor recognizes five distinct levels, from the "expressive" creativity of children's drawings (where final product is unimportant) to the "emergentive" creativity of significant production.

The jungle looks impenetrable. But as a matter of fact, however scholars quibble over definitions, most of us recognize creativity when it appears. Creativity is the opposite of copying, imitating. It is something new. The Sistine Chapel ceiling and *Hamlet* are creative achievements; so were Franklin's lightning rod, Watt's steam engine, the first kidney machine and the first heart transplant. Political and social developments can be creative: Magna Carta in the thirteenth century, day care centers and cooperative medicine in the twentieth. And a child is creative when he produces—in wood, paint, words, movement, clay—a genuine expression of himself.

Central to all creative activity is a special kind of perception, the ability to look freshly at an object or a problem and see it not in terms of familiar categories but (the phrase is Matthew Arnold's) *as in itself it really is.* Carl Rogers calls this "openness to experience." When Cézanne painted an apple, when Claes Oldenburg constructed his plastic hamburger, monumentally banal, it was as if no one had ever seen an apple or a hamburger before. An original scientist, too, needs an innocent eye. If a man wants to become a creative chemist, say, he should learn all he can about chemistry—and then refuse to believe any of it. (History provides abundant illustrations of this principle. For a century before Lavoisier demolished the phlogiston theory, scientists kept turning up clues to the true nature of combustion. But only Lavoisier began from scratch, as if no one had ever before considered what happens when matter burns.) The clear-eyed child in "The Emperor's New Clothes" had creative perception—and so does every child until he learns to see what he's supposed to see.

Along with a special kind of perceiving goes a special capacity for absorption. If you've watched a three-year-old building a teetery block tower or trying to sink a cork, you know exactly what I mean. It's as if all the rest of the world had fallen away, so that there's no mother, no dinnertime, *nothing* left except the utterly fascinating NOW. Discovering a problem, immersing oneself in it, trying out possibilities, rejecting false starts, battering away until a solution emerges—all this is a fundamentally creative process that carries with it its own reward, a satisfaction variously described as "the Eureka feeling" or simply "*Aha!*" Leonardo mastering the problems of perspective, Martha Graham evolving the vocabulary of modern dance, J. D. Watson solving the mystery of DNA—all these activities are alike in kind. And they differ chiefly in degree from the explorations of the child who takes a ball of clay or a dry cell and says to himself, "What if . . . ?"

Students of creativity generally cite as its distinguishing characteristics *fluency* (lots of ideas), *flexibility* (different kinds of ideas), *redefinition* (turning the idea upside down or sideways to see how it looks) and *elaboration* (carrying an idea as far as it will go). One standard test of creativity, for example, asks for suggestions of different ways in which bricks might be used. Some respondents confine themselves to a single narrow path: build a house, build a factory, build a school. . . . Others open up a cornucopia of possibilities: make a paperweight, drive a nail, grind for red powder, build a board-and-brick bookcase, put in the oven and use as a bed warmer. . . . Adults who cross categories in this way, inventing striking new uses, are in the minority. But give a roomful of average six-year-olds a really good challenge, like "What different things can you do with this plastic detergent bottle?" and you'll be amazed at the variety of uses they find. In the hands of an inventive child, the bottle becomes a boat, a doll, a puppet, a bird feeder. It can be a bubble-blowing machine (filled with soap solution). Cut off the top, it's a planter, a sandbox scoop. If you squeeze it, it's a noisemaker—or a means of air-propelling paper boats across water.

The creative trying-things-out that enters into most childhood play is not always playful in the adult sense of the word (that is, lighthearted, diverting). Indispensable to creativity is a willingness to take risks. It's easy to see how this spirit informs the work of, say, Robert Oppenheimer in physics and Samuel Beckett in the theater. The activity of a creative child often shows a similar courage—not the Purple Heart variety but a testing of limits, a willingness to stake everything. In a remarkable book about his teaching experience at a New Zealand school, Elwyn Richardson describes a group of children coiling their first clay pots. Most of the youngsters were content with modest bowls, but one boy, Trevor, had another goal: a truly giant pot. Higher and higher rose his coils; the pot reached a height of eighteen inches, so tall he had to hold the sides to prevent sagging. Still, for the massiveness he wanted he'd have to . . . Suddenly the whole pot slumped to the table. But for its maker, Richardson reports, the project was "a tremendous success. He was overjoyed. Then he began again, with caution, and a pot rose that was firm and solid but not as high as the one that had thrilled him and the others a short time before."

What kind of individual, child or adult, joyfully accepts both the risk and the instructive failure? Obviously, one not concerned with what others will think or say, whether he'll be laughed at. The creative person is not deliberately nonconformist. He doesn't look to see what the rest are up to, then decide to do something different. He's genuinely independent because he trusts himself. Most children start out with faith in their own capacities (think of the firmness with which a two-year-old says, "*Me* do it!") but end up persuaded, through restraint or criticism, that evidently others know better.

Studies show that creative persons are curious, flexible, inventive, spontaneous, playful, observant and free. More than most, they have what Erich Fromm calls "a capacity to be puzzled" and to enjoy the puzzles they find. Now these are also the characteristics of healthy children. So it's not surprising that experts agree on a further matter of immense importance to parents: creativity is part of the general human heritage though, as Abraham Maslow says, "it does very frequently get lost, or covered up, or twisted or inhibited . . . and then the job is of uncovering what all babies are, in principle, born with."

To say that all children are creative is not, of course, to say that all are or can be *equally* creative. Some children are born with a gift—for music, let's say, or mathematics. A favorable environment may cause the gift to blossom into greatness. But the most favorable environment in the world won't make a creative musical genius out of a child with a tin ear. So it's necessary at the outset to distinguish between two kinds of creativity—the special talent variety, which depends upon genes and chromosomes, and the instinctive urge to learn, grow, develop, which exists in every individual. Creativity in this sense is a drive toward wholeness and integration, toward realizing all one's potentialities. (Maslow calls it self-actualizing.) Its product is not a poem or a painting but a human being fully alive.

What about the relationship between creativity and intelligence? Except in mathematics, where creative gift goes hand in hand with superior intelligence, there seems no necessary correlation. When the University of Minnesota tested elementary school children for both intelligence and originality, 70 percent of the most creative children failed to distinguish themselves on standard intelligence tests. In other words, if you relied on intelligence tests alone, seven out of ten highly creative individuals would be missed. (It's instructive to remember that one of Thomas Edison's teachers wrote his mother to say the boy was "inattentive, indolent, and his brain seriously addled.")

This surprising result is perhaps best explained by J. P. Guilford's distinction between convergent and divergent thinking. IQ tests assess convergent thinking: memory, recognition, ability to analyze and to reason. A typical problem of this sort would be that familiar parlor-game puzzler involving three sheep, three wolves and three shepherds, all of whom must be transported across a river by canoe. The catch is, the canoe holds only two passengers at a time. How do you get all nine safely across? (You can't take a sheep and a wolf together—or leave sheep and wolves together on either side unless a shepherd is present.) The solution depends on pure reasoning.

Now consider this problem.

Without letting your pencil leave the paper, draw four lines in such a way that they pass through each dot.

Here the solution comes not through reasoning but with a kind of intuitive flash, the realization that lines needn't be restricted to the area bounded by the dots.

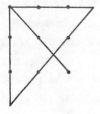

This kind of *divergent* thinking—exploratory, venturesome, free-wheeling—characterizes all creative activity. It has little to do with high IQ. When psychologist Donald F. MacKinnon tested (at the Institute of Personality Research) a group of architects nominated by experts as the most creative in their field, he found an extraordinarily wide spectrum of intelligence: IQ scores ranged from very low to very high, with a mean of 113.15. His conclusion: "Above a certain required minimum level of intelligence, which varies from field to field and in some instances may be surprisingly low, being more intelligent does not guarantee a corresponding increase in creativeness. It simply is not true that the more intelligent person is necessarily the more creative one." Intelligence is one factor in creativity, yes. More important, MacKinnon feels, are a high degree of self-acceptance and confidence, sheer energy, and a whole-hearted commitment to the chosen task.

For a parent, the most significant implication of MacKinnon's study is this: that test scores and school performance provide only one index of capacity. A child with a middle-range IQ may be highly creative. Furthermore, though both imaginative and intellectual growth are influenced by genetic inheritance (brain, sense organs, nervous system), it's clear that a stimulating and accepting environment can enhance creativity as a repressive one can destroy it.

Since roughly 1957, when Russia's Sputnik shook up the American intellectual establishment, educators have become increasingly interested in the possibility of training for creativity. Many universities—and businesses—now offer courses in creative thinking, with measurable results. In a typical project, at the University of Buffalo, two groups of students were carefully matched for age, sex and IQ; one group was given a creative problem-solving course, the other a graded series of academic tasks not related to creative thinking. Before and after the experiment, all students were tested for their ability to generate useful, novel ideas and for those personality traits generally associated with creativity (for example, dominance, self-control, need to achieve). The trained students showed notable improvement on both counts, the control group did not. Furthermore, the course had proved equally helpful to students with low and high initial creative ability, and to those with low and high IQ. This is absolutely in line with J. P. Guilford's assertion that "like most behavior, creative activity probably represents to some extent many learned skills. There may be limitations set on these skills by heredity, but I am convinced that through learning one can extend these skills within those limitations."

Of similar experiments conducted with young children, R. S. Crutchfield's work in teaching problem-solving skills is particularly interesting. To test his assumption that *every* child, regardless of age, sex, intelligence or socioeconomic background, can improve his creative thinking capacities, Crutchfield and his associates devised a set of detective-style problems. For example: a man falls into a stone pit with steep sides that offer no foothold for climbing. There is nothing in the pit but a few rocks. Luckily he has drinking water: a small waterfall flows down the side of the pit and out through a hole in the bottom. How can the man get out of the pit? Later problems, involving jewel robberies and spy chases, present increasing degrees of difficulty.

For four weeks, Crutchfield guided 267 fifth-graders through his problem-solving course while another 214, the control group, did busy work. Tests administered after this period showed that the "trained" children, in relation to the untrained, now asked twice as many relevant questions while working on a problem, were more sensitive to significant clues and factual discrepancies, generated more and better ideas, were more persistent in reaching a solution. The "trained" group also performed better on creativity tests of an entirely different sort, Torrance's divergent thinking tests (which ask open-ended questions like, "What changes would you make in this toy dog so it would be more fun to play with?"). Eighteen months later, the difference between trained and untrained was still impressive. It's notable, too, that improvement showed at all IQ levels. In fact, training overrode the effect of intelligence. At course's end, the low IQ children (below 100) surpassed the high IQ children (above 115) in problem-solving skills.

At this point, perhaps, I should record a personal bias. I am not, as teacher or parent, much interested in creativity courses. I wouldn't enroll my child in such a course or urge it upon other parents. Not because creativity courses are bad, but because they seem to me limited and artificial. The best encouragement of creativity is not instruction in problem solving but a home environment so rich, so open and so stimulating that the child can't help but grow as a creative human being. Whatever makes him more *alive* will also make him more creative. What interests me in connection with problem-solving courses is the evidence that creative power is not a fixed, immutable quality determined at birth, but something that can be cultivated. (The same, of course, is true of IQ. Instead of saying X has an IQ of 110, we should probably say, an IQ of 90 to 125—depending on circumstances.)

So far I have written as if every parent naturally regards creativity as a desirable goal in child raising. Since that may be too large an assumption, something should be said about the importance of creative power. The social need seems to me self-evident. Enormous problems—of population growth, environment, transportation, housing, education, food supply—await solutions; answers must come, not from existing knowledge, but from application of knowledge in new ways. Furthermore, the *rate* of change is now so rapid that genuinely creative adaptation has become almost a condition of survival. It is no longer possible to equip a child with skills for the future. Who knows what skills will be needed? What new occupations will emerge, which old ones will become obsolete? Twenty-five years ago, a graduate engineer was trained for a lifetime's career. Today he can't hope to continue more than ten years without updating his knowledge and techniques. How will individuals in the future make use of increased leisure—in passive entertainment, chemical escapes from boredom . . . or fruitful activity? For the space and nuclear age, we need what Abraham Maslow has called "a new kind of human being who is comfortable with change . . . who is able to improvise, who is able to face with confidence, strength and courage a situation of which he has absolutely no forewarning."

From the standpoint of individual development too, creativity would seem indispensable to full humanity. What, after all, does a parent wish for his child? Most of us would begin with vague formulations. "Happiness." "Success." And what does that involve? The child's confidence in himself, certainly, in his ability to cope. Self acceptance (and a willingness to accept others who are different). Adaptability. Ability to concentrate, persist, work through difficulties. The joy of finding what he does best—of doing anything really well.

Now all these are part of the creative spirit. Creativity is an attitude; it springs from the impulse of every human being to communicate in some appropriate form his own, absolutely unique experience—unique because there has never, since the beginning of time, been anybody just like him. Every child longs, in effect, to put his thumbprint on the page, to scrawl his message on the world's surface: I WAS HERE. When he succeeds, he feels a special joy and wholeness. If he fails—if, for example, he is constantly thwarted by adults telling him what to do and how to do it—then he is cut off from one of life's ultimate satisfactions. "In the most profound sense," says Carl Rogers, "to be creative is to fulfil oneself as a person." Whatever makes an individual more creative will also make him a better citizen, a better friend, a better parent, a better biologist or poet, a better anything. Because education for creativity is nothing less than education for life.

What Is Creativity? Can It Be Cultivated?

READING LIST

ANDERSON, HAROLD H., ed., *Creativity and Its Cultivation*, Harper, 1959.

——, ed., *Creativity in Childhood and Adolescence*, Science and Behavior Books, 1965.

ANDREWS, M. F., ed., *Creativity and Psychological Health*, Syracuse University Press, 1961.

BARRON, FRANK, *Creative Person and Creative Process*, Holt, 1969.

——, *Creativity and Psychological Health*, Van Nostrand, 1963.

BRIM, ORVILLE G., RICHARD S. CRUTCHFIELD, and WAYNE H. HOLTZMAN, *Intelligence: Perspectives, 1965*, Harcourt, 1966.

BRITTAIN, W. LAMBERT, ed., *Creativity and Art Education*, National Art Education Association, 1964.

BROWN, GEORGE ISAAC, *Human Teaching for Human Learning*, Viking, 1971.

BURTON, WILLIAM, *Creativity: Step Beyond*, National Education Association, 1964.

CAUDWELL, H., *The Creative Impulse*, Macmillan, 1951.

DE BONO, EDWARD, *About Think*, Jonathan Cape, 1972.

——, *The Dog-Exercising Machine: A Study of Children as Inventors*, Penguin, 1970.

FINE, BENJAMIN, *Stretching Their Minds*, Dutton, 1964.

FOWLER, HARRY, *Curiosity and Exploratory Behavior*, Macmillan, 1965.

GETZELS, JACOB, and PHILIP W. JACKSON, *Creativity and Intelligence*, Wiley, 1962.

GHISELIN, BREWSTER, ed., *The Creative Process*, University of California Press, 1952.

GOWAN, JOHN, *Annotated Bibliography on Creative TV and Giftedness*, n.d.

GRUBER, HOWARD E., GLENN TERRELL, and MICHAEL WERTHEIMER, eds., *Contemporary Approaches to Creative Thinking*, Atherton, 1962.

GUILFORD, J. P., *Personality*, McGraw, 1959.

HARTMAN, GERTRUDE, and ANN SHUMAKER, eds., *Creative Expression*, E. M. Hale, 1939.

HOURD, M. L., and G. E. COOPER, *Coming into Their Own*, Heinemann, 1959.

KAGAN, JEROME, ed., *Creativity and Learning*, Beacon Press, 1968.

KNELLER, GEORGE, *The Art and Science of Creativity*, Holt, 1965.

KOESTLER, ARTHUR, *The Act of Creation*, Dell, 1967.

LOWENFELD, VIKTOR, *Creative and Mental Growth*, Macmillan, 1964.

MAC KINNON, DONALD W., *The Creative Person*, University of California Press, 1962.

MARKSBERRY, MARY LEE, *Foundations of Creativity*, Harper, 1963.

MASLOW, ABRAHAM H., *The Farther Reaches of Human Nature*, Viking, 1971.

——, *Motivation and Personality*, Harper, 1954.

——, *Toward a Psychology of Being*, Van Nostrand, 1968.

MC KELLAR, PETER, *Imagination and Thinking*, Cohen & West, 1957.

MEARNS, HUGH, *Creative Power*, Dover, 1960.

MIEL, ALICE, *Creativity in Teaching: Invitations and Instances*, Wadsworth, 1961.

MOUSTAKAS, CLARK, *Creativity and Conformity*, Van Nostrand, 1967.

MYERS, R. E., and E. P. TORRANCE, *Can You Imagine?*, Perceptive Publications, 1963.

NEWELL, A., *et al.*, *The Processes of Creative Thinking*, Rand Corporation, 1959.

PARNES, SIDNEY, and HAROLD HARDING, *A Source Book for Creative Thinking*, Scribner, 1962.

PATRICK, CATHARINE, *What Is Creative Thinking?*, Philosophical Library, 1955.

ROGERS, CARL R., *On Becoming A Person*, Houghton, 1961.

RUBIN, LOUIS J., ed., *Nurturing Classroom Creativity*, Ventura County Secondary Schools, 1960.

RUGG, HAROLD, *Imagination*, Harper, 1963.

SMITH, JAMES A., *Setting Conditions for Creative Teaching in the Elementary School*, Allyn, 1966.

SMITH, PAUL, ed., *Creativity: An Examination of the Creative Process*, Hastings House, 1959.

STEIN, MORRIS I., and SHIRLEY HEINZE, *Creativity and the Individual*, Free Press, 1960. (Annotated bibliography.)

TAYLOR, CALVIN W., *Creativity, Progress and Potential*, McGraw, 1964.

TORRANCE, E. P., F. B. BAKER, and J. E. BOWERS, *Explorations in Creative Thinking in the Early School Years*, Minneapolis Bureau of Educational Research, 1959.

TORRANCE, E. P., *Guiding Creative Talent*, Prentice-Hall, 1962.

———, *Rewarding Creative Behavior*, Prentice-Hall, 1965.

WILT, MIRIAM E., *Creativity in the Elementary School*, Appleton, 1959.

YOCHIM, LOUISE, *Perceptual Growth in Creativity*, International Text Book, 1967.

ZIRBES, LAURA, *Spurs to Creative Thinking*, Putnam, 1959.

2

Perspective for Parents

There's no magic formula for creativity. How could one provide rules for spontaneity, freedom and personal growth? It's possible, though, to make suggestions about the kind of environment in which creative impulses are most likely to flower. Here are suggestions intended not as a blueprint but as a stimulus to your own adventures in creativity.

Help Your Child to Observe

Teach him to really look and see—the mysterious bubbles in a spring pond, the symmetry of a snowflake, the blade of grass that forces its way through asphalt, the pattern of television antennae against the sky. . . . All healthy children begin with an enormous interest in the world about them, a freshness and luminosity of vision. A four-year-old, marveling at the blurred ribbons of color in a grease puddle, bends closer: "It's a dead rainbow!" A five-year-old whose foot has fallen asleep wriggles in amazement: "My toes feel like ginger ale!" A three-year-old studies the night sky as if it were the first sky ever and announces solemnly, "Well. I see night is navy blue." We all remember moments like that. A phrase from the seventeenth century poet Henry Vaughan comes to mind: the child feeling "through all [his] fleshly dress Bright shoots of everlastingness."

With years, many children seem to lose this faculty completely. It's as if they never looked closely at anything anymore, never touched or listened or smelled. "Last Sunday we went for a drive and had a picnic at this really nice place. We did all kinds of fun things and really had a ball." That's a twelve-year-old writing a letter. Did he smell egg sandwiches in the car, hear milk sloshing in the thermos? Was the road lined with billboards or poplar trees? Did he play Baseball or Statues or Kick the Can? The whole rich world of sense experience seems to have evaporated, leaving dusty labels, stereotyped judgments ("nice," "fun," "had a ball") and an impoverished imagination. In art class, such a child automatically paints fire red and skies blue—though as a matter of fact, flames are seldom red (yellow shot with blue is closer) and skies may be virtually any color.

Parents can help keep a child's senses alive by providing a generous range of experiences and time in which to savor them. It's never too early to begin. Child care experts now tell us what many mothers have discovered for themselves—that even in the first weeks of life babies respond to color, movement, sound. It's been demonstrated that a newborn will look more often at a facelike representation than at a random arrangement of eyes, nose and mouth, and that even day-old infants discriminate between a variety of sounds and odors. So a three-month-old baby needs something more to look at than the ceiling. Fluttering strips of colored cloth, crumpled aluminum foil, shiny paper, a mirror, can be suspended above his crib. He needs the stimulation of sound, whether it's his mother's voice or a ticking clock. One eminent pediatrician recommends a texture pad, a patchwork-style square of different fabric surfaces to stimulate an infant's awareness of variety as he moves or scratches at it. "The more the child sees and hears," Piaget observes, "the more he wants to see and hear." Sensory stimulation, in short, is an important avenue of growth.

The first years of life are properly the most curious—the most reaching, stretching, expanding. It's important, then, not to discourage exploration by a barrage of thou-shalt-nots. *Don't touch the turtle, it's dirty. Don't splash in the water, you'll wet your clothes. Don't stand there watching that caterpillar, it's bedtime. Don't, don't, don't.* An overbold child may need gentle restraint. A timid one perhaps will take nudging. And all children, at times, need to have their attention *directed* by an adult who shares their interest and joy in learning. Sit with a three-year-old under a tree and listen to a summer silence, you'll find it full of sounds. There's a lawnmower . . . a branch cracking . . . a jet overhead . . . was that a bluejay calling? You can play, "I see something that's shiny and has two wheels. . . ." It's a game, yes. It's also a form of what Clark Moustakas calls "authentic education, [where] the emphasis is on direct primary experience, using one's own senses, perceiving reality freshly and naïvely, and spontaneously encountering life."

One incident, from a book mentioned earlier, will dramatize the imaginative stimulus that comes from close observation. Elwyn Richardson's first teaching success in his primitive rural school came through potting. Delighted with the children's work in clay, he moved on to linocutting, but was dismayed by an unexpected outpouring of the commonplace—boats, coral islands, airplanes, spitting bullets, cowboys, cliché images utterly unrelated to the children's own experience. Direct criticism, he decided, was not the answer. So he began regular nature walks to the river, occasions when children might study water snail eggs on a stone or the quivering delicacy of fern fronds. Sometimes he gave special assignments: Go and find several beautiful stones. Turn on the tap. Look down a crack in the concrete. Listen to the sounds of the swamp. . . .

Without any prompting from their teacher, the youngsters began introducing into their linocuts phenomena observed on their outings; the drawings took on precision and grace. A similar development occurred in writing. To begin with, children had churned out false, stilted rhymes barren of feeling or reality:

.   The thrush sings all day
    But doesn't have any pay.
    He flies in the bush.
    His color is bright
    But you cannot see him at night.
    They aren't very nice to us.

After the nature walks, the real looking at real birds, a twelve-year-old produced a small miracle:

The blue heron stands in the early world,
Looking like a freezing blue cloud in the morning.

"All children," Richardson concludes, "have in them a gift of seeing directly and a talent for expressing their vision with truth and power. This talent or gift is a large part of what I mean by creativity. It is there in all children . . . but it will not come to the surface unless it is recognized and encouraged."

Encourage the Keeping of Records

There is more than one way to preserve a special moment—tape, paper, film. For a young family, a moderate-priced cassette recorder is a splendid investment. You can record a toddler's first spontaneous songs and stories and, later, a nursery-schooler's more self-conscious narratives. Ten minutes or ten years later, children love listening to their own taped voices. In our family, one all-time favorite tape features a four-year-old telling a story over her Rice Krispies (with pauses for crunching). "Once in the woods was a little bear Tiny, over the bridge and out he walked. His name was Tiny because he was so little. His mother didn't know what to do. She gave him juice and milk and cereal and he ate juice and milk and cereal and tried exercising every morning in the dawn. The sun shone and all his friends sang a song:

> The dawn is in the sky so cleverly shining,
> The dawn is in the sky so cleverly shining,
> And everyone here likes you and likes me."

And so on, until the bear comes upon a huge pot of honey and gobbles it up—after which he's known as Big Tiny.

Preschoolers also enjoy having their stories made into books which they can illustrate themselves. Use large sheets of unlined paper for this, giving a separate page to each step of the action. Then, as you read the story back to its author, he works busily with crayons or paint, showing just how Tiny Bear ate his cereal and what the cleverly shining sun looked like. He can make a decorated cover, too, out of colored paper. Staple the pages together or punch holes and tie with yarn. The result is a book a child can read all by himself—and will read, over and over. Sometimes children prefer to reverse this procedure: make pictures first, then talk about them as a parent transcribes.

Keeping a poetry book is another valuable kind of recording. Though writing poems seems to adults a highly specialized activity, many children, if encouraged to express what they feel and think, compose poems as naturally as they skip or sing. A feeling for rhythm, after all, is instinctive, part of the way human beings tick. The heart beats rhythmically, the lungs inflate and deflate, we walk and swing our arms rhythmically . . . and young children frequently invent chants or nonsense rhymes for the sheer pleasure of the beat. A child just beginning to talk says "nightie night," "bye bye," not "night" and "bye." Later, he delights in the strong pulse of "Eenie meenie minie moe" or "Tom, Tom, the piper's son." Young children also have a flair for metaphor, seeing unexpected likenesses. "When I ski down a big hill, the air's like peppermint in my mouth." "Make a fire, Daddy, so it can fly up into the sky and make the sun and stars." The last example comes from a collection of children's poetic utterances made by the Russian poet Kornei Chukovsky who concludes, "beginning with the age of two, every child becomes for a short period of time a linguistic genius."

Whether every child is a linguistic genius or not, it's true that any child makes observations worth recording—and some will be genuinely poetic. In this country, Kenneth Koch has been notably successful at stimulating children to make poems of their wishes, dreams and fanciful lies.

And Richard Lewis has gathered from many countries evidence of the sudden vision that comes to a child whose senses are alive:

> It was midnight
> The sky was dark black
> The stars were threepenny bits
> The sea was making a sound
> Like a silk dress.

In a Canadian school, I was shown a book of poems composed by a third-grader who, because of a learning handicap, can neither read nor write. What he can do is compose poems, which he dictates to his teacher:

> When the night grows dim
> Ghosts appear.
> They shellac the sky
> With their milky white
> Then disappear into the night.

These examples are, admittedly, unusual, evidence of special gift. But I can recall magical poems produced by children whose most obvious talents were, say, athletic or mathematical.

> Do leaves have shadows?
> That is the question
> That I may mention.
> Poor folks have tension,
> Old folks have pension.
> As the hawk flies

> Over the corn field
> Do leaves have shadows?
> That is the question.

The ten-year-old author of that poem was not a poetic genius, but a bright, funny, extroverted youngster whose interest in language had been systematically encouraged.

Personal photographic recording can also begin early. At five or six, a child can operate a simple press-the-button camera. This trains his eye and hand, provides a fresh incentive for exploring. A first-grader might like to start a Family Book featuring his best shots with captions and commentary. (Many will be headless figures or close views of feet and knees. No matter.) An outdoor child can photograph discoveries like a meadowlark's nest, a strange log washed up on a beach; an indoor child will enjoy arranging dolls or stuffed animals for a group portrait.

Learning to write opens up a new possibility, the absolutely private journal. One of the best gifts I know for a child over six is a tempting hard-cover notebook in which he can record things seen, felt, wondered over. (*Not* a commercial diary with key. What of any interest can the owner write in the allotted three lines per day?) Cover the notebook with attractive fabric or contact paper to make it special. As the journal keeper gets older, he'll want to design his own covers or experiment with simple bookbinding.

Record keeping of the kind I've suggested can become a profound source of creative life. In the first place, it sharpens awareness. A child accustomed to writing or dictating his observations *sees* in a different way. He thinks through to exactly what he observes, feels, believes; he becomes less inclined to usual answers, stock response. It develops his self-esteem, pride in the self as maker. It makes him comfortable with language, refines his feeling for the precise meaning or color of a word. ("I like that part about the sandy hills," a five-year-old announced judiciously after I'd read her story back to her. "Only I want it *bumpy* sandy hills.") It may have decidedly therapeutic benefits, as a way of letting off steam. (I think of what John Ciardi once said, "An ulcer is an unwritten poem"—and of the way my own daughters would rush in, breathless from some great experience, with "I need a pencil!") It helps a child discover who and what he is, keeps him continuously in touch with the person he was. What wouldn't most adults give for a true record—not a school report or a parental account—of what they felt at age six? Pursued throughout the growing years, the habit of recording induces that openness which Maslow describes as typical of creative persons: a "lack of fear of their own insides, of their own impulses, emotions, thoughts. . . . More of themselves is available for use, for enjoyment and for creative purposes. They waste less of their time and energy protecting themselves against themselves."

Create an Environment That Is Rich and Personal

One striking characteristic of Britain's innovative primary schools—every observer comments on this—is their emphasis on beauty and personal style. Corridors glow with displays of children's work; individual classrooms dazzle with the students' own productions in clay, paint, fabric and paper collage, needlework, wood construction, calligraphy, bookbinding. Most parents would agree that such a setting invites joyous participation in creating—yet many of the same parents decorate a child's room according to purely adult standards. A common phenomenon is the little girl's boudoir which suggests nothing so much as Mother playing house: walls of palest pink, much ruffle and lace, tastefully disposed costume dolls (the kind that can't be undressed or played with), elaborately framed pictures of Miss Muffet types, plywood cutouts of Disney characters. The effect of such a room is to discourage any messy activity and ultimately perhaps any making.

The ideal child's room is decorative, yes (and remember that children generally prefer strong colors to pastels). It's also one that expresses the child. Why shouldn't a four-year-old have some say in the decoration of his room? He's not old enough to choose wallpaper; the cowboys and ballet dancers that enchant him now would be a blight later on. But he can make his own pictures, changing the display regularly. He might enjoy painting, on a long roll of shelf paper, a "mural" that can be tacked or taped to the wall. A good big tree branch—let the child choose his own and paint it if he likes—can be firmly anchored with clay or plaster of Paris in a pot, where it will inspire all sorts of projects. In spring he can decorate it with paper flowers and butterflies; in fall, with leaves and fruit. It can be an egg tree in April, a Christmas tree in December. Small stuffed animals can nestle there; birds of paper, cloth or straw can twirl on threads attached to a twig. It will also come in handy as a prop for play-acting. Another happy addition to a child's room is a good-sized display box which, like the Japanese *tokonoma*, can hold a single interesting object—a pebble he's found, a puppet he's made.

Besides the child's own work, consider putting up some appropriate masterpieces. Handsome, inexpensive art reproductions are available from museums, galleries and many bookstores. Mondrian's elegant abstractions, Jackson Pollock's turbulent splashes and swirls, Klee's fanciful humor—children respond to these as well as to the more familiar world of Degas or Renoir. Paintings of animals are always welcomed—and, of course, paintings of children. Though any list is bound to be personal, here are pictures that offer a child an experience, visual and emotional, to grow on:

  *Avercamp, *A Scene on the Ice*
   Bellows, *Lady Jean*
  *Botticelli, *Madonna and Child with Angels*

*Breughel, *Children's Games*
   The Numbering at Bethlehem
   Fall of Icarus
*Bronzino, *A Young Woman and Her Little Boy*
*Brown, *Bareback Riders*
 Chagall, *I and the Village*
   The Birthday
   The Green Violinist
   Lovers Over the City
*Cassatt, *Mother and Child*
*David, *The Rest on the Flight into Egypt*
 Degas, *Four Dancers*
 Dürer, *Young Hare*
 Goya, *Don Manuel Osorio*
 Hicks, Edward, *The Cornell Farm
   The Peaceable Kingdom
*Holbein, *Edward VI as a Child*
 Klee, *Carnival in the Mountains*
   Child on the Steps
   Landscape with Yellow Birds
 Marc, *Blue Horses*
 Matisse, *The Sadness of the King*
   Margherita with Black Cat
   The Goldfish
 Picasso, *Girl with Pigeon*
   Maria with Sailor Doll
   Paul as Pierrot
   Paul Sketching
   **The Family of Saltimbanques*
 Rousseau, **The Equatorial Jungle*
   The Sleeping Gypsy
   The Football Players

Raphael, *Saint George and the Dragon*
   The Small Cowper Madonna
Renoir, *Girl with a Hoop*
   Girl with a Watering Can
Romney, *Miss Willoughby*
Savage, *The Washington Family*

Reproductions of starred paintings are obtainable by mail from the National Gallery of Art (Washington, D.C.) at 35 cents for a high-quality 11 by 14 print—an astonishingly good buy. Many are also available in a larger size (16 by 20 to 22 by 28) at $3.00 each, or on a handsome laminated plaque (11 by 14) with clear plastic or linen finish, edges beveled and gilded, and a hanging device attached to the back, at $2.50 each. The National Gallery also offers splendid portfolios of prints suitable for framing; particularly good for a child's room is their Portfolio No. 3, *Portraits of Children* (twelve prints—$3.00). This contains many of the paintings listed above, also some Titian, Rembrandt and Cranach. (Orders mailed to a single address in the United States are sent postage paid. Make check or money order to NGA Publications Fund. The Gallery will also send, free, a catalog of all prints, color slides, books, and sculpture reproductions.)

Keep Alive the Child's Natural Curiosity

"Every question," I once read, "possesses a power not found in the answer. A man grows in wisdom by learning to ask the right questions." The truth of this principle is abundantly illustrated in the history of science and invention. (Darwin's genius lay in asking, "Can the principle of selection, which we have seen so potent in the hands of man, apply under nature?") It's also evident in the history of any individual child. The years of most rapid intellectual growth, from birth to about age six, correspond with the years of eager, incessant questioning. "Was it not then,"

Tolstoi writes, "that I acquired all that now sustains me? And I gained so much and so quickly that during the rest of my life I did not acquire a hundredth part of it. From myself as a five-year-old to myself as I now am there is only one step. The distance between myself as an infant and myself at present is tremendous."

Some of the questions young children ask are serious, important and obviously "useful." *What makes rain?* Others seem nonsensical. *Why is purple?* If, however, you want a child to develop the skill of question asking (and it *is* a skill), treat all questions respectfully. Particularly unusual ones.

In theory this principle is easy to accept. Unusual questions. Of course. Imagination, ingenuity, curiosity . . . naturally we welcome it. The trouble is that often the questions come when you're least prepared to answer—or they are *so* unusual, so unthinkable, that you slam the door on them without thinking. The first questions about sex, for example. They seldom come during a quiet hour at home when you can sit down and explain, lovingly and carefully, how babies are born. They come on a crowded bus or at the dinner table. The question about why people don't fall off the round earth comes five minutes before guests are due, with the living room still a mess and the hall rug to vacuum.

In the nature of things, it's often not possible to drop everything and attend to a child's question. But it is, or should be, possible to treat every question seriously. If it's ill-timed, simply say that you can't go into it this minute, but later you'll explain —or help him find out for himself. As an example of poor handling, I recall an excruciating cocktail party incident. Our host's three-year-old daughter had been brought in to meet the guests. She trotted cheerfully up to a friendly-looking grandfather type and asked loudly, "Have you got a penis?" The man looked somewhat taken aback, but not horrified. I got the impression that he was about to say *yes* (in which case surely none of the guests would have been embarrassed or surprised). But the child's mother rushed over. "Joan, of course the gentleman has no peanuts. If you want peanuts, go to the kitchen." "Not *peanuts*." The child's voice rose. "*Penis*. Has he got a *penis*?" For answer, she got a smart smack on the bottom. Then she was dragged howling from the room to a furious accompaniment of "You're a bad, bad girl. You're going straight to your room—and don't you dare come out!" Leaving aside for the moment the matter of how such handling affects sexual attitudes, what has this child learned about asking questions?

In addition to taking questions seriously, parents should resist the temptation to force-feed information. As Paul Tillich observed, the fatal error in teaching is "to throw answers like stones at the heads of those who have not yet asked the questions." What children need, they will ask for; what they ask for, they can use. You can see this principle at work in any "open" classroom where reading and writing instruction is geared to the child's readiness. In a typical situation, six-year-olds will be making books (about tigers, football, electricity . . .). When a child needs a new word —one he can't spell—he goes to the teacher. She writes it down, the child copies it and transfers it to his list or "word box." At the Huron School in Toronto, for instance, one little boy showed me the cards in his box. He had just added "St. Mark's Square" to a collection that included "luna moth," "marzipan," and "supersonic jet." With some pride he announced, "All these words come in handy."

Parents and teachers often behave as if their whole job were to transmit pieces of correct information and eliminate mistaken ideas. Ask an eight-year-old why he goes to school, he'll say, "To learn things." Of course it's easier to teach facts than to train thinking—but the ultimate aim of education should be to teach children how to find the facts for themselves.

If a six-year-old asks, "What makes flowers grow?" you can say, "Soil, water, air and sunlight." Period. Or you can launch him on a series of simple experiments from which the answer will emerge. To introduce him to the idea of scientific controls, you might have him plant bean seeds in two different pots—one

with moist soil, one with dry. After a few days of watering one
pot only, he'll have discovered a crucial fact about germination:
seeds won't sprout without water. If he's still curious, let him
figure out ways to discover whether light is necessary for sprout-
ing (NO) and for continued growth (YES). Suggest an inquiry
into the effect of temperature. Can he find a hot place for one
pot of seeds, a cold one for another, an average-room-temperature
spot for a third? What happens to seeds kept in a very hot or
cold place? A child of eight or ten may be able to devise a technique for finding out whether germination requires air, and
whether roots grow in one direction only. A very young child will
be thrilled by the drama of a plant reaching toward a single
source of light, or a celery stalk drawing up through its veins
the colored water from a glass. Activity of this sort is not just
"learning things." It's education. The root meaning of education,
after all, is to bring out (*e-ducare*), not merely to put in. A
child is a lamp to light, not a vessel to fill.

Education for creative life involves keeping alive the questioning spirit. A child should never be made to feel silly for
asking, just because the answer—*you* think—is obvious, or because there's no answer possible.

Avoid Premature Differentiation of Sex Roles

A creative person is a complete person. The creative man
keeps alive that side of his nature—sensitive, gentle, compassionate, poetic—which society generally labels "feminine"; the
creative woman is not afraid to be hardheaded, aggressive and
tough ("masculine"). One conclusion of Donald MacKinnon's
studies of notably creative men is that, whatever their professional field, such men score high on the femininity scale of
standard personality tests. It seems safe to guess that similar
investigations of creative women would show a high "masculine"

component in their natures. Think of Sarah Bernhardt, Maria Callas, Louise Nevelson, Anna Freud . . . and Germaine Greer. As for why this should be so: everything we know about creativity suggests that it springs from a special openness to feelings—all feelings—and a refusal to change what one *is* in the interest of what one is *supposed to be.*

Parents concerned with creative wholeness, then, should try not to impose stereotyped images of male and female. If you say to a weeping four-year-old, "Be a man!" you're communicating the notion that real men don't feel (or express) the softer emotions. If you say to a girl who fights back, "Be a little lady!" you're perpetuating a view of women as delicate and helpless—perhaps doing violence to the spirit of a child who *wants* to defend herself. Though the unisex drift of youth culture and the efforts of Women's Liberation have enlarged traditional sex-role concepts, young children still encounter from many sources rigid views of "boyish" and "girlish." You can't do much about television commercials which represent men as conquering the world while women rejoice in the latest floor wax. But you can, in choosing books, try to modify a world view which casts boys in an active role (climbing, exploring, taking chances) while girls bake cookies with Mother. The preschooler who enjoys *Mike Mulligan and His Steam Shovel* might also respond sympathetically to *William and His Doll.* Little girls who suffer with Sara Crewe can triumph with the battling heroine of Edward Ardizzone's *Diana and Her Rhinoceros.* For older children, *Martin's Father* (Margrit Eichler) features a boy who shares household chores as well as outdoor adventures with his father, and *Pippi Longstocking* a gloriously unconventional girl who manages teachers, bullying boys and officious policemen with equal aplomb.

In the area of toys and play, too, parents can do a great deal to keep the options open, giving children the opportunity to experience a wide range of activity and feeling. Little boys enjoy baking cookies just as much as girls do—until someone tells them it's sissy. They also like dancing and beadwork and playing house. (Why should a doll be any more "unmanly" for a boy than a stuffed rabbit? Boys need to nurture and show affection just as girls do.) And little girls enjoy hammering, collecting insects, raising hamsters, studying magnets and gyroscopes and crystals. Parents who mechanically label toys as pink or blue— tea sets for girls, trucks for boys—block off whole areas of human experience and limit creative growth.

Encourage Reasonable Independence

One of the most striking characteristics of creative individuals is their self-sufficiency. Donald MacKinnon observes, of his highly creative subjects, that most had parents who showed "an extraordinary respect for the child and confidence in his ability to do what was appropriate. They did not hesitate to grant him rather unusual freedom in exploring his universe."

Such freedom is truly useful, of course, only to the child who trusts himself. And self-trust, conviction of personal worth and effectiveness, develops chiefly through successful experiences in coping. The first such experience occurs long before rational thought, in infancy, when a baby discovers that his cry brings food. He has *affected* his universe. Later, the child discovers other exhilarating powers. He can throw or retrieve a toy . . . he can push a chair to the cupboard, climb on it and get a cookie . . . he can tie his own shoelaces, go shopping for Mother, ride a two-wheel bike, prepare a meal, take an after-school job.

If you want your child to be independent, you have constantly to stand back and let him do things by himself. That he may at first do them badly is irrelevant. Errors can be very instructive. Furthermore, he learns only by performing *real* tasks. Ruth Benedict, the anthropologist, tells of a three-year-old Papago Indian child asked to close a heavy door. The child pushed again and again; the door didn't move. "No one jumped to the child's assistance," Dr. Benedict reports. "No one took the responsibility away from her. On the other hand, there was no impatience, for after all the child was small. They sat gravely waiting until the child succeeded and her grandfather thanked her. It was assumed that the task would not be asked of her unless she could perform it, and having been asked, the responsibility was hers alone just as if she were a grown woman." Children—Indian or American— are not fooled by pretend jobs. A little girl who's given flour and water to make a cake which no one eats enjoys no important satisfaction. But a little girl who's allowed to set the dinner table knows she's made a contribution to the life of the family. The "ego identity" of the young, Erik Erikson observes, "gains real strength only from wholehearted and consistent recognition of real accomplishment." When that occurs—when a child knows he's done something well on his own—he's like the little boy ecstatic at a restaurant waiter's asking *him* for his order: "Look, Mommy, I'm real, I'm *real!*"

"But—" the careful parent wonders, "what about actual physical dangers? Because I want her to be independent, do I let a three-year-old set the table, knowing she might drop a glass and break it? Allow a four-year-old to handle a hammer?" I think the answer has to go something like this. Obviously you don't allow children to take risks they're not ready for. A three-year-old can't cross a busy street by himself. As far as possible, you prepare a child for ordinary dangers. (In the case of street crossing, by explaining to a preschooler that cars can hurt people, and later by teaching him to obey traffic lights and look both ways before starting across.) But the moment comes when you have to let him go. Life is a chancy business. Nothing we do can change that. Shouldn't we, then, teach youngsters to assess the chances intelligently?

Consider Charles Lindbergh's response to his boys' request for permission to climb an awesomely tall tree. "How are you going up?" he asked. Scott, the twelve-year-old, pointed. First this limb, then that. "You're going to get stuck there, aren't you?" Lindbergh prodded. The boys sadly agreed. Only when they had calculated and theoretically tested various routes up the tree did their father give his consent. Then, to a watching friend, he said, "They must learn to take calculated risks. As long as they figure out everything ahead of time and just don't go off half-cocked."

A protective parent's reaction to this story is likely to be, "Lindbergh was lucky. Those kids could've taken a twenty-foot fall." True. It is also true that to some extent children act out our expectations. If we hover over them—"Don't ski, you might break a leg; don't swim, you might drown"—they *feel* fragile. I once watched, on a TV documentary, as a three-year-old Eskimo child expertly cut seal blubber with his father's knife. His mother didn't look anxious or even particularly interested, and surely her calm had much to do with the boy's assurance. Children who take risks are exposed to accidents, surely. That's usually not too high a price to pay for the freedom to venture and grow.

Every human being, Abraham Maslow has said, carries within him two sets of conflicting forces—the desire for security and the desire for growth. "One set clings to safety and defensiveness through fear, making him afraid to take chances, afraid to jeopardize what he already has." The other "impels him forward towards wholeness of Self and uniqueness of Self, toward confidence in the face of the external world at the same time that he can accept his deepest, real, unconscious Self." The process of healthy growth becomes therefore "a never ending series of free choice situations, confronting every individual at every point throughout his life, in which he must choose between the delights of safety and growth, dependence and independence, regression and progression, immaturity and maturity."

Give Your Child Practice in Decision Making

To make choices wisely, a child needs experience in choosing. Even a three-year-old can make some decisions for himself. At this age, it's best to present alternatives. "Shall we watch *Sesame Street* or go to the park?" An eight-year-old needs more freedom: "What would you like to do this afternoon?" If his choice disappoints you—he decides to curl up with comic books rather than join the family on a museum visit—remember that the *process* of choosing may, in the early years, be more important than particular choices made.

Parents can nourish independent decision making by being question-oriented rather than answer-oriented. Your child says, "Rusty's giving up his newspaper route. Think I should take it over?" Instead of simply expressing your opinion ("It's time you earned some money" or "You've got too much going already"), help him see the questions within The Question. At what time would papers be delivered? Can he regularly be home from school by then—or is he prepared to rise daily at that hour? How useful would the work experience be? Is he willing to accept responsibility in any weather? Could he line up a substitute for emergencies? How would he use the money? And so forth. This takes a lot longer than YES or NO. It's worth doing because it goes beyond the immediate need; it prepares the child to act next time on his own.

Another useful technique for developing problem-solving skills is making a family game of "What if?" One person poses a problem. It may be wildly unlikely ("How would you cook a fresh-caught fish in the wilderness if you had matches but no pan?") or practical and possible ("What if you'd taken the wrong subway in a strange city and had no money left?" "What if you found that your best friend had cheated or stolen some-

thing from a store?"). Then everyone takes a turn at proposing
a solution to the dilemma—or explaining why someone else's
idea won't work. This sort of thing gives children invaluable
practice in the fundamental techniques of decision making—
starting from what's given, imagining the consequences of this
or that course of action, weighing advantages against disadvantages, and choosing on the basis of what matters most.

Be Tolerant of Error

Being *right*, at age two or ten, is not very important. Being
venturesome is. If a child is to grow in creative power, he needs
the assurance that he can afford to take chances and make mistakes. Generally speaking, you don't have to encourage children to experiment. You have only to refrain from discouraging
their natural impulse to try something new and see what happens. I once visited a friend whose eight-year-old daughter had
been baking in the kitchen. When Alice brought us a platter of
cupcakes, her mother inspected them severely. "What on earth
have you done with the icing?" The child beamed. "Oh, it was
a bit runny, so I stirred in some flour. Look—now it's thick as
fudge."

Now icing made with flour is admittedly not tasty. Since an
aspiring cook needs to know about the different thickening
agents—what works where—Alice's mother might well have converted a trivial failure into a valuable learning experience. She
might have explained that just adding more icing sugar would
have done the trick. Or she might have suggested ways of
salvaging the cupcakes—cutting away the fudgy icing and using
the remains for trifle. Instead, she delivered a lecture, sharply
impatient, on following instructions. "Why didn't you do it the
regular way? Why didn't you come and ask me? Have you any
idea what nuts cost? And butter?" Alice will be more careful

next time, no doubt—and less ready to indulge a spirit which, when you think of it, differs only in degree from the try-and-see attitude which led to the realization that penicillin had antibiotic properties, or that 2-4-D, a plant-growth hormone, might be used to kill weeds.

Proverbial wisdom in Western thought emphasizes caution. "Better safe than sorry." "A bird in the hand is worth two in the bush." But if a child never ventures into the bush, how will he know what's there? Should he hold onto a sparrow when he might find a phoenix?

Psychological safety and psychological freedom, which Carl Rogers calls the fundamental prerequisites of creativity, are possible only in an atmosphere where the individual is free to fail. Parents should, I think, say less about error and more about possibility—particularly if a child is timid or overly disciplined. When a little girl, making her first apron, accidentally slashes the fabric, you can say, "Well, *now* you've ruined it!" (convincing her that she's too awkward to sew). Or you can show her how a flower appliqued over the tear will make the finished garment even prettier. One of my favorite book dedications (in Chester I. Barnard's *Functions of the Executive*) goes: "To my father—at a crisis in my youth he taught me the wisdom of choice. To try and fail is at least to learn; to fail to try is to suffer the inestimable loss of what might have been."

Never Hold Back the Child Who Is Ready

Sometimes it's the most conscientious parents who straitjacket a child by imposing on his natural impulses an artificial timetable. Having read somewhere that the small muscles don't develop before five, they insist that a four-year-old stick to crayons even though this particular child loves pencils and manages them well. Or they've heard that early reading is bad

socially ("What will he do later in school?") and physically
("The eye muscles aren't ready"). The truth is that the "right"
age to learn reading, for example, varies from child to child,
depending on intelligence, temperament, environment, motivation. A youngster growing up in a bookish household may be
ready to read at four, though his friend, in an athletically
oriented family, won't be interested for several more years. (But
his friend is ready to ski.)

To everything there is a season. This is as true in intellectual
development as in the area of physical growth. Embryologists
tell us that if the fetal eye or the liver or the heart does not develop at its appointed time, its form is permanently modified
and the whole hierarchy of organs is disturbed. Similarly with
life skills. Prevent a child from doing what he's ready to do and
you not only impede his development, you create attitudes
detrimental to growth. He likes letters at two, though he's "too
young"? Put bright-colored magnetic letters on the refrigerator
door, where he can make a game of them. And now, at three, he
wants to know what the signs say? Tell him. At four and a half,
he'll be sounding out words in books, delighted with his new
powers. As for what will happen to the precocious reader in
first grade . . . Give children a zest for life, a joy in mastery,
and they will cope with what comes.

Respect the Child's Privacy and Need
to Be Quiet

The most tempting playroom I ever saw had a room-within-
a-room. Or, to be more exact, a house-within-a-room. The main
play area was bright, open, chock full of materials—clay and
paint and books and toys and dress-up clothes. One corner,
though, was occupied by a fiberboard playhouse just large
enough for a child. It had a real door, one tiny window, a pillow

for the floor . . . nothing else. And I thought, looking at it, how pleasant it must be for a five-year-old, excited and exhausted from active play, to creep in there and just sit. Even the most energetic children want, at moments, to do nothing whatsoever. Attics and lofts (for those lucky enough to have them), closets, crawl spaces under stairways—children have always loved dark hidden places and, if necessary, will create them under a dining room table or behind a chair. Some modern architects meet this need by utilizing dead space— above a closet, say—for "reading platforms." The fascination of *The Secret Garden*, for many young readers, is the vision of an adult-proof hiding place. Such secret places may be used for reading or playing; or they may be just sit-and-think places, and that's a good use too.

American culture has always been frenetic about anything that looks like idleness. Since the days of the *New England Primer* we've placed a disproportionate emphasis on keeping busy lest the devil find work for idle hands to do. Fathers come home from a day's labor and relax by remodeling the kitchen. Mothers use their free hours to take courses, organize committees, rally support for candidates. Both look askance at the child who's not *obviously* occupied. But every child needs, at times, to withdraw into himself; to realize his creative potential, he must learn to be alone.

History supplies abundant examples of outstanding achievement following periods of passive incubation. For parents concerned about a child who dreams and dawdles, Benjamin Fine, former Education Editor of the New York *Times*, poses a salutary can-you-imagine: "Isaac, stop wasting time. How long are you going to sit under that apple tree?" "Ben, stop playing with that kite immediately and get to work!" If you want children to develop as complete human beings, Fine observes, you must permit them "the freedom to waste time, to play, to moon, to make mistakes, to read junk if they want to read junk, to relax, to kick off their shoes."

Avoid False Distinctions Between Work and Play

Sophisticated adults make sharp distinctions between work (something you do because you must) and play (something you freely choose to do; entertainment). No such division exists in primitive societies—or among children. A Xincantecan Indian sculpting a clay animal is neither working nor playing; the same might be said of a child constructing a tree house. Children begin life with a healthy joy in mastery, whatever the nature of the problem being mastered. What a pity, then, to give them the idea that this pleasurable activity is in fact drudgery, work.

In his account of schoolteaching experiences, Elwyn Richardson gives a marvelous example of his pupils' freedom from the traditional work-play dichotomy. Having decided to introduce them to potting, Richardson organized crews to prepare materials. All day the children—ages six to eleven—labored—digging clay, filling heavy sacks, trundling them up to the school, mixing and purifying the clay, building the kiln . . . and rejoicing in their incredible, their unlooked-for liberation. "Hooray, no work!" Another example comes from a British mathematician who reports listening to two eight-year-olds playing during school recess. When a jet plane flew overhead, the boys' talk turned to aerophysics. They discussed Mach numbers, aerodynamics, the relative merits of pure jet versus turbojet. Suddenly the school bell rang out. "Time to go back to work," sighed one. "We have to go in and learn to count by fives."

In this respect children are often wiser than their parents: a task that challenges, invites and satisfies is neither work nor play. It's *life*.

Help Your Child to Deepen and Enlarge
His Interests

If you want children to follow, you must begin where they are. As a brilliant illustration of this principle, I think of a dance class I watched in Toronto, taught by a German pantomimist, Til Thiele. Her pupils on this occasion were four- and five-year-olds, lively and more or less undisciplined. The little girls burst into the room full of high spirits—racing, chasing, playing tag. Frau Thiele didn't clap her hands for order or announce that class was about to start; she watched. Only when the children began hopping about on the checkerboard-patterned linoleum did she move forward. "Look—this way we can make a dance!" Then, with quiet authority, she proceeded to demonstrate a pattern for their random hops. The game turned into a simple dance, one foot on the white square and two feet on the black. Within minutes, the mob had become a *group*, a dozen delighted and fascinated little dancers following their teacher's lead.

There is no use trying to impose interests on children. We've all seen dismal examples: the musical parent who drags an unwilling child to concerts, the literary one who insists that his offspring read particular books. But if you begin with the child's own interest, showing him how it can be deepened and enlarged, you contribute to his total personal growth. Is he intrigued by the sand dollar he found on the beach? Take him to the library to explore the wonderfully illustrated books on shells. Help him start a collection. Perhaps there's a science museum you might visit. Does he like playing with clay? Find out if there's a potter's studio nearby. Show him the pre-Columbian sculpture in art books or galleries—the simple, immensely dignified pots, the strange little animals and human figures. . . .

It's not *what* interests a child that matters; it's how fully he explores it. I remember when my five-year-old daughter fell in love with horses. The passion began during a farm visit; for some time after that, we made regular Sunday excursions to pat horses' heads, feed apples and occasionally, thrillingly, to ride. Horse stories came next. *Billy and Blaze, High Courage, The Blind Colt, King of the Wind, My Friend Flicka, Little Vic*— we read them all. Whatever their literary value, those books were a rich *experience*. We had progressed to materials thoroughly didactic—breeds of horses, development of the horse from earlier prototypes—when suddenly ballet struck. Rona came home from a movie, *The Red Shoes*, in love with dance. We abandoned eohippus for Margot Fonteyn, the five basic positions, recordings of *Swan Lake* and biographies of Anna Pavlova.

My daughter never became a horse breeder or a ballerina. But she learned, from those early passions, the pleasure of knowing, of living deeply into a subject until it becomes part of the self.

Work Towards the Establishment of Values and Standards

To be creative, an individual has first to be free. Self-expression comes before discipline; when you give a child paints and a brush you don't ask him to turn out a picture suitable for framing. But ultimately, if work is to have value and the worker is to grow, there must be standards of performance, a criterion by which this is seen to be better than that.

Now this whole matter of standards is delicate, tricky. I've heard teachers say, of children's painting or writing, "Oh, I never criticize. It kills the creativity." My own feeling is this: If you criticize by applying impossible standards of excellence, that is discouraging. If you criticize by comparing one child's work with another's, that is destructive. But if you never criticize at all, accepting everything the child produces as of equal value, then you indeed "kill the creativity" by eliminating challenge. Children are not fooled by false enthusiasm and empty praise. An art supervisor describes a typical school experience: a teacher walking through art class "lifting every piece and gushing oohs and aahs in the most public sort of way. Any scratch or blob was loudly praised for its freshness, vitality or spontaneity." One boy, observing this indiscriminate approval, playfully turned his back on his paper and sloshed away, eyes shut, with loaded brush. Sure enough, when Teacher saw his painting she *loved* it.

Helpful criticism, the kind a child can grow on, evaluates in terms of the child's own capacity. It asks not, "Are you as good as the next fellow?" but "Is this the very best *you* can do?" Creative freedom is not license. If a child's work seems to you always sloppy rather than uninhibited, ask him to make something special: a picture you can put in a frame, a birthday present for Grandma. That way he learns the difference between casual wild free things and finished work.

It's important to time critical suggestions carefully, to present them within a context of warmth and acceptance. To an eight-year-old who has made her first doll dress with an impossibly small neck opening, you wouldn't say, "How on earth do you expect to get that over her head?" but "Oh, it's lovely. What neat little stitches. Now, I wonder . . ." To a painter just old enough to understand the fundamentals of perspective you might say, "Your picture's so gay it makes me feel good, just looking. But shouldn't the house be smaller than the man? Because the house is a long ways away." As a model of the attitude which builds standards and pride in workmanship, consider these random teacher comments recorded by Marilyn Hapgood, a sensitive observer of the English primary schools:

Off you go now, and come back and show me when you've finished these three.

That's rather nice, isn't it? He's done it very carefully.

I'll see you in a minute, darling, would you just wait?

Now just see if you could find out what twelve more would be?

Martin, get on, would you?

Jolly good, now you bring your book about the Normans and let me have a look at that, would you?

Have a look now and tell me who you think is the tallest person.

You *told* her. I wanted her to find out. Now you take her and show her where 3 feet 10 inches are on the measuring tape. You can help her.

I should do some printing with other colors if I were you.

Oh, lovely writing; good girl.

Well, that's very good, because every time you've added twelve more. That's really your twelve times table, isn't it?

I should put them in a little egg crate; you won't drop them then.

Clever girl to find it.

You're just watching, Caroline? You're doing an art picture. Could I have a look at it then?

Don't interrupt when I'm speaking to Martin, please.

And what have you been doing this morning? This book's full —it's marvellous, isn't it?

The tone here is an attractive blend of gentleness and authority; there's humor, enthusiasm, and a brisk no-nonsense quality. What pupil wouldn't wish to be praised by such a teacher? What child wouldn't exert himself, just a little more than he'd thought possible, to meet the standards implicit in her most casual remarks?

Show the Child That You Value His Work

The parent who files a report card, but crumples up a painting after a perfunctory "That's nice" has made a judgment few children miss. Of course you can't keep every drawing, admire every wood and wire construction. But no work should ever be destroyed before a child's eyes. (In our family, once it became apparent that the volume of art work was too great for any scrapbook, we started a suitcase for each child's things-to-be-saved. Those suitcases are now a jumble-chest of treasures— letters from camp, papier-mâché puppets, a spool knitting potholder, drawings and paintings and occasional unclassifiables like a nursery school report. We still look through them regularly, each grown daughter discovering again the child she was.)

Special achievements should be recognized. If children have practiced a play, you can help plan a full-scale performance in the living room, with programs and refreshments for the family. If a child is building miniature houses and vehicles, give him a big table where he can develop, undisturbed, his own little town. A child who has been experimenting seriously with electricity or magnetism should be given a chance to see a real lab (where, almost certainly, you can find someone to answer his questions). Children can be encouraged to make and mail their own greeting cards. A specially nice drawing can be xeroxed —any child old enough to drop a nickel in the slot is thrilled by the magical reproduction of his work—and shared with friends. Put up a bulletin board in the child's room large enough to hold all the work he wants to show. (Commercial boards are generally far too small. You can make a good one by covering a sheet of fiberboard with burlap in natural or bright color.) The very best paintings can be put up about the house along with other "real" pictures. A useful hanging device is the inexpensive

Braquette, which clamps a sheet of glass over the picture for effective display. Or you can buy painted metal strips, in various colors, which clamp around drawings to provide an instant frame.

A final caveat. One way in which parents show their serious interest in children's work is, very simply, by not treating it as secondary to adult convenience. By and large, the adult world is time-bound: there are places to go, things to do, at particular hours. Obviously a whole household can't be kept waiting because one member is busy constructing a pendulum. If, however, a child is deeply, truly absorbed in a task, he should not be disturbed for considerations that are in the long run more trivial. When an eight-year-old is excited about a painting or trying out a tune on his recorder, it may be more important to let him continue than to have him wash up and meet a family visitor. (The parent who constantly interrupts a child's work is often the same one who, ten years later, complains that a teen-ager never finishes anything, lacks commitment and purpose.)

Creativity thrives in a home where the child's creations are genuinely and clearly valued. "What is honored in a country," as Plato said long ago, "will be cultivated there."

Perspective for Parents

BOOKS ON CHILD DEVELOPMENT AND CHILD CARE

ABRAHAMSON, DAVID, *The Emotional Care of Your Child*, Trident, 1969. A child psychiatrist illustrates his discussion of emotional growth—and problems—with clinical case histories.

ASSOCIATION FOR CHILDBOOK EDUCATION INTERNATIONAL, *Feelings and Learning*, n.d.

ASCD YEARBOOK, *Perceiving, Behaving, Becoming*, National Education Association, 1962.

BARUCH, DOROTHY W., *Parents and Children Go to School*, Scott, 1939.

BETTELHEIM, BRUNO, *Dialogues with Mothers*, Free Press, 1962. Though individual dialogues deal with special problems (giving up the bottle, hitting back, kissing), Dr. Bettelheim's overall theme, firmly handled, is the dilemma of the modern American parent, so belabored with advice and admonition that he hardly dares trust his own sound instincts lest it be "bad for the child."

BEYER, EVELYN, *Teaching Young Children*, Pegasus, 1968. Primarily concerned with nursery school, this book will help parents evaluate their children's school programs and experiences. Good general suggestions on building desirable attitudes in preschoolers—and concrete help for indoor and outdoor play. Warm, cheerful, anecdotal.

BOWLBY, JOHN, *Child Care and the Growth of Love*, Penguin, 1965. Bowlby's thesis, impressively documented, is that the quality of parental care received in the first years of life (particularly a warm, intimate, and continuous mother-child relationship) vitally affects an individual's future mental health.

BURNETT, DOROTHY K., *Your Preschool Child: Making the Most of the Years from Two to Seven*, Holt, 1961. The author of this delightful book reports that she is not a psychologist, a nursery school teacher or an artsy craftsy type but that, having survived two children, she knows "exactly how embarrassed, frustrated, stupid, well-meaning, exasperated and desperately tired parents can feel." For such parents, she offers a cornucopia of ingenious ways-to-cope and things-to-do. Play ideas for all seasons, first aid for birthday-party planners, tricks for travel and entertaining sick children. . . . Practical and fun.

CENTRAL ADVISORY COUNCIL FOR EDUCATION (England) REPORT, *Children and their Primary Schools*, Her Majesty's Stationery Office, 1967. This historic report on Britain's innovative open schools contains much useful and suggestive material on the child's emotional, physical and psychological development and on the encouraging of awareness, curiosity, imagination.

CHESS, STELLA, ALEXANDER THOMAS, and HERBERT BIRCH, *Your Child Is a Person*, Viking, 1965. "A Psychological Approach to Parenthood Without Guilt": reassurance for parents whose children fail to conform to supposedly ideal "norms," and for those who nervously imagine that they and they alone are responsible for their child's emotional and intellectual development. The authors emphasize the enormous differences between individual children and the *many* types of good parenting. A sound corrective for books that urge total acceptance of everything a child does. ("The pat formula of unlimited love and acceptance ignores the child's need to face life and adapt to the fact that, while he may be unique, he is only one of many human beings in the world. Parents who try to follow this formula may find themselves acting a part instead of being themselves.")

DODSON, FITZHUGH, *How to Parent*, New American Library, 1971. One of the best all-round guides to living and growing with children; if I had to choose only one book for a new parent, it would be this. A psychologist and psychological consultant to his own nursery school, Dr. Dodson brings to his subject a scholarly knowledge of child development research and a parent's practical instincts for what works. An immensely readable volume.

ERIKSON, ERIK H., *Childhood and Society*, W. W. Norton, 1963. One of the really great books on child development and childhood problems. Erikson's brilliant analysis of the life cycle as offering at each stage opportunities for new strengths and integration provides a unique angle of vision for parents.

FRAIBERG, SELMA H., *The Magic Years*, Scribner, 1959. The imaginative world of early childhood, explored with style, humor, insight and affection.

GESELL, ARNOLD, and FRANCES L. ILG, *The Child from Five to Ten*, Harper, 1946. Behavior profiles of typical eating, sleeping and social patterns of children from year to year, plus practical guidance suggestions.

———, *Infant and Child in the Culture of Today*, Harper, 1943. Though Gesell's norms should not be taken as absolutes, parents will be fascinated by his charting of week-by-week growth patterns.

GRUENBERG, SIDONIE MATSNER, *The New Encyclopedia of Child Care and Guidance*, Doubleday, 1968. A splendid, comprehensive guide to every aspect of child life. Alphabetized and cross-indexed (so that the entry under "spoiled child," for example, guides you also to *comforting, crying, permissiveness* and the chapters, in the book's second half, on What the New Psychology Means to Parents and What We Know About the Development of Healthy Personalities in Children).

HARTUP, WILLARD, and N. SMOTHERGILL, *The Young Child, Reviews of Research*, National Association for the Education of Young Children, 1967. The place to look if you want to find out what has been written recently about any particular early childhood problem.

HOMAN, WILLIAM E., *Child Sense*, Basic Books, 1969. A pediatrician's book, down-to-earth and practical.

HYMES, JAMES L., *A Child Development Point of View*, Prentice-Hall, 1955.

ILG, FRANCES, and LOUISE AMES, *Child Behavior*, Harper, 1955. Two associates of the Gesell Institute of Child Development consider behavior problems and developmental needs in relation to the natural cycle of growth.

ISAACS, NATHAN, *The Growth of Understanding in the Young Child: A Brief Introduction to Piaget's Work*, London Educational Supply Association, 1961.

ISAACS, SUSAN, *The Nursery Years: The Mind of the Child from Birth to Six Years*, Schocken, 1968. A brilliant, meticulous study of child development by a pioneer of the modern British nursery school movement.

JONES, EVE, *The Intelligent Parents' Guide to Raising Children*, Free Press, 1959. Takes parents from the hospital door to the teen-ager's first car. The latter portions of this book have been outdated by the world's swift turning, but the material on young children remains helpful and sound.

KASSIRER, EVE, ed., *What's What for Children*, Citizen's Committee on Children (Ottawa). A parents' guide to music, art, books, drama, creative writing, pets, toys. Brief introductory essays with very useful lists and bibliography. Order from 221 Donald St., Ottawa, Ontario.

LEEPER, SARAH H., RUTH J. DALES, DORA SIKES SKIPPER, and RALPH L. WITHERSPOON, *Good Schools for Young Children*, Macmillan, 1968.

LE SHAN, EDA, *How to Survive Parenthood*, Random House, 1965. Written with warmth, charm, wit and deep humanity, this book combines sweet reasonableness with an evident love and respect for children—and for life. (The needs of *parents* receive attention along with the demands of their offspring.)

MONTESSORI, MARIA, *The Absorbent Mind*, Holt, 1967. A plea for the providing of an environment which offers "an education from birth" and "the true cultivation of the human individual from the very beginning." An analysis of the child's physical and psychological development during the critical first six years in relation to the child's growing mastery of motor skills, social adjustments, work habits and language.

MOUSTAKAS, CLARK, and M. BERSON, *The Young Child in School*, Morrow, 1956.

MULLER, PHILIPPE, *The Tasks of Childhood*, trans. Anita Mason, McGraw, 1969. An overview of the best current thinking on child care and development, which takes as its chief focus the concept of the various developmental tasks which children must master in their progress toward maturity.

PIAGET, JEAN, *The Language and Thought of the Child*, World, 1955. A classic study of intellectual development in the early years.

———, *Play, Dreams and Imitation in Childhood*, Norton, 1962.

PICKARD, P. M., *The Activity of Children*, Humanities Press, 1968. A crisp British guide to the ways in which parents can help children help themselves. A good companion to *The Tasks of Childhood*, since it pays considerable attention to the ways in which "growing points" can be recognized and utilized to further maturation.

PIERS, MARIA, *Growing Up with Children*, Quadrangle Books, 1966.

REPORT OF THE PROVINCIAL COMMITTEE ON AIMS AND OBJECTIVES
OF EDUCATION IN THE SCHOOLS OF ONTARIO, *Living and Learning*, Ontario Department of Education, 1969. An enlightened—and strikingly handsome—government report defending the rights of children "to be treated as human beings—exquisite, complex, and elegant in their diversity." The sections on "Today's Child," "The Learning Experience" and "On Aims of Education" are particularly suggestive.

RUSSELL, DAVID H., *Children's Thinking*, Ginn, 1956. A formidably complete study of the child's intellectual development (how children form concepts of the self, time, etc.) with emphasis on types of critical and creative thinking. One section considers techniques by which children's thinking can be improved.

SHARP, EVELYN, *Thinking Is Child's Play*, Dutton, 1969. Based largely on the work of Piaget and Jerome Bruner, this book explains how the young learn to think and provides mind-stretching exercises.

SPOCK, BENJAMIN, *Baby and Child Care*, Pocket Books, 1972. The parents' bible, concentrating largely on physical matters but written out of a wider wisdom and concern.

———, *Dr. Spock Talks with Mothers*, Houghton, 1961. Retaining the warm, chatty tone of the magazine articles on which the book is based, Dr. Spock deals with discipline, behavior problems, fears and anxieties—and basic physical considerations (diet, exercise, sleep, etc.).

STERN, CATHERINE, and TONI S. GOULD, *Early Years of Childhood*, Harper, 1955. Steering a careful course between permissiveness and authoritarianism, the authors suggest effective approaches to The Poor Sleeper, The Poor Eater, The Timid Child, The Tyrant, The Slow Learner.

STONE, L. I., and JOSEPH CHURCH, *Childhood and Adolescence*,

Random House, 1957. A truly comprehensive and scholarly study of child development.

TAYLOR, BARBARA J., A *Child Goes Forth*, Brigham Young University, 1972. Designed as a curriculum guide for preschool teachers, this book contains useful suggestions as to the kinds of knowledges children should acquire between three and six—about families, houses, weather, seasons, holidays, modes of transportation, birds, animals, elementary science and arithmetic.

TODD, VIVIAN E., and HELEN HEFFERNAN, *The Years Before School: Guiding Preschool Children*, Macmillan, 1970. Primarily for nursery school teachers, but full of suggestions for guiding the play and learning experiences of two-, three- and four-year-olds. Typical chapters deal with "Furthering Physical Development," "Learning to Participate in the Culture," "Building Science Concepts," "Developing Verbal Communication."

WINN, MARIE, and MARY ANN PORCHER, *The Playgroup Book*, Penguin, 1969. A marvelously detailed and practical guide to life with the two-to-fives—play, science, art, music, books, and excursions, with instructions for making all kinds of useful equipment like easels and puppet stages.

WINNICOTT, D. W., *The Child, the Family and the Outside World*, Pelican, 1964. A distinguished pediatrician and child psychiatrist writes in a relaxed, intimate and cheerful way about everything from "Why Do Babies Cry?" to "Aspects of Juvenile Delinquency." Like a British Dr. Spock, helpful and reassuring.

WITMER, HELEN L., ed., and RUTH KOTINSKY, *Personality in the Making* (White House Conference), Harper, 1952. Considers the influence of congenital characteristics, physical limitations, parent-child relations, income level and racial or social discrimination on a child's psychosocial development.

WOODWARD, O. M., *The Earliest Years*, Pergamon Press, 1966.

WOLFE, ANNA W., and SUZANNE SZASZ, *Helping Your Child's Emotional Growth*, Doubleday, 1954. Brief essays, many pictures, on such themes as sudden shyness, bedtime fears, another baby in the family, grandparents.

YARDLEY, ALICE, *Senses and Sensitivity*, Evans, 1970. Simply written but deeply understanding, a book about nourishing the whole child, helping him "to become all that he is capable of becoming." Chapters on such matters as the education of taste, the body as instrument, the foundations of belief.

3

Play Is Serious Business:
Toys and Playthings for the Growing Child

At the kindergarten sand table, Janet is building. The dry sand won't hold a shape. How much water will make it just right, not crumbly but not too gooshy either? She stirs, pats, piles, sighs with satisfaction as the castle takes form. Carrie gallops past on a broom handle. "Out of my way, everybody! I'm a mustang!" Steve's working on a puzzle; he needs a curvy green piece. Laura and Mike have set up a hospital. Laura, pronounced dead just a few minutes ago, is now a nurse giving shots and taking temperatures. Lee hangs by her heels on the parallel bars. A group of five-year-olds, preparing for a game of Snow White, argue passionately over who gets to be witch.

These children are involved in a common activity—they are *playing*—but the motives and meaning of their play differ as much as the children themselves. Janet is learning about the world —about shape, density, texture. Carrie's working off steam. Steve wrestles with a spatial problem, an intellectual challenge. Laura and Mike, enacting the fascinating rituals of sickness, express old fears and new awareness. Lee is finding out what her body can do. And the squabbling cast of Snow White is experimenting with a very grown-up kind of play, one involving compromise and co-operation.

A child's play is not diversion but the most serious business of his life. When an adult plays—at golf, dancing, chess—he turns aside from his "real" work to relax; the refreshing activity is very properly called re-creation. But a child's play is a continuous act of creation. Running or digging, building or pretending, the child creates *himself*: he discovers who he is, what he can do, how things work, where he fits into the total scheme. This truth has not always been recognized. A colonial American school charter (1784) includes, for instance, a typical prohibition: "the students shall be indulged with nothing which the world calls play . . . for those who play when they are young will play when they are old." Two centuries of educational research has brought the wheel full circle. "Deeply absorbing play," writes Arnold Gesell, Yale's eminent child development specialist, "seems to be essential for full mental growth. Children who are capable of such intense play are most likely to give a good account of themselves when they are grown up."

Parents inclined to regard play as idle amusement might well reflect on recent studies having to do with its role in both animal and human development. Rats confined throughout infancy to bare cages later show signs of profound disturbance, while those given a rich environment and play materials become lively and emotionally stable adults. Human babies are similarly dependent on play stimulus. In a series of dramatic experiments at Middle Eastern orphanages, Dr. Wayne Dennis found that infants given adequate physical care but no playthings (and no opportunities to play with adults) were strikingly late in mastering elementary physical skills. Between the ages of one and two, fewer than half these children could sit unsupported; none could walk. When, however, "backward" babies about seven months old were given a variety of objects to look at and handle, they made great forward leaps physically and socially. (Dr. Dennis estimates that these children made four times the average gain in development as a result of play experience.)

In the United States, the entire Head Start program is based on a new view of the difference between children of middle-class and low-income parents: children from privileged homes are much "brighter" by age three or four, it's thought, because they receive more sensory and intellectual stimulus and more play materials. (In a fascinating application of this theory, Florida some years ago instituted a pilot program which sent lay teachers into poor homes to show mothers how to play with their babies.)

All young animals play. The kitten chasing a ball, the puppy chewing a stick, the baby sucking on his fist or reaching for a rattle—all spontaneously, with curious deep absorption, try out their powers. Watch a three-year-old hammering pegs, a six-year-old wobbling on his first two-wheeler, and you're struck by the fact that such play is a kind of *work*—something the child wants to do, and also something he *must* do. Children envy—how can they not?—what seems the absolute freedom and power of adults. And when they rush out, mornings, to play, they're impelled not only by a desire for fun, but by a drive for mastery, over themselves and the physical world.

Adults, accustomed to thinking in terms of end results, may be puzzled by a child's casual destruction of the block tower he's labored to build. But for a playing child it's the process that matters, the exercise of control. Play, as Lawrence Frank observes, "is the way the child learns what no one can teach him," that he can act for himself. Every time he makes or masters or affects his environment, his self-esteem grows—and with it, his confidence. No wonder, then, that after a particularly difficult or exhausting game, children appear—the description is Maria Montessori's—"satisfied, rested and happy, with the look of those who have experienced some great joy."

In Play, a Child Learns About the World

A conscientious parent, once alerted to the notion that play is a kind of learning, may become obsessed with educational toys. His school-age children get electrified quiz games and 3D stereo viewers ("See Japan, Fish Life, Moon Landing *right in your own living room*"). His preschooler owns a spelling-counting board.

Even the baby inhabits a special "enriched environment" crib equipped with spinning wheels, sand timers, voice-activated mobiles and a tank of live fish. Such well-intentioned earnestness is often self-defeating (a lively eight-year-old gets the ho-hums on a second viewing of Fish Life) and pointless. In a crib wired for light and sound, says Harvard pediatrician Richard Feinbloom, babies may acquire some skills earlier, but "they cannot do much with their precocious acquisition."

Children make their most important play discoveries without any special equipment at all. An infant learns, by chewing, that fingers are Me but the rubber duck is Not-Me; by feeling, the difference between hard and sharp and rough and smooth and sticky and warm. A one-year-old playing Peekaboo makes the truly momentous discovery of what psychologists call "object permanence": out of sight does not mean *lost* or *gone*. Toddlers messing with sand and water learn that the cup fits into the bowl but not vice versa, that balls float and stones sink. A five-year-old finds that a tall tower requires a solid block base; big blocks on top of little blocks equals trouble. Young painters learn how to keep colors separate on the page, and how to make colors by blending. Young sculptors discover that certain kinds of clay figures require wire armatures, and so on. "It is in such activities as these," says the English educationist P. M. Pickard, "that children, whatever their age, are grounded in physics, in mathematics, in art. They calculate, estimate, test gravity, weight, capacity, volume, light refraction."

For a child, *any* experience may be educational. All a parent has to do to promote growth is to make a variety of experiences available. Real learning—it's an obvious truth, but it bears repetition —is grounded in firsthand experience. Children may talk knowledgeably about jet propulsion and electromagnetic forces without any real understanding at all; they juggle phrases. But a child who has tinkered with even such simple apparatus as a dry cell or a bar magnet *knows* something about the physical universe. The cycle of learning moves from particular to symbolic to abstract. The child's appetite for play constitutes an instinctive recognition of this process: only through doing will he learn, and only through learning can he surmount his youthful dependence, becoming his own man in a world no longer frightening because now it is intelligible, understood.

In Play a Child Develops Mastery—
Physical as Well as Emotional

Human babies are born helpless. The newborn calf staggers to its feet; the newborn chimpanzee clings to its mother by its own strength and within a month stands upright. In man, however, the initial disproportion between brain weight and body mass makes for a relatively long period of total dependence. Even a year after birth, a child would surely die if no one looked after him.

Throughout that first year, the infant moves toward control of his own body and the physical environment. He learns to focus his eyes; to grasp, shake, bang, drop and retrieve objects; to make sounds that produce desired results (like food, change of place). All these developments occur in play. Through play the baby moves from passivity to activity; being tossed in the air by adults is fun, tossing a ball is even more fun because now *he's* agent. Freud, in *Beyond the Pleasure Principle*, describes this fundamental joy in mastery as revealed in the play of an eighteen-month-old boy. The child, generally "good" in spite of his mother's frequent absences, was obsessed by a single troublesome game: flinging into corners or under furniture every toy he laid hands on. This activity he accompanied by "an expression of interest and gratification," a long-drawn-out "Go-one!"

What made the game so satisfying? Freud puzzled over that until the child introduced a significant variation—throwing into his crib a wooden reel attached to a string and then drawing it

back with a joyful "*There!*" Of course. The boy was playing dis-
appearance and return, assuring himself that the vanished object
(toy—or mother) *would* come back, and that he could control
the situation, turn passivity into activity. In real life the mother
came and went as she chose, the child waited. In play, as Erik
Erikson says, he "has the mother by a string. He makes her go
away, even throws her away, and then makes her come back at
his pleasure."

Much of children's play is inspired by precisely this need—to
do to others (especially adults) what is usually done to them. So
the toddler runs away and hides from his mother, reversing the
usual order of events ("Good-bye, darling, be a good boy while
Mummy's gone"); experiencing control in the play situation, he
masters his fear of loss or abandonment. A four-year-old gets
down on the floor and barks ferociously—becoming a bad dog who
frightens four-year-olds. He jabs his doll with a make-believe
hypodermic needle; now he's the doctor giving shots. A school-
age child will act out the classroom experience over and over
again; if his teacher is authoritarian, he does a lot of play-ordering
and play-punishing. In all of these ways, children assimilate their
experience and master their actual helplessness by conjuring up
pleasurable fantasies of power. (The Monopoly craze which hit
America during the great economic depression of the thirties
illustrates a similar pattern on a grown-up level. From a reality
of breadlines and no jobs, adults turned to games which made
possible a paper mastery of economic forces.)

Play makes possible the mastery of primitive anxieties. ("Like
a sufferer passing his tongue over an aching tooth," George
Steiner observes of traditional street and playground games, "the
child provokes fear and even pain in order to test his control
over that which he fears. The death pantomimes of children,
the night runs through ambushing, clawing shadows are rehears-
als for the terrors of adult daylight and for the inconceivable
obviousness of death.") It is also the child's way of dealing with
forbidden wishes. A child wants to please his parents, and be

like them. But that involves giving up important satisfactions. Big boys don't hit, scream, break things or make messes; they don't, they most definitely don't wet their pants.

Now the fact that children relinquish certain activities doesn't mean they've stopped wanting to do those things. And what a child wants, he wants very badly. So he must either repress the unacceptable desire (in which case it goes underground, perhaps breaking out later in damaging ways)—or express it in the most acceptable avenue open to him, through play. This is where mud and water come in; they appeal, not only through sheer sensuous delight, but because of their unconscious associations.

A child begins with intense interest in his own body products. Since he's not allowed to play with this fascinating material, mud and clay—the squishier the better—become a special pleasure. (Listen to the conversation of nursery schoolers rolling clay and you'll almost certainly hear bathroom talk.) Water too is endlessly interesting: pouring, filling, emptying, splashing, children obscurely work out feelings about physiological processes. (Every child knows the experience of "making water" himself, withholding, releasing and, in boys, directing the stream.) One basic meaning of water play appears in games involving wetting dolls. A little girl still struggling with her own uncertain controls will repeat constantly the sequence of bottle-feeding, diaper-soaking and, very likely, a vigorous final *thwack*. "Look at your pants. Naughty, naughty!"

Fruitful play leads in the direction of physical as well as emotional development. Working with erector sets or lace-up and button toys, children achieve small-muscle coordination. Outdoors—climbing, jumping, swinging, sliding, racing, chasing, they discover what the large muscles can do. The desire to control the body and, through the body, the environment, is strong in these early years. Watch a timid preschooler approaching a high slide. At first, even the steps terrify. He goes up one step, retreats. Two steps, three, four . . . now getting back again is scary. Still, the slide remains something he needs to conquer. With support, he returns again and again. There will be, probably, a weeping session at the top before he finally lets go. When he does manage that, the joy of success is wholly disproportionate to the pleasure of a short ride; it's the pleasure of mastery over self.

To achieve this kind of satisfaction, confidence in a well-coordinated body response, children will show phenomenal persistence in returning to a self-assigned task. I think of a photograph in *Design for Play*, a book about model playgrounds: a junky vacant lot, with a girl swinging between low-hanging wires, serenely joyful. What makes the moment memorable is the fact that she has one leg in a toe-to-thigh cast, and a pair of crutches slung over her shoulder. "This little girl," the caption reads, "actually broke her leg playing on these wires but could not resist returning to the challenge."

Mastery of a physical challenge is frequently followed by obsessive repetition which guarantees the skill. (Gesell calls such compulsive redoings "benign and probably beneficial seizures." The toddler who has just learned to climb stairs will climb them all morning.) The next step, for many children, is to complicate the just-achieved task, make it harder still. The youngster who has learned to swing from a rail wants to walk it; having successfully graduated from tricycle to two-wheeler, he must ride no hands with feet on the handlebars. Adults who try to discourage such derring-do with "You could crack your head open!" miss the point. The point is the risk. As street games like Ghosties and Murder in the Dark demonstrate, most children enjoy play that involves a substantial element of fear, and that tests the limits of their own capacities.

In Play a Child Practices Adult Roles and
Absorbs the Dominant Values of His Culture

A child observing the mysterious behavior of adults, says psychologist Margaret Lowenfeld, "is in the position of a behaviorist, an archaeologist or an anthropologist among a people speaking a language which is unknown to him." Why does Mother move in such a cross, snappy way when guests are coming to dinner? What makes Father use one voice for the telephone, a different voice talking to Mother and still another one for him? The child hasn't the faintest idea. But he imitates what he observes (often with devastating accuracy) and, through imitation, arrives at certain private understandings.

Playing grown-up, the child tries on different roles—teacher, policeman, truckdriver, nurse, storekeeper, cowboy. In this way he gains not only understanding but also some genuine skills. Playing house, in the beginning, is making mud pies. Later on, the pretend-cook helps stir the batter or punch bread dough. Later still, he makes his own tart out of some leftover pie crust . . . and so on, up to the first made-it-myself cake. From hammering pegs to building a cabinet is a long learning; the young carpenter achieves it happily through play. All children long to know what their parents' work *means*, and to reenact it in play. If a parent's work role is one familiar to most children (dentist, bus driver), no special introduction is necessary. But if, for instance, Father or Mother practices law, a profession with which the young normally have no contact whatsoever, the child should have a chance to visit the office or courtroom, see what goes on there (and perhaps bring home some business stationery to play lawyer with).

In play, too, the young absorb their parents' notions of how-we-behave. Anthropologist Martha Wolfenstein describes how play practices condition French children to accept the social values of their culture. Parisian children are taken regularly to a park for strictly disciplined, solitary play. The adult sits on a bench; his child typically plays directly in front of him, often with the pathway sand. His pail is *his*. If a nearby child reaches for it— or if he himself picks up someone else's pail—the guardian intervenes promptly. (*Give it back. Bad boy.*) French children are expected to play with other members of their family, regardless of age difference. If two near-age little strangers gravitate toward each other as children will, the concerned mothers rise silently from their benches, separate the pair and return their charges to solitary though adjacent play. Any form of physical aggression is sharply discouraged—and ended, if necessary, by adult intervention. So is shouting and running and getting dirty. (An elegantly clad French child will squat carefully over the sand, so that only his hands become soiled. Periodically, he shows them to his mother, she cleans them, he goes back to play.)

By just such practices, no doubt, the French are conditioned to family solidarity, respect for property, extreme restraint and a high tolerance for solitary diversions (like café-sitting). American play practices, on the other hand, encourage sharing, outgoing behavior, self-expression and gregariousness. Play is in effect "a tradition, a form of regularized and ritualized behavior that reproduces the regulations of society in miniature. Children learn the rules of the adult world they will inhabit from the rules of their play as children. Both the best and the worst aspects of a society are first learned in play."

On a somewhat more abstract level of speculation, play specialists have suggested that national inventiveness and drive may be directly or indirectly influenced by the kind of toys generally in use. The life-size preschool toys of Denmark and the United States, for example, give children a comfortable, reassuring toy world; this, and the popularity of "unstructured" playthings like blocks, may well stimulate creative energy. The miniature toys of Germany, on the other hand, may encourage manipulativeness if not grandiose dreams of mastery. And the relative absence of toys in very poor countries (India, the Arab nations) may result in a high proportion of individuals whose self-image is depressed, and who assume that they have no hope of affecting their environment.

In Play Children Learn Cooperation
and Compromise

A child's first play is egocentric and solitary. Given a rattle or a spoon, the six-monther doesn't look for playmates. Banging, sucking, throwing is diversion enough. Gradually he learns to enjoy a rudimentary form of interaction like Peekaboo or I-Throw, You-Pick-It-Up. But it's not until about two years that a child derives any special pleasure from the company of other children. Even then, another toddler is apt to be treated like another plaything—poked, prodded, explored. Sharing is unthinkable to a child who has just discovered *I* and *Mine*.

Toward the end of the third year, parallel play (side by side but separate) shades into truly social interaction. Now jumping is more fun if there's someone else to jump with. "Let's *both* be airplanes" and—a real step forward—"You be the store man and I buy the hot dogs." Even the most elementary social play contributes to a new sense of what's required in group living. Peggy can't always give the orders. "You've *been* the mother. Now it's *my turn*." Sharing is seen as enlargement, not diminution. "You bring your dump truck and I'll get my bulldozer. We can make a big road." Adults still have to intervene occasionally ("Maybe if you asked nicely, Mark would let you use his shovel"), but three-year-olds learn on their own, through play, *what works*. Other kids don't like it when you grab. Tell somebody how you feel instead of hitting him and he'll still be your friend. Waiting, respecting others' rights (and defending your own), not crying over little things—these hard lessons are made easier in a play context.

School marks the beginning of a new stage in social relationships. Now children want to play in groups (though the chief connection is with the group, not with other members). There is lots of racing around together, much emphasis on mastering skills like rope jumping and riding a two-wheeler, but little zest for competitive games. (Psychologist Ruth Hartley observes that a six-year-old has to learn to work *with* others before he starts working *against* them.) Another year, though, and the group becomes a gang with a passionate interest in rules and regulations. (Seven is the great age for clubs with charters elaborate enough for the United Nations.) Along with rules comes a new concept of fairness, "being a good sport," and consequently, interest in team and board games.

Though team games are contests, the pleasure of Giant Steps or Red Rover has little to do with winning. Children like games involving luck, fresh starts, magical rhymes, lots of high moments. The most popular ones, as Iona and Peter Opie point out, are ceremonies rather than competitions, reassuring rituals in which relationships are clearly defined. "A child can exert himself without having to think whether he is a popular person, and can find himself being a useful partner to someone of whom he is ordinarily afraid." As team games give players a sense of secure companionship, board games provide experiences in friendly rivalry (again contained by rules). Even a simple game like Old Maid prepares children for the importance of luck as well as strategy in human affairs—and demonstrates the need for rules. "You can't play tennis without a net," Robert Frost once commented; the realization that rules don't destroy fun, but make it more possible, is one that first comes to many children as they bend over a domino board.

Beyond the Toy Box

Some of the best play experiences don't involve toys at all. Up until this century, children didn't need toys: the whole world was a playground. In the cities, fascinating adult activities took place in plain view. A child could wander down the block to watch a blacksmith shoe a horse, a butcher dissect a carcass. The streets, still relatively free of traffic, were good for games, and the sidewalks for roller skating or hopscotch. Now the streets are forbidden. ("Hold my hand. Don't dig by that tree. Don't throw your ball, you'll break a window.") The city child's only playground is likely to be an asphalt compound ringed with iron fences and stocked with equipment frustrating or dangerous—whirls where he can take a bad fall climbing on or off, jungle gyms correctly sized for ten-year-olds but not for those older or younger, swings that hurtle through the air like unguided missiles and slides where a whole line of impatient children stand waiting their turns.

In suburbia, things are not much better. Gone are the woodpiles, rainbarrels, sheds, cellar doors, basements and attics and clotheslines that once offered exercise and adventure. A country yard now is a grass plot anxiously tended. No racing around there, no games that might scuff the Kentucky blue back to bare earth. Rocks and trees to climb are in short supply. Still, some basic materials are everywhere available—and important to creative growth.

Mud, Water, Sand

A report from the new scientifically planned towns of West Germany casts fascinating light on children's most basic play needs. In a government-sponsored study of over five thousand children's drawings, it appeared that the young saw their bright modern communities as concrete fortresses of order and boredom. (A thirteen-year-old in one model town drew himself and his friends walking, single file, down a traffic line in the middle of the road. Behind the boys, a car dutifully steers along the same line.) What these children really enjoyed, the drawings revealed, was playing by puddles, trash cans and storm drains; studying trains and factory smokestacks; poking around in construction debris . . . being in contact with *real things*.

The West German report dramatizes an important truth: whatever sophisticated entertainments are available, every child needs experience with what Margaret Lowenfeld calls "inchoate materials"—substances which, being formless, give free rein to the imagination.

The emotional importance of mud and water play has been mentioned. These materials also afford valuable learning experiences. Consider the properties of water which adults take for granted. It takes the shape of its container. It can be clear, dirty, colored (and can make things clean or dirty). Emerging from a hose, it has force and direction, can make rain, cool the air. Boats and corks float on it, tin soldiers sink. And so on. These are amazing discoveries for children. In the early years, then, they should have plenty of chances to do what one four-year-old calls "puddling around." In the bathtub or out, children enjoy water play with plastic cups and funnels, squeeze bottles, sprinklers, spoons, straws, sponges, rubber dolls and doll clothes to wash. Bubbles are always fun—sloshing bubble bath in the tub, or whipping up soap flakes in a pan. "Painting" with water and a big brush is satisfying to under-fours. Though this sort of activity is pretty messy indoors, it can be made manageable in a kitchen if you swathe the young splasher in a plastic apron (or an old shower curtain with an over-the-head opening) and protect the floor with newspaper padding laid over plastic. Anyhow, cleaning up puddles can also be fun.

Sand, like water, becomes more interesting with the right equipment. All kinds of discarded kitchen tools do nicely here— measurers and containers, plus sifters and shakers. Once a child reaches the sand-construction stage, he'll want small toys to give his landscapes conviction—plastic people and animals, cars to run about the sand streets, trucks to cart and dump. If sand is hard to come by, just plain mud will do.

In any of these activities, try not to make children overanxious about getting dirty or messy. There will be plenty of opportunities to teach fastidiousness; the civilized world closes in soon enough. Water, sand and mud are for freedom.

Dress-up and Dramatic Play Materials

One way a child discovers his own identity is by pretending to be somebody else. From three on, children begin, in play, to experiment with adult roles. Earthbound boys become astronauts; a timid girl turns into Joan of Arc or the Wicked Witch of the West. Though such transformations can be accomplished with a minimum of props, a dress-up box provides a valuable stimulus to imaginative play. It's possible, of course, to buy costumes—sleazy Batman suits, overpriced fairy princess gowns. But the discards of any clothes closet (or the ratty furs and out-of-style garments found at church rummage sales) are a treasure trove for children.

Collect: suits and dresses, especially evening gowns; hats, all kinds; shawls and scarves; purses and gloves; shoes; costume jewelry and sunglasses or old spectacle frames; odd lengths of fabric; cardboard, aluminum foil, felt bits and glittery things for such accessories as crowns and helmets. Some materials can be purchased only at particular holiday seasons: at Christmas lay in a supply of tinsel and small bells, at Halloween of masks (both cover-the-face types and simple eye visors) and easy-to-wash-off children's makeup. Try making, perhaps with the child's help, wings (butterfly, fairy) out of bent wire and crepe paper, and for animal games a pin-on tail or floppy ears. An eye patch may come in handy, for pirates. Don't forget to include items specially attractive to boys—boots, army castoffs, badges. An old razor (without blade, naturally) and a shaving brush is a useful piece of equipment. So is anything associated with Father's work —a wrench, a lunchbox, an old attaché case, a book of samples.

Kitchen Adventures

The kitchen is a popular play area, not only because Mother's often there too, but because it's full of *stuff*. Toddlers are happy just banging pots; older children can operate such thrilling gadgets as egg slicers, cheese graters, food grinders, beaters and whisks. A kitchen has *containers*; milk cartons and oatmeal boxes offer all sorts of possibilities (blocks, drums, noisemakers —with rice or dried beans inside—and trains). A kitchen has manipulable foodstuffs: macaroni to string, dried beans and seeds for collages, corn meal to sift. A kitchen has things-to-grow: children can sprout dry legumes in a glass of earth and watch roots form, or start a real plant (sweet potato, carrot or pineapple top, avocado pit, orange or lemon seed). Above all, a kitchen is a place to cook and stir. Most mothers discover for themselves such traditional child-helper pleasures as cutting cookies, stirring icing (and licking the spoon). A new one, immensely satisfying, is making Crunchy Granola, a dry cereal mix that's fun to produce and more wholesome than sugary commercial products. Here's a basic recipe, one children will enjoy varying as they become expert cereal makers:

Mix together with the hands in a very large bowl:

> 5 c. rolled oats
> 1 c. wheat flakes
> 1 c. rye flakes

    1½ c. unsweetened coconut
    1 c. wheat germ
    ½ c. sesame seeds
    1 c. ground roasted soybeans
    1 c. sunflower seeds
    1 c. nuts (flaked almonds, broken cashews)
    1 c. soy flour
    1 c. powdered noninstant milk
    2 tsp. sea salt

(All of these ingredients can be purchased at health food stores. But a good granola can be made using just the rolled oats, coconut, wheat germ and sesame seeds.)
Now heat together in a pan:

    1 c. honey
    ½ c. soybean or peanut oil
    1 tsp. vanilla

Mix thoroughly, spread in three pans and roast slowly in 250-degree oven, taking out pans frequently to stir. When nicely browned, return to bowl and mix raisins generously throughout.

One specially nice feature of granola making is that a three-year-old can do the fun part (hand-mixing) all by himself; he can also, supervised, pour soybeans into the blender and press the magic grinding button. Children will enjoy making their own decorated cereal containers for keeping or giving. (Oatmeal boxes, and coffee cans with snap-on plastic lids, can be covered with paper or fabric and made special.)

Outdoor Treasures

If you're lucky enough to have a garden, flowers (petals and seed pods) make fanciful dolls. My children found that ripe quinces made fascinating heads for old-lady dolls. (Draw the features with ball-point pen or felt marker; as the quince withers,

the face ages convincingly.) Hollyhocks made glorious Scarlett
O'Hara skirts for tiny dolls, I remember—and geranium petals,
glued to drawings, turned into fairy hats. Your child will discover other possibilities. Then there are acorns, good for making
birds, animals, and miniature cups or hats; pebbles for mosaics
or doll house paths; small stones that can be transformed, with
felt pen and fabric scraps, into human or animal figures; shells
for jewelry making, sand scoops, ashtrays, collages; berries to dry
and string. A good stick has a thousand lives—spyglass, cane,
earth stirrer, rifle, hobbyhorse, sword, wand. . . .

Fascinating Junk

"Anything can be used for anything," my five-year-old daughter once announced—not knowing she had formulated an important principle. By and large, it's true: to a child with a
developed eye and practiced hand, nothing is useless. Consider
the empty wooden spool. In combination with other spools or
blocks, it's good for building. Paint it for stringing, either as a
necklace or, more elaborately, a jointed doll. Decorate and hammer in four nails at one end, you have a knitting device that,
by a simple process of looping yarn over the nails, turns out fine
fat "knitted" coils. Use it for wheels on a small box wagon, as
a dollhouse table. Make a toy lawnmower (wire handle, spool
roller). Glue four or five spools together for a telescope. Use a
spool as the nose-bridge for a pair of binoculars made from empty
toilet-paper rolls. (Preschoolers will take these proudly on birdwatching expeditions.) Use it as the smokestack of a locomotive.
Paint horizontal stripes on it and spin it, top fashion, from a
pencil. Wind it tightly with an attached cord, you've got a yo-yo.
Dip one end in paint, you've got a stamper that prints a circle design. Why would anyone throw away a spool?

So many common household objects are equally versatile that
a list would be endless. Some of the best are: corks, plastic pill

containers, typewriter ribbon spools, shirt and notepaper card-board, jar and bottle tops, toothpicks, clothespins, foil pans, paper bags, rope, string, straws, buttons, golf tees, ball bearings, marbles, watches that don't tick and record turntables that don't spin, plastic detergent bottles, egg cartons, popsicle sticks, paper and plastic cups, boxes of all kinds—wood, metal, cardboard. Before you discard anything, ask yourself (better yet, ask your child), "Now, what would this be good for?" Incidentally, in collecting good junk, don't overlook the possibilities of hardware departments—nuts and bolts, pulleys, springs and latches. And of free materials good for playing store or office—mail-order catalogs, maps (from service stations), brochures about foreign countries (travel agencies) and old wallpaper books (paint stores). Specialty stores are often glad to dispose of boxes, all shapes and sizes.

How you store junk affects its usefulness. I don't like toy chests; they so quickly become, as Fitzhugh Dodson says, just a place to dump things in, "a vast archaeological scrap heap with odds and ends dating back to the Pleistocene era." To keep materials readily available, tempting, and inspiring creative play, the child will need a handy storage place. Then, in a what-can-I-do moment, he can sort through his possessions and see what they suggest. An old chest of drawers, with dividers, is ideal, or one of the inexpensive small-parts cabinets sold in hardware departments.

What makes a good toy?

A Good Toy Is Adapted to the Child's Age, Developmental Needs and Personality

A parent buying shoes for his child takes pains to insure a correct fit. The same parent buying toys often behaves as if, in this matter, no problem of fit existed. Moved by confused memories of his own childhood, perhaps, he buys Lincoln Logs for a three-year-old. (At this stage, a child is happy to stack and build with blocks. He's not ready to fit pieces together in predetermined patterns.) He gives his two-year-old a bride doll—it's so pretty—when what she'd really like is a rubber baby to bathe. (Two-year-olds have no romantic-sentimental interest in weddings, can't manage the buttons on a gown.)

Because play is a kind of life education, toys should be chosen to correspond with a child's learning and mastering needs at any particular time. The just-toilet-trained youngster needs play materials to be messy with (clay, crayons, paint). A seven-year-old newly interested in group play is ready for board games involving self-discipline and rules. At any age, children need toys the right size. As a rule, the younger the child the larger his beads, blocks, crayons, dolls should be. Small children don't find miniatures "cute," are too clumsy-fingered to manipulate the dinky toys older siblings enjoy. A six-year-old will be thrilled by a playmate doll her own size; an eleven-year-old, if she's still playing dolls, wants a six- or thirteen-inch model.

Though children develop at different rates, all children pass through the same stages, face the same developmental tasks. Certain kinds of experience seem necessary if a child is to master these tasks, which may be physical (small-muscle coordination) or emotional (learning to share). The result is that a child who misses sand play, for instance, or running-chasing games at the logical age will later on try to make up for the loss. (When London's adventure playgrounds first opened, teen-age girls were observed happily making sand pies. P. M. Pickard, of the Maria Grey College of Education, speculates that this was probably an activity they'd missed along the way.)

Improper timing is not disastrous. But giving play materials for which a child is not ready—a chemistry set to a nine-year-old, a heddle loom to a girl who hasn't yet mastered spool knitting . . . this may actually discourage native inclination. Giving a toy too late (unless it's an all-ages pleasure like balls and blocks) is simply wasteful. What can a four-year-old do with a wheeled wooden duck on a string?

Age and stage are important. Equally important is the question: what is this child like? What's fun *for him?*" Though a good toy may well extend the range of a child's interests, it shouldn't represent a direction utterly foreign. An ant farm—a live colony in a see-through plastic box—is a fascinating object of study. But there's no use giving it to a lace and ruffles sort of girl who's queasy about bugs. (Try to interest such a child in observing insects outdoors by all means. Don't expect her to keep them on her shelf.) An exceptionally active, vigorous, outdoorsy child does not want a jigsaw puzzle consisting of five hundred tiny pieces. And while one can lead a timid child to a unicycle, twenty cannot make him ride.

A Good Toy Inspires Active Play

Genuine, satisfying play calls forth a child's energies and imagination. A good toy requires that the owner *do* something —push, pull, climb, build, fit, combine, dissect, pretend. Give a child a bucket of blocks, he can hardly wait to get to work. Give him a mechanical robot and he'll wind it up enthusiastically the first half-dozen times. But watching a toy work is boring. That's the reason children so often destroy mechanical toys. Taking them apart, seeing what makes them go, is the most interesting prospect they afford. (One appealing type of mechanical toy is the music box or clock with fully visible works in plastic housing.)

Consider, for instance, the battery-powered "mystery locomotive" produced by one major manufacturer. "Just put in two 'D' batteries," says the ad for this item, "and watch this puffer-belly chug away. Smokestack smokes . . . headlight glows . . .

whistle sounds." The play here is in the toy, not the child. He'd have a lot more fun with a simple wheeled engine to push or ride. Or take the Tell-a-Tale Machine, complete with story cartridges. This imitation television set ("high-quality plastic") comes with a Sleeping Beauty roll and a Little Red Riding Hood roll. Insert the roll, turn on the light, press the button . . . and guess what? The pictures unfold before your very eyes, "accompanied by the story in words." This is the sort of thing inventive children construct on their own with a shoebox, a flashlight, and a roll of shelf paper on which they've made a series of drawings to be rolled past a cutout box "screen." The advertising copy for Tell-a-Tale emphasizes its "remote control" feature. Now, however appealing this might be to the middle-aged who want to switch channels without getting up, it holds small attraction for the young. Children will become passive spectators if we force that role on them. But what really pleases is active involvement.

I remember in this connection a revealing conversation between two five-year-olds. The time was just after Christmas; my daughter and a friend were comparing treasures. "I got a talking doll," the friend announced proudly. "Did you get a talking doll?"

Joyce, looking a little dashed, shook her head. "What does your doll say?"

Her friend checked the batteries in Talking Tillie's formidable hardware stomach and turned a key. "Can you dig it?" said a recorded voice. "Let's cut a rug."

Joyce listened solemnly to all seventeen of Tillie's observations. Then she gave her baby doll a reassuring hug. "*My* doll," she whispered, "can say *anything*."

A Good Toy Is Sturdy and Well Constructed

No self-respecting cook would embark on a *Cordon Bleu* dinner without the right pans and whisks. No cabinetmaker would attempt a job using third-rate "economy" tools. Why should a child be expected to play happily (and play is the child's work) with shoddy toys? If a toy is not sturdy enough to take all the uses to which it can reasonably be put, if it has moving parts that don't move properly, attachments that don't fit, then it's worse than useless: it's frustrating, even damaging. "Play materials which are not appropriate or honest," says psychologist Ruth Hartley, "may teach a child to destroy rather than construct"; the natural response to a balky or easily broken toy is rage.

Miniature sewing machines, whether operated by hand batteries or electricity, are a prime example of the exasperating fraud. (Consider the complicated mechanism required for stitching and you'll see how unlikely it is that a machine in the four- to twenty-dollar price range will work well.) Much better, if a child wants to sew, invest in needles, fabric, good scissors— and let the electric machine wait until he's old enough for a grown-up model. A well-constructed hand printing set will in the long run give more satisfaction—and more scope—than a toy typewriter that sticks. If a two-dollar plastic telephone promises to ring, light up and deliver recorded messages, it's promising too much (to say nothing of the fact that most children would prefer to compose their own messages). Get a rugged instrument in wood, metal or polyethylene (not shatter-type) plastic and let the child's imagination supply the action.

Beware the kit. A kit, by definition, is a collection of inferior materials attractively packaged and vastly overpriced. Particularly around Christmas time, toy manufacturers go kit-crazy.

Here in one convenient package is everything you need to weave, paint, stitch leather, play doctor, bake cakes. . . . The trouble is, such bright distractions are mostly container, cardboard, directions and junk. A typical nurse kit contains a stethoscope, a thermometer, a box of Band-Aids, a pillbox (pillbox!), a cheap cotton headband, a blunt scissors, brittle plastic eyeglass frames and a cardboard watch. You can collect most of this stuff around the house—and children will enjoy thinking up ways to make a stethoscope. (Two spools and a thick cord? A length of rubber tubing and a small funnel?) Assemble your own sewing, knitting or embroidery kits from a good needlework department. Make up a carpentry kit from a hardware store and spare your child the exasperation of those prepackaged fakes—blunt saws, stiff clumsy pliers, hammers that won't drive a nail.

Children want *real* things. That's why they like playing with kitchen pots and office staplers—sturdy, well-designed equipment that works. (One way to meet this need is to buy good secondhand tools or machines. Instead of an inefficient toy typewriter—easily damaged and unfixable if broken—look for an old standard at garage sales or an office supply store that takes used machines in trade.)

A Good Toy Supports—at Least Does Not Violate—Socially Desirable Attitudes

When you give your child a toy (as, presumably, when you make any gift) you are saying, "I like this. I expect you to like it too." So the choice of toys is no frivolous matter; it's one of the many ways in which parents communicate values and standards. A good set of felt-tip markers says one thing (Express yourself); a paint-by-numbers set says something else (Do as you're told and stay inside the lines). You can give a baby doll with bottle, blanket, carriage and so forth and provide the opportunity for early loving-and-caring experiences. Or you can present your daughter with Dawn's beauty pageant, an all-American spectacular which includes doll contestants, a dinner-jacketed male escort doll, a jeweled scepter for the winner and a pink plastic stage. What view of womanhood (and real achievement) does that suggest?

Dolls are images of humanity, and that's how children see them. So I couldn't myself buy a doll that seemed deliberately grotesque, or a black doll that wasn't a dignified representation of black humanity. I also wouldn't give a ten-year-old dolls embodying the ideals of precocious teen-age sexuality: Barbie and Ken gyrating to hard-rock rhythms on a motorized stage. Before I bought Shoppin' Sheryl (who pushes a shopping cart, reaches out with magnetized hand to pluck items off shelves and then chugs along to the Check Out Counter), I'd ask myself what this compulsive shopper said to a child about the role of adult women. And then I *wouldn't* buy her.

The question of war toys is one every parent must decide for himself. According to expert opinion, cops and robbers (or cowboys and Indians) is a perfectly healthy way to work off aggression—unless, of course, a child is obsessively preoccupied with shoot-ups, will play nothing else. Certainly a toddler's zestful "Bang bang you're dead!" is innocent diversion. (*Bang* is a noise, and what is *dead?*) In some rural areas, guns are a part of daily life and so, presumably, toy rifles are as natural to children as toy tractors. If, however, parents abhor physical violence, they surely need not provide their progeny with guns. My own position is this: if my children passionately longed for a "fighting" game, I'd consider an Old West set or a medieval castle complete with moat, drawbridge, defending and attacking knights—something that could be set firmly in a historical context and supported perhaps by reading. My feelings about modern warfare wouldn't permit a gift of miniature machine guns.

Though guns may be an open question, I don't see how conscientious parents can allow, let alone give, toys that deliberately stimulate brutality and sadism. The James Bond craze brought in its wake a host of such marvels as the Laser-beam Torture Machine and the private eye doll whose trick shoe concealed a weapon in the toe. ("Swish! Sudden kick springs out knife!") Though these particular items seem to have vanished, toy stores still do a thriving business in horror. One manufacturer's line includes a bizarre variety of torture kits (Hanging Cage, Pendulum, Pain Parlor) and a do-it-yourself guillotine complete with detachable doll head and a basket to catch it in. Such toys don't even help the child rid himself of aggression because they involve no physical activity.

And what, with drug addiction a growing source of anxiety, is one to say of a candy-filled syringe that comes with a button for the owner: "Hippy Sippy says, I'll try anything once"?

A Good Toy Lends Itself to More Than One Use

The best possible toy for a child between two and ten is a very large box. A box is, according to mood, a house, a car, a boat, an airplane, a store counter, a fort, a train, a robot, a bed, a kitchen stove. It can be pushed and pulled, crawled into, carried and driven. (Note: most liquor stores will give you, free, any number of lidded cardboard cartons, exceptionally sturdy and uniform in size. Painted, they make dandy multipurpose additions to a child's room.) A box can be *anything*. In that respect it's like the natural play settings children everywhere delight in (rocks, trees, caves) and utterly unlike the typical overcomplex mass-produced toy that does only one thing.

The more a toy is prestructured (designed to be played with in a particular way), the more it inhibits imagination and creativity. How many different games can you play with a jack-in-the-box? Children can be wonderfully ingenious, mind you, in circumventing adult intentions. A friend once told me how her six-year-old had "ruined" an expensive toy, a music box that played "All around the cobbler's bench" and contained a felt weasel that popped out on cue. And how was this costly creation ruined? Why, the boy tore out the weasel to make a puppet, removed the mechanism to see how it worked—and used the stripped box for his rock collection. In a way, something of a triumph.

Adults choosing toys are often attracted by simulated realistic detail, like a fire engine with hoses, horn, brakes, jacks and ladder—none of which work. The more such empty extras a toy possesses, says David Aaron, an eminent "playscape" designer, "the more the child is forced to recognize that the toy is a bore and, what is worse, a fake. A toy of value cannot be a fake. It is a thing with possibilities."

Left to themselves, with simple materials, children will explore and expand a plaything's imaginative potential. Furthermore, a really satisfactory toy will be returned to again and again over the years, used in different ways. For example: when my first daughter was very small I bought her a Woman in the Shoe toy. This consisted of a sturdy wooden shoe on wheels, with movable tongue and holes for lacing practice. The shoe was closed at the top by a panel with various-shaped holes through which one could drop block "children." At eighteen months, Rona pulled the toy by its shoelaces, wagon style. At two, she liked dropping the children into their "house" and then taking them for rides. At three, a nursery-schooler, she worked busily with holes and cord, learning to tie shoelaces like the big kids. Seven years later, that shoe was still in use, a vehicle now for the miniature animals in a circus game she played with her little sister. The same sort of continuous adaptation occurs in the way children play with sand. A toddler mostly fills and dumps, running the grains happily through his fingers; a two-year-old will add water and pat into shapes; a six-year-old has graduated to castles and a ten-year-old may spend hours creating a sand city complete with bridges, tunnels and canals.

In general, the vaguer the symbols, the more useful the toy. That's why blocks are good, and dolls with facial expressions not too precisely defined.

A Good Toy Affords Challenge
Without Frustration

My daughter was six when a friend, knowing her interest in handiwork, gave her a Swedish loom. A small tabletop model of beautiful white birch, it was a perfect miniature of the treadle looms used by craftsmen, with a geared crank to shift threads after each shuttle. Joyce looked at the bright yarns, the photographs of scarves and belts in the accompanying booklet. What joy! But threading the loom was an impossible task for six-year-old fingers. Even after we did that for her, she found the actual weaving too difficult and too slow. The loom, with its half-inch of uncertainly woven fabric, gathered dust. When I last saw it, it had been dismantled and the slats used for a dollhouse bed.

Two years later, when Joyce was eight, that loom would have been perfect, challenging without intimidating. Offered prematurely, it served only to discourage and to convince the recipient that weaving was dull work. Children enjoy complexity, but the complexity must not be *overwhelming*. The trick in choosing toys is to find those that, in Lawrence Frank's nice phrase, are "just on the margin of the child's growing capacities," that excite his imagination and stretch his skills. It is wasting a child's time to give him playthings that demand a sophistication beyond his years—or not to give him opportunities for using and extending those skills he already possesses. B. F. Skinner has shown that pigeons learn best through success, that is, by performing a series of tasks carefully graduated in difficulty so that mistakes are minimized. Though many of Skinner's pigeon-principles seem questionable as applied to human beings, this one is instructive. Children move forward most confidently if, at every step of the way, they encounter projects just difficult *enough.*

A Good Toy Fits *Human* Needs, Not Rigid Stereotypes of Masculine and Feminine

During the first years of life, boys and girls obviously have the same developmental needs and parents, recognizing this, generally offer the same toys to both. After all, there's nothing either girlish or boyish about a cradle gym. When the child reaches three or four, though, there's a tendency to choose toys along pink or blue lines. Now girls get tea-sets and dolls and pianos and nurse kits and cooking implements; boys get wheeled vehicles of all sorts, carpentry sets, drums and doctor kits and construction toys. Is it any wonder that, ten years later, so many boys prove deficient in verbal skills, so many girls are weak in problem solving—and in personal ambition? (In the year when a woman first entered the United States presidential primaries, a major toy manufacturer brought out "a different game for girls eight to thirteen: "What Shall I Be? The exciting game of career girls." Options presented are ballerina, teacher, nurse, model, actress, airline stewardess—all thoroughly safe conventional female roles (several downright unrealistic for the average girl).

One fruitful result of the Women's Liberation movement has been a greatly increased awareness of the way in which young children are conditioned and limited by narrow, artificial sex-role divisions. Why shouldn't a boy play with stuffed animals and dolls? He needs to express love and tenderness as much as any girl does. Since, chances are, he will one day be a father but will not be an astronaut, he might better practice with a baby bathinette than with a space capsule. Hairdressing, design and cookery are respected male professions, but from the toys commonly given to little boys one might suppose they were all destined for truck-driving careers. As for girls: they face a world of greatly expanded opportunity. There's scarcely a trade or profession, now, from which women are barred. If girls are to take advantage of this new freedom, they need to play with (try out) chemistry sets, hammers, microscopes, electrical apparatus . . . the full range of human skill-developers. Without that experience, how can they meaningfully choose? (Elizabeth Koontz, of the U. S. Department of Labor, has suggested that women would be particularly well suited as upholsterers, optical mechanics, tool-and-die makers, repair specialists for machines and electrical appliances. Few girls have play experiences that would in any way lead to such occupations.)

In the long run, boys and girls have the same goals: to become whole persons, participating fully in the life around them and making their most fruitful contribution to society. So they need much the same kinds of toys.

A Good Toy Is Safe

This seems almost too obvious to mention. Since, however, stores still stock darts that blind, caps that explode, BB guns that maim, and electrical gadgets that shock or burn, it perhaps needs emphasis. Particularly with chemical and electrical equipment, suggested age levels should be carefully studied. Even then, common sense may rule out the manufacturer's notion of appropriateness. (One plastic casting set currently on the market reaches an internal temperature of 660 degrees—and is recommended for children ages five to eight.)

Of course, some toys perfectly "safe" in themselves are not safe for younger children. Bright wooden beads for stringing, safe for a four-year-old, might be lethal for a two-year-old given to putting objects in his mouth.

Age and Stage List of Suggested Play Materials

Playthings are listed under the earliest age at which they become useful. Of course some, like blocks, will be enjoyed for years.

THE FIRST YEAR

Here, in what Piaget calls the sensorimotor phase of human development, the infant progresses from instinctual reflexes (closing the hand around an object placed in it, for example) to coordinated, controlled muscle movements. Through exploration of his environment he proceeds to "practice play," delighted repetition of an action which he himself has caused. So he needs:

Things to Look At
  Crib mobiles and bright dangling objects
  Wood or plastic-framed steel mirror
  Cloth or heavy cardboard picture books

Things to Touch, Grasp, Shake, Manipulate
  Rattles (4 months+)
  Small soft animals or dolls (4 months+)
  Soft rubber squeeze toys (1 year)
  Ball (woolly, or foam with contoured shape) (4 months+)
  Plastic disks on chain, plastic spoons (4 months+)
  Smooth clothespin
  Household sponge
  Floating bath toys (6 months+)
  Plastic beads and blocks
  Nesting and stacking color toys (9 months+)

Things to Listen to
Ticking clock
Music box or musical mobile
Wind chimes

Things to Taste and Chew
Rubber or plastic teething rings (5 months)
Hard rubber bones and rings from pet department

TWELVE TO TWENTY-FOUR MONTHS

A creeping, crawling, staggering, walking, climbing period in the course of which, to use Erik Erikson's terms, the child either develops basic trust and confidence or, if discouraged from active inquiry, lapses into self-doubt. Now he wants:

Things That Move
Pull and push toys, preferably those that clatter or jangle
Large, foot-propelled riding toys (tractor, locomotive, horse, etc.)
Small rocking chair

Things to Build with and Manipulate
Nesting blocks
Drop-the-block-through-the-hole type toys
Pounding bench (hammer and pegs)
Mud and sand equipment (pail, shovel, spoons, scoops, molds)
Bean bag

Things to Love
Soft dolls and stuffed animals

TWO TO THREE YEARS

The child adds to earlier interests a passion for "symbolic play," just-pretending, which helps him assimilate new knowledges (as practice play helped him assimilate new physical skills).

Things for Make-Believe

Dolls, doll accessories (blankets, bed, carriage, tea set, telephone)

Housekeeping materials (toy broom, dusters, pots and pans, little table and chairs, iron)

Wheeled vehicles (fire engine, cars, trucks large and small)

Dress-up clothes

Things to Make the Fingers Work

Large beads to string ($2\frac{1}{2}$ years+)

Books and toys that involve buttoning, lacing, fitting interlocking parts (3)

Good sturdy blocks (2+)

Blunt scissors and construction paper (3)

Small rubber balls

Dress-me dolls with zippers, buckles, snaps, etc.

Blackboard and chalk

Crayons, fingerpaints, clay

Soap bubbles

Thinking Things

Wooden puzzles with big pieces ($2\frac{1}{2}$+)

Lift-out puzzles with easily identifiable objects that can be removed, played with and refitted

Lotto cards for simple matching (3)

Plastic or metal letters and numbers; magnetized ones are nice to use on the refrigerator door ($2\frac{1}{2}$+)

THREE TO FOUR

Three is a plateau of relative calm, cheerfulness, cooperation and sociability. The three-year-old has discovered that patience sometimes works better than furious attack; he knows the power of language. Now he will work, serious-careful, at any skill promising a surer control of his world. He wants materials he can use in his own way (sand, clay, blocks, wood) and also those he can use in distinctively adult ways. Carrying over many of the toddler toys, he also enjoys:

Felt pens
Poster paints, fingerpaints, easel
Color and shape and design materials (bits of interesting-shaped plastic or felt that adhere to a larger picture surface, pregummed paper mosaic pieces)
Block-printing equipment
Solid child-size hammer, large nails, soft wood
Wagon, wheelbarrow, tricycle
Simple music makers (drum, tambourine, castanets, triangle, rhythm sticks, maracas)
Phonograph and records
Materials for playing house, store, train

FOUR TO FIVE

Four is off-balance again, struggling to be "big." Four is tempestuous and extreme (Gesell's label is "out of bounds"), battering at whatever opposes his will. His imagination and energy reach new heights. He needs play materials that take up this energy and direct it constructively.

Workbench with saw, vise, screwdriver, wrench
Fit-together construction toys (Tinkertoy, etc.)
Miniature people, animals, vehicles for block play
Dress-ups for particular occupations (nurse, policeman, astronaut, fireman, carpenter)
Board games, simple (Snakes and Ladders)
Puzzles, picture lotto
Cooking equipment
Kite

Wheels, all kinds: trucks, bulldozers, tractors, trains
Scooter
Punching bag
Flashlight

FIVE TO SIX

The kindergartener is a Responsible Citizen. He handles tools, problems, his own emotions with new assurance; he makes plans. For him, the best play involves other children and a clear relationship with the real world. New strong interests are:

Science materials (magnet, magnifying glass, flashlight, stethoscope, clocks and cars with see-through mechanism)
Cameras, simple Instamatic
Modeling materials that dry or bake to a permanent finish
Dolls with convincing accessories
Dollhouses with furniture, people
Miniature forts, filling stations, farms
Crafts involving small-muscle coordination (loop looms, spool knitting, simple sewing, stringing beads)
Jigsaw puzzles
Skipping rope, roller skates, ice skates

SIX TO SEVEN

Six is active and social, eager for those skills which confer status in the group. "Toys" become less important than the paraphernalia of sports and games.

Skipping rope
Two-wheel bicycle
Baseball equipment
Fishing tackle
Jacks, marbles, tops
Board games, dominoes

Doctor and nurse accessories
Trains with tracks, switches, signals
Paper dolls
Puppets and puppet theater
Marionettes
Pedometer, stilts
Croquet set
Gyroscope
Field glasses
Craft materials, moderately advanced (Formafilm)
Simple Erector sets

SEVEN TO EIGHT

Seven-year-olds like systems and rules, admire physical prowess. They engage in elaborate imaginative play, more sustained than earlier "let's pretend" and welcome realistic equipment suitable for astronauts or queens. A few intense interests often now replace the earlier range of activities.

Costumes and accessories of all sorts
Board games depending on skill as well as luck (checkers, Monopoly)
Card games
Puzzles and skill-testers, yo-yo
Simple magic tricks
Walkie-talkie
Collector's equipment (coin folders, butterfly net, stamp books)
Model airplanes

EIGHT TO TEN

This is an age of passionate interest in how-things-work and how-to-make-things. It's the time, as Ruth Hartley says, for "table-top physics and kitchen chemistry." Play materials now should call forth energy, inventiveness, independence and orderly, systematic activity.

Craft materials, fairly advanced (weaving, embroidery, leatherwork, metalcraft, woodcarving)
More difficult board games (Parcheesi, chess)
Magic stunts and tricks
Compass
Materials for electromagnetic experiments
Plywood, coping saw, plane
Plastic and paper sculpture materials
Telescope, microscope
Pocket knife
Sports supplies (tennis, Ping-pong, badminton)
Model car kits

Play Is Serious Business

AARON, DAVID with BONNIE WINAWER, *Child's Play*, Harper, 1965. A lively, engaging and insightful book on the role of play in the child's life, with particular emphasis on playgrounds and their equipment. The author is a sculptor and designer; splendid photographs.

ARNOLD, ARNOLD, *Your Child's Play*, Essandess, 1968. A toy and industrial designer, the author brings to his study of play a concrete knowledge both of children and of the play value built into (or out of) common toys.

ASSOCIATION FOR CHILDHOOD EDUCATION INTERNATIONAL: pamphlets available from ACEI, 3615 Wisconsin Ave., N.W., Washington, D.C. 20016.

> *Basic Propositions for Early Childhood Education*, 1965.
> *Characteristics of Early Childhood Education*, 1968.
> *Creating with Materials for Work and Play*, 1969.
> *Early Childhood: Crucial Years for Learning*, 1966.
> *Kindergarten*, 1967.
> *Play—Children's Business; Guide to Selection of Toys and Games*, 1963.
> *Play Is Valid*, 1968.
> *Playgrounds for City Children*, 1969.
> *What Are Kindergartens For?*, 1961.
> *What Are Nursery Schools For?*, 1964.

BANCROFT, JESSIE H., *Games*, Macmillan, 1955.

BOETTIGER, ELIZABETH, *Children Play, Indoors & Out*, Dutton, 1938.

CAPLAN, FRANK and THERESA, *The Power of Play*, Doubleday, 1973. The founders of Creative Playthings apply their philosophy of play to a consideration of children's toys.

CRAFT, RUTH, *Play School Ideas*, British Broadcasting Corporation, 1971. A bookload of home adventures for the young —finger plays, craft projects, games, experiments. If you don't know how to make a junkopotamus, or a dried-coconut snowstorm shaker, or an aquarium or a bird pudding . . . you need this book.

DARROW, HELEN F., *Independent Activities for Creative Learning*, Columbia University, 1961.

DATTNER, RICHARD, *Design for Play*, Van Nostrand, 1969. Written out of the special knowledges of a playground and play-equipment designer. Erudite, readable, with good photographs.

DE MILLE, RICHARD, *Put Your Mother on the Ceiling: Children's Imagination Games*, Walker, 1967.

FARINA, ALBERT M., SOL H. FURBER, and JOSEPH M. SMITH, *Growth Through Play*, Prentice-Hall, 1959.

GARRISON, CHARLOTTE M., *Permanent Play Materials for Young Children*, Scribner, 1926.

GERI, FRANK H., *Illustrated Games and Rhythms for Children: Primary Grades*, Prentice-Hall, 1955.

GREGG, ELIZABETH M. and members of the Boston Children's Medical Center, *What to Do When There's Nothing to Do*, Dell, 1968. A real (and inexpensive) treasure house: 601 tested play ideas from infancy on up. Things for rainy days, sick-a-bed days, cranky child and cranky mother days, indoors and out.

GROSS, KARL, *The Play of Man*, Appleton, 1901.

HARTLEY, RUTH E., and ROBERT M. GOLDENSON, *The Complete Book of Children's Play*, Crowell, 1970. A splendidly helpful guide not only to toys and play materials, but to the whole spectrum of experiences that enrich a growing child's life. Includes a useful bibliography of books, records, hobby information sources and parent reading.

HUIZINGA, J., *Homo Ludens*, Beacon, 1955. The philosophy and psychology of play.

JOHNSON, HARRIET, *The Art of Block Building*, Day, 1933.

JOHNSON, JUNE, *Home Play for the Preschool Child*, Harper, 1957.

KEPLER, HAZEL, *The Child and His Play*, Funk, 1952.

KRAUS, RICHARD, *Play Activities for Boys and Girls*, McGraw, 1957.

LEHMAN, H. C., and P. A. WITTY, *The Psychology of Play Activities*, Barnes, 1927.

LOWENFELD, MARGARET, *Play in Childhood*, Wiley, 1967. An analysis of children's play, supported with illustrations from the author's experience as Psychological Director of the Institute of Child Psychology, London.

MATTERSON, ELIZABETH, *Play and Playthings for the Preschool Child*, Penguin, 1967. A clear, practical and well-illustrated book on active and imaginative play, with instructions for making all kinds of playthings from simple materials.

MELLOR, EDNA, *Education Through Experience in the Infant School Years*, Basil Blackwell, 1967.

MILLAR, SUSANNA, *The Psychology of Play*, Penguin, 1968.

MOLONY, EILEEN, *How To Form a Playgroup*, British Broadcasting Corporation, 1970.

MULAC, MARGARET E., *Fun and Games*, Harper, 1956.

NATIONAL ASSOCIATION FOR THE EDUCATION OF YOUNG CHILDREN, pamphlets available from NAEYC, 1834 Connecticut Ave., N.W., Washington, D.C.
  One Giant Step, 1968.
  Play and Playgrounds, 1970.
  The Good Life for Infants and Toddlers, 1970.
  Water, Sand and Mud as Play Materials, 1959.

NATIONAL KINDERGARTEN ASSOCIATION: *pamphlets available from* NKA, 8 West 40th St., New York, N.Y., 10018.

About Kindergartens.
Kindergarten Teaching: The Open Door.
Stevie's Kindergarten Day.
We Are Only Five Once.
What! Science in the Kindergarten?

OPIE, IONA and PETER, *Children's Games in Street and Playground*, Clarendon Press, 1969. A rich collection of traditional games as played in all parts of the British Isles.

RADLER, D. H., and NEWELL C. KEPHART, *Success Through Play*, Harper, 1960. How to help children develop perceptual and motor skills through games.

ROGERS, JAMES E., *Child and Play*, Appleton, 1932.

SLOVENKO, RALPH, and J. KNIGHT, *Motivations in Play, Games and Sports*, Charles Thomas, 1967.

WYLIE, JOANNE, *A Creative Guide for Preschool Teachers*, Western, 1966.

4

"I Made It Myself!"—
Paint, Crayons, Clay and So Forth

"Art," a friend once said to me, "is a frill. It's fine if you're talented. But my son is the scientific type. I want him to learn something *useful*."

This attitude, very common, stems from a basic misconception about the place of art in a child's life. In providing art experiences for your child, you are not trying to make him a painter or a sculptor; you are satisfying a fundamental human impulse. I think of a photograph in Kenneth Jameson's *Art and the Young Child:* a twenty-month-old girl, naked as she was born, crouching before the huge pad of paper she has just found on the lawn. There are other treasures too, new to her but not at all intimidating—brushes, paint. Can of paint in one hand, brush in the other—fascinated, absorbed, and confident, she is painting away.

The impulse *to be a maker* manifests itself early and dies hard. Adults who profess indifference to the arts flock to hobby stores for macrame supplies and beads to string. My friend the art-is-a-frill critic owns a bottle cutter. ("Transform ordinary bottles into beautiful drinking glasses.") Now it is certainly not economy which sends hobbyists to the workbench; the average do-it-yourself mosaic table costs rather more than a commercial model. Nor is it, I think, a desire for the finished product, the stenciled wooden box or shaky mobile. What tempts is the activity itself. The desire to create is as deep-rooted as the desire to learn, and both are aspects of the same need, instinctive as breathing—the need to experience.

"When your child's art is frustrated," writes Viktor Lowenfeld, "all the qualities which may later make him another Edison or Marconi or Einstein may become inhibited." Paint, clay, wood, cloth, paper are all means by which the child explores and organizes his world. Drawing his kitten, he experiences warmth, softness, fluff, quick movement, sweet furry smell; he says what he could never express with a preschooler's vocabulary. He paints fear in a haircut, joy at a birthday party, a whirl of conflicting emotions in the portrait of baby sister. Every "successful" art experience (the success is in the realized experience, not the final product) increases his sureness and mastery. So fostering a child's art is, as Lowenfeld insists, one important way of promoting "his growth and development, his ability to adjust to new situations, in fact, his happiness as a human being."

How can experiences at an easel, for instance, promote happiness? Well, consider first of all a supercautious four-year-old. Perhaps he has never painted before. If he comes from a home where neatness is important, he's understandably nervous. (Paint spills. Brushes drip.) Cautiously, he reaches for a brush, dips it into the nearest container and touches it gently to paper. A spot, a red spot. Amazing. He tries again. No one stops him. Two, three spots. He swings his arm, and there's a wide red stroke; back and forth, a glorious spreading patch of color. *He* made it. He can unmake it too, scrubbing the brush recklessly over the entire page, obliterating lines and spots in a red sea. These initial discoveries are happy accidents. But next time he approaches the easel, he's in command. Now he *chooses* his color and *directs* his strokes. "This is a bulldozer," he says happily, "scooping up dirt." No matter that adults see only an amorphous red blot. He *feels* a bulldozer.

Or consider the timid child, the one for whom playgrounds are agony because he's less well coordinated and less confident than the rest. He paints the high slide, which he has often approached but never conquered. The pictured slide, two slashing strokes, is pure terror: an impossibly steep incline, a precipitous drop. Now, tongue nervously licking his lower lip, he paints a figure struggling up the ladder. The ladder is huge, the figure tiny. It has no legs to speak of, but the hands are carefully drawn, with extra clutching fingers. Painting this private nightmare, the child seems overwhelmed with anxiety. Then he stands back, contemplates his work with obvious satisfaction, and scampers off. Does he rush out and conquer the slide? Not necessarily. Probably not. But in expressing his fear, he has partially conquered that. It is unexpressed fears that can cripple and, through the energy used up in repression, stunt creative growth. "The emotional intensity of a young child's life," says a British government report on infant schools, "reaches its zenith about the end of the third year. At this age, every emotion the child undergoes is felt with a vividness and strength that is never again experienced either in later childhood or in adult life." His rages, terrors, jealousy and love far outrun his command of language—but they speak with remarkable clarity in his art.

Though art may be a kind of therapy—and, indeed, is often so used with emotionally disturbed children—it's much more than release. It's a special, feeling kind of learning. Discovering how to make an oval head symbol, or how to roll clay into a snake, is like acquiring a new word. And it becomes, like a new word, an added means of control, a way of assimilating experience. Working at collages, a young artist learns about texture. With mobiles, he makes discoveries about size, shape, balance; what pleases the eye and what confuses. He learns boldness with fingerpaint, patience with printing and whittling. In all of the arts, he learns respect for materials. (He can't use transparent watercolor as if it were poster paint, or papier-mâché as if it were clay.) And in all the arts, if he is wisely guided, he learns the most important human lesson: that he can produce something of value by finding and expressing *himself*. Not by copying. Not by doing what he's told. But by saying, in whatever medium he chooses, "This is what *I* see, feel, imagine. THIS IS ME."

At the very mention of "guidance," some parents will be alarmed. "But I don't know anything about art." "I can't draw a straight line. How could I *guide?*" Take comfort. To launch a child in the creative arts, you need no special knowledges, only an informed attitude—and an awareness of what *not* to do. Parents can help in these ways.

Provide Good Materials and Tools

Children need a place to work and things to work with. It's as simple as that.

If your child has a room of his own with a scrubbable floor, that's marvelous. You can then provide him with a standing easel (three feet is about the right height) with a rack at the lower edge to hold paint. If an easel's out of the question, use a sheet of plywood leaning against the back of a straight chair. A low work table is very handy—for clay, cut-and-paste, woodworking . . . and indeed for painting too. Children who apply paint very generously often find that it runs at an easel and will control it better on a flat surface. Low shelves or a set of drawers should be arranged so that materials are easy to get at and well ordered. Nothing is more discouraging to enthusiasm than a jumbled-up collection of broken crayons stuck with bits of plasticene, or paper that's crumpled. Cutlery dividers—ordinary small boxes, for that matter—will keep the chalk separate from the felt pens and the miscellaneous collage materials. With encouragement, a child will come to take pride in keeping his art materials in some sort of order and ready for use. A stool, a wastebasket, a painting smock (Father's old shirt, worn backwards) and the stage is set.

This is the ideal. If a permanent work area is impossible, next best is a free corner of the kitchen, with one spot—almost everyone can spare *one* cupboard or drawer—given over to art materials. Another, less attractive possibility, is a carton of supplies and tools that can be brought out as needed.

Children vary as much in art readiness as in physical readiness. So new materials should be offered cautiously at first. One three-year-old, given fingerpaint, will swirl it purposefully on paper, enjoying the good feeling and the astonishing bold results. Another smears it over his arms and face, puddles it on the floor, maybe tastes to see if it's as good as it looks. He's not ready to paint—though he might use crayons constructively. Of two same-age children, one uses clay to roll or model, another breaks it up and throws the pieces about. Certainly children should be encouraged to use materials in new ways—using, say, the tip of a brush handle to get a fine line, or combining crayons with chalk. Common sense will tell you when the child's experimenting reveals not imagination but simple immaturity.

In choosing art materials, a parent enjoys a special advantage over all but the most perceptive teachers: knowledge of this particular child. An unusually aggressive youngster may need, really need clay—to pound, squeeze, roll and twist. Thick rich poster paint will be good for him too; probably not chalk (it breaks easily) or pencil. A tense rigid child will not enjoy fingerpaint, but may be loosened up with collages (where there's a nice balance of clean-cut and messy paste). Ultimately, as children grow in the joy of making, they should have a chance to experiment with all kinds of materials and tools (not just brushes for paint, but sponges, lollipop sticks, potato printers). It goes without saying that materials and tools should be in good condition. You wouldn't attempt to cut out a dress pattern on a coffee table, with manicure scissors. How can a child work happily with a brush that sheds bristles or clay that's crumbly-dry? Poster paint should be creamy and deep-toned, fingerpaint slippery and smooth. Fabric bits for collage should be clean and ironed, with no suggestion of ragbag.

Remember That the Child Needs Freedom—
Within Limits

Children are born free. In a totally accepting environment, they unfold as naturally as Japanese water flowers. Since, however, few parents are perfectly accepting (or perfectly patient), even a three-year-old is likely to have acquired his share of doubts, inhibitions, self-consciousness and fear. By three he's heard, "Don't eat with your fingers" "Would you try not to make so much noise?" "Look at the mess you're making!" "*Finish up!*" Now these injunctions, however necessary to civilized life, all work against the art spirit. So the child given paint or clay often needs reassurance. He needs to feel that in this activity there is no *right* or *wrong*.

Natalie Robinson Cole, a gifted teacher, describes her methods of freeing the art that is in the child. Before she introduces a class to painting, she talks a little about old-fashioned art teaching aimed at getting children to draw an apple exactly as it looks. That sort of literal representation, she insists, has nothing to do with real painting. "Our picture is beautiful only as we go *way deep down inside* and bring it up *our own honest way*. We can paint a beautiful picture without painting *anything* —just working with line and color!" So her pupils begin with great joyous swooshes of the brush, splashes and dashes of pure color that communicates what they feel. Only very gradually do they move on to painting what they *see*. But though this activity is wonderfully free, it's disciplined too. A child choosing a color is cautioned, "Wait until you find the one that gives you just the right feeling inside." Good work habits are gently suggested. "By the way, why should we be careful not to spill our color?" Though the emphasis is on freedom, "letting it come as easy as breathing," there's a calm assumption of control too. "Let's make our lines *say* something. Then we won't have to pile a lot of lines on top of one another hoping to *fool* people."

Liberating natural art impulses does not mean *anything goes*. The child should learn respect for his tools. Brushes must be washed after each new color and wiped on a cloth; if not, reds and blues turn muddy brown. Felt pens must be recapped promptly so as not to dry out. Modeling clay, unless oil-based (like plasticene), has to be carefully wrapped in plastic or it turns brittle. Children who begin this way can, within a few years, handle quite sophisticated equipment. Mrs. Cole's pupils, for instance, in the fourth grade produce stunning block prints using a razor-edge knife. Listening to her crisp, firm instructions, one understands why, in all her years of teaching, there have been no linocutting accidents. "Feel this linoleum. Now feel your hand. Which is harder? If this cutter will go through the linoleum like nobody's business, what do you think it will do to your hand?" So, *"the left hand must go behind the cutter!"* (And anybody who forgets has cut his last piece of linoleum in *that* class.)

Good work habits in the arts are like good work habits in any other area—with one significant exception. No child should ever be pushed to finish a project. Adults, accustomed to thinking in terms of end results, look for products. They would like that painting completed (nice for Aunt Ethel's Christmas present) —or they imagine that if it isn't completed, the child's moral fiber is somehow weakened. (He's developing slipshod ways.) Nonsense. A child is finished when he's lost interest, when he's tired, when the work satisfies him, when he's learned as much as he can from this activity, when he's carried the project as far as he can . . . in short, when he has had a complete *experience*. A very young child, after half an hour's hard painting, will sometimes obliterate everything he's done. That's all right too.

When my first daughter was three, she produced around Christmas time a lovely drawing of Mary and "the baby Jesus lying sweetly in the hay." What a fine greeting card that would make, I thought. How *impressive*. I sat Rona down at the table with a folded stack of colored paper and, like the greedy miller in *Rumpelstiltskin* ordering the farmer's daughter to spin straw into gold, I put her to work. The first few cards came easily enough—though with a distinct falling off in verve. By the time we got to card number ten—I blush to remember—she was in tears and I, all perspective lost, was imploring, "Please, dear, just one more bundle of hay!"

It was a long time before Rona reached for her crayons again.

Beware of Models, Copying, Demonstration

Every child is unique. I've said that before, but it bears repeating. One great value of the arts is that they offer each child a means to express his unique experience, to work out what he has seen, thought, felt. How can adult models help him to do that? What coloring books and demonstrations can do—often with melancholy efficiency—is pervert and ultimately destroy the child's own way. He stops dreaming purple cows. He learns how to make the "nice picture" we've all seen a thousand times: box house with four windows, central chimney and curly smoke; stick-figure child rigid on one side, tree or flower on the other. Blue strip above (sky); green strip of grass below.

Years ago, Viktor Lowenfeld, a pioneer in children's art education, carried out an intriguing experiment in the influence of adult stereotypes. A small group of children was invited to draw birds—any birds. The result was a marvelous variety of wobbly, feathery, winged and beaked creatures original and live. Next the children were given coloring books in which birds were represented by the familiar V symbol of abstracted flight. Two weeks later the same group was asked, once again, to draw birds. Wiser now, subdued to one color, most turned out V's.

"But—" a parent may object, "my child *loves* coloring books."

Of course. Coloring books provide easy, mindless activity—minimum investment, maximum result. In that respect, they're a little like TV. But it's a rare child who wouldn't give up Saturday morning cartoons for a chance *to do something real* with his family. And it's hard to imagine a child who wouldn't get more satisfaction from making his own picture than from filling in the spaces of someone else's. The habitual use of coloring books and paint-by-numbers sets creates a crippling dependency. The child comes to believe that he can't draw; he loses the confidence and joy that comes with truly creative work. This is equally true of mosaic kits, preprinted cloth doll materials with stuffing and the "right" embroidery thread and clay that comes with cookie cutter molds.

What about helping children solve a particular art problem? "My car doesn't look right." This sort of lament, incidentally, is not likely to come from a three- or four-year-old whose independence has been encouraged. When he moves his brush, he *feels* car and as far as he's concerned, he's *painted* car. But around six or seven, children become more aware of the usual expectations, art as representation, and so, sometimes, worried about their lack of skill.

As an example of apt handling in such situations, I recall a kindergarten clay-table crisis. A five-year-old who had been struggling with his clay ball suddenly burst into tears. "I can't make my turtle!" Now I don't doubt that his teacher could have modeled a turtle for him in three minutes. The child would then, probably, have played happily with the turtle, either forgetting that *he* wanted to make one or concluding that he couldn't produce anything nearly so fine. (Meantime, all the other five-year-olds would have been demanding turtles.) The teacher didn't touch the clay. "Do you have a turtle at home?" she asked. The child nodded, snuffling. "Show me what he's like. *Show me with your hands*." The child stopped snuffling. His fingers described an arc in the air. "He has a round humpy back, like this. . . . And his head pokes *here*" (small scooping motion) "and his tail pokes *here*." "What happens if you turn him over?" The child lay down on the floor and mimed frantically wiggling appendages. "Oh, that's lovely!" his teacher said. "*Now* make him." The result was a comic triumph, a clay turtle so lively one almost expected him to move.

If you help a child do what, unassisted, he might do on his own, you deprive him of a growing experience. Only one kind of assistance, it seems to me, is really justified: the demonstration of techniques. Most children have to be shown how to mix colors (though the child who discovers on his own that blue and yellow make green experiences a moment of pure magic). They aren't likely to hit on the technique of using slip (liquid clay) to attach pieces of clay sculpture, or on the use of a wire armature. In general, no help should be offered unless the child, temporarily stymied in his work, asks for it. If he's a reader, he can perhaps be referred to a practical arts and crafts book (see Bibliography). If a demonstration is really in order—say, the use of coils to build up a clay pot—a parent might roll a few sample coils, then scrunch them up and let the young artist proceed on his own.

See That the Child Has an Abundance of Rich Experiences

"Children cannot create out of a vacuum," says Natalie Cole. "They must have something to say and be fired to say it." The child who asks, "What shall I draw?" may or may not suffer from a poverty of imagination. Almost certainly he entertains narrow, rigid notions of the subjects suitable for art. Give him a topic— *Paint a tree*—and he may never get out of the woods. What he needs is the assurance that anything which interests him is material for art—as for conversation. (No child ever asks, "What shall I talk about?") Finding a broken bird's egg on the grass, skipping double dutch, carrying groceries home. . . . A quarrel, a playground triumph, a new teacher, a case of mumps, a wrecking ball swinging, a scary moment in *Treasure Island*—these are all *subjects*. The way to stimulate a child's imagination is to insure a variety of rich, active experiences.

Sometimes young children need a little help getting started. Donald and Barbara Herberholz, in a collection of "motivations" for drawing, painting and modeling, suggest five useful types of stimuli: Direct Happenings, Roundabout Happenings, Imagination Stretchers, Point-of-View Changers and Cluster Activities. A Direct Happening is something the child *does*. He plays Indian, he goes to the zoo, he flies a kite or picks flowers. A Roundabout is experience at second hand, but not necessarily the less vivid for that: he watches a film about spiders, listens to a recorded Christmas carol. Imagination Stretchers are fantasy flights (If I were a sky diver) and Point-of-View Changers are deliberate exercises in the unusual (drawing on a long horizontal strip of paper, on a tall vertical strip, on a circle, on concrete with chalk . . .). Cluster Activities are joint projects, like a "summer fun" mural, with different children contributing their private images of joy.

With any one of these motivations, a child may work more zestfully, live more intensely into the experience, if the parent asks leading questions. On the Direct Happening, "walking in the rain," for example, the Herberholzes suggest focusing questions like Did you carry an umbrella? And did the wind tug at it? What color is your raincoat? How about boots? Did you splash in puddles? Stick your tongue out to catch a raindrop? And so on. Long before you get to the last question, the paintbrush will be moving.

Criticism and Praise: Don't Impose Adult Standards of Neatness and Realism

In the early years, a young artist doesn't set out to reproduce the visible world. He paints to paint. I think of the parent who observed his five-year-old covering a sheet of paper with purple dots. "What are you painting?" he asked. "Spots." (Busily working, brush tipped to paper.) Father persisted. "Yes, but what *are* they?" The child turned, and with an expression in which compassion, amazement and impatience were marvelously blended repeated, "Spots, Daddy. SPOTS."

Often, as a child works, a subject appears by happy accident. Here's a transcript from a three-year-old monologue at the easel. "This is all red. I'm making it redder and redder. Look, here's a worm. I just think it's a caterpillar worm. No, it's a lawnmower and it's mowing. I'm going to paint the whole paper. This is my wagon . . ." and so on, as new strokes produced fresh possibilities. Asking a three-year-old, "What are you painting?" is quite beside the point. He won't know till he's through. Even the often-recommended, tactful, "Tell me about your picture" may create uncomfortable pressure. (If he could tell you about it, the child probably wouldn't be painting at all. He'd be talking.) Children are easily confused or discouraged by the adult expectation that a picture should mean or look like something. At two or three, a child manipulates paint and clay as materials, not symbols. If you want to comment on a swirl of color, the safest remark is something like, "What a lovely sunshiny yellow!" or "I like the way you swoop your brush." In other words, concentrate on the child's experience rather than on the finished work.

Gradually, out of the young child's swirls and scribbles there emerge recognizable forms. Free arm movements create ovals which the artist discovers with surprise and pleasure. A *head*. He learns to *make* ovals, by design, and soon his additions—random eyes and mouths—mark a new sophistication. He's making *people* (mostly himself). Next, arms and legs shoot out of the face. Somewhere between ages three and five, a line joining the two legs creates a body. At this point some parents may be tempted to move in. Time to give the little fellow a helping hand. "No, Stevie, the body should be bigger than the head. And grass is green, not purple." This sort of criticism is quite beside the point. The child doesn't aim at photographic likeness (and couldn't get it if he did). Color, size and proportion are *feelings* to him. So a little girl's painted wedding may show an enormous bride and a groom no bigger than her bouquet. In terms of the way she feels about weddings, that's about right.

Should a parent, then, never make suggestions? That depends. If a child habitually works very small, scrunching up a drawing in the center of his paper, you might encourage him to work more freely. (I like Natalie Cole's formula, "Fill the whole space beautifully!") If he paints the same subject over and over, offering him a new medium—say, wood or clay rather than paint—may stimulate new experiences. (Not, "Why don't you do something else for a change?") If his drawings seem always slaphappy, unrealized, you can ask questions that prompt him to feel more deeply into the picture. "Is there a cake with candles at this birthday party? How about balloons?" Generally speaking, children will ask for the help they need. When a ten-year-old is ready to grow in a new direction—"How can I make the trees look far away?"—that's the moment to offer elementary comments on perspective ("the farther away things are, the smaller they look") or direct him to the library for a good drawing book.

Encouraging a child's art is always appropriate. Judging and applauding, however, is tricky. Children love praise, naturally; but if every daub and scribble is greeted with cries of joy, they soon lose interest in their parents' fake delight. To be meaningful, praise must be judicious. And how can you be judicious if you really know nothing about art, have never before paid attention to children's work and honestly feel that all-those-paintings-look-alike-to-me? I have two suggestions. One is, take the time to look through any collection of children's drawings and paintings. (Most books listed at the end of this chapter are gloriously illustrated.) That will give you an idea of what can be expected at various ages, and of what children's art looks like at its most exciting. The other course is simpler, more intuitive. If a picture or a clay sculpture makes you smile with pure pleasure, if something about it makes you feel, "That's my kid, all right. It's *just* like him!"—then that's a time to clap.

A last caution. Excessive praise, even if well founded, can be damaging. A child who sees that Mummy is thrilled with his bicycle picture may switch to an assembly-line production, more and more bicycles. Some children are made dependent by praise, working for that rather than the joy of doing. Some become overly competitive. A good test is: does this recognition and enthusiasm strengthen the child, help him to go forward in his own best way—or does it actually distort and weaken his creative drive?

A Guide to Arts and Crafts for Children

It's customary to make distinctions between art (imaginative activity for its own sake) and craft (which emphasizes the discipline of a particular material and aims at an end product). So painting is commonly called an art and pottery or photography a craft. But anyone familiar with the photographs of Ansel Adams, or with Mayan pots, knows that these constitute art of a high order—while much earnest painting is not art at all. So for purposes of this chapter, I've made no attempt to distinguish. As practiced by the creative child, embroidery, collage and puppetry may all be arts.

Painting

BEGINNINGS

A child can enjoy painting experiences before he's old enough to handle real paint. Between two and three, he's perfectly happy painting with water and a large (one-inch) brush. A hardware or pastry brush is just right. Outdoors on wall or driveway, indoors on a blackboard, the wet areas will *look* different. In winter, let him try snow painting. Add food coloring to a tin of water; the child can swab colored water on snow with a brush, or dribble it in patterns. If he's fairly well coordinated—and if you're exceptionally tolerant of mess—you can let him try "real" painting at floor level. Spread the kitchen floor thickly with newspapers. Set out a low, flat-bottomed container of poster paint, the wide brush and some big sheets of paper—wrapping paper or brown bags opened out. For that matter, the child can paint directly on the newspaper. At this stage he has no interest in "pictures" or finished results. The activity is the thing.

FINGERPAINT

Fingerpaint, an intensely sensuous material, is an ideal medium to introduce when the social pressures of toilet training and table manners have only recently begun to crimp a three-year-old's style. In fingerpainting, children enjoy the pleasures of legitimate messing and of free rhythmic movement. Also—at an age when small muscle control permits few triumphs with crayons—they're able to produce quite spectacular effects.

You can buy fingerpaint at any hobby or art supply store. Much cheaper, and just as satisfactory, are these homemade mixtures:

I. Supereasy fingerpaint

    Mix   1 c. flour
          4 Tbsp. salt
          ⅞ c. cold water
          Few drops food coloring

This produces a nice goppy paste good for smearing directly
on smooth surfaces. Younger children (two to five) can be safely
allowed to "paint" the floor or the kitchen counter with this mix,
which wipes up easily. For a somewhat more professional-type
paint, try one of the following.

II. Laundry starch paint

    Dissolve ½ c. of powdered laundry starch in cold water
    until it's the consistency of thick cream. *Gradually* pour
    this mix into 4 c. boiling water, stirring all the while. Re-
    move from heat, add ¼ c. *soap flakes* (not soap powder
    or detergent) and a few drops of either food coloring or
    powdered poster paint.

III. Cornstarch paint

    Mix in a heavy pan 2 heaping Tbsp. cornstarch with ¼ c.
    cold water; stir till smooth. Add 2 c. water, stir well and
    bring to a boil. Beat into the mixture 1 Tbsp. soap flakes.
    Cool, add food coloring or powdered poster paint.

    NOTE: flour and starch paints will ferment in time unless
    you add a preservative such as oil of cloves or glycerine.
    Store in small covered jars (baby food containers are per-
    fect) in the refrigerator.

    Any glossy surface invites fingerpaint. Formica, porcelain and
plastic tabletops are all good. So is a piece of solid-color oilcloth
or an aluminum cookie sheet. For older children (who may think
table-painting babyish), shiny shelf paper is ideal. Other good
(nonabsorbent) papers are: glazed butcher paper, shirt card-
boards, gift wrapping paper, glossy cardboard boxes.

PROCEDURE

Fingerpainting is messy, so children should be well swaddled in smocks or shower curtain ponchos. If paper is used, wet the entire surface with a sponge, smoothing the paper down as you go to prevent wrinkles and air bubbles. Pour a heaping table-spoonful of fingerpaint directly onto the wet paper. The child places his hands palms down in the paint and then swirls it over the paper. Knuckles, fingers and the heel of the hand can be used too, of course. Experienced painters may want to try out special effects, introducing other colors or stamping with found objects (wooden spools, jar tops, and so forth).

Encourage large free arm movements—up and down and around and around, zig and zag, loops and waves and wiggles and pats. A musical background—something dreamy like a Brahms waltz or frolicking like a Corelli Gigue—may inspire fresh pat-terns.

Paintings to be kept should be dried carefully, taped or tacked to a newspaper-covered board. (They will be *very* wet.) If they crinkle badly in drying, press with a warm iron on the reverse side. The resulting decorated paper makes attractive cov-ering material for notebooks (the child's own, or the family tele-phone book) and small boxes; preschoolers will be thrilled to see grown-ups *using* their work.

Though fingerpainting is wonderfully liberating and contrib-utes to confidence, coordination and finger strength, its growth value is limited. It does not offer great scope or challenge, and should not be regarded as a substitute for brush painting.

POSTER PAINT (ALSO CALLED TEMPERA OR SHOW CARD PAINT)

The best all-round medium for children's painting. Oil paint is much too difficult, watercolor tricky to control (before about age ten) and commercial paint sets—half-inch squares of hard color set in tin cups—are mostly frustrating. Good poster paint is a tempting consistency (like thick cream), flows smoothly from the brush, and comes in brilliant colors. Since, unlike watercolor, it's opaque, the child can paint over parts of his work; he can also mix colors in a jar or on the painting itself.

You can buy store paint in either liquid or powdered form. The liquid costs a bit more, but it's ready to use and richer in color. Get red, yellow, blue, black and white. (Black will dull any color; with the other, primary tones the child can mix what he needs.

> Yellow + blue = green
> Yellow + red = orange
> Orange + black + blue = brown
> Red + blue = purple
> Red + blue + yellow = gray

Brushes for young children should be fairly stiff, one-half to one and a half inches wide. Paper can be—almost anything. Construction paper, old wallpaper books, wrapping paper, magazine pages (interesting effects with these), even newspaper: all are useful. Painting paper should be clipped to an easel or tacked to a board so that the painter has a firm, nonslippery surface to work on. Since few households can afford a brush for every color (the ideal arrangement), you must provide tins of clean water and paint cloths, making sure that the child understands: wash the brush after each new color or you'll muddy up the whole lot. Most easels have special paint-holding compartments. For table painting, set out colors in baby food jars (filled only to the depth of the brush bristles) or in glass furniture casters.

Though children don't need instruction in how to paint, they do need some guidance in handling materials:

▪ Put plenty of paint on the brush, then tap it lightly against the paint container to control drip.

▪ Hold, don't grip, the brush above the ferrule so that it

moves freely. Pressing hard, scrubbing back and forth, is hard on both brush and painting.

■Clean brushes between colors by rinsing, then wiping on cloth or paper. After painting, lay cleaned brushes flat in a box or upended in a jar. Don't leave them in water; it loosens the glue in the handle. Don't leave them in a jar with bristles pressed against the bottom; that spoils the shape.

Effects can be varied by (1) changing the texture of the painting surface (corrugated paper, paper that's been rubbed with candle wax or crayon so that the waxy portion rejects the paint (2) applying paint with something other than a brush—twig, cork, pipe cleaner, sponge, cloth, eye dropper, fingers. A particularly interesting technique is string painting. For this, the child folds a piece of paper in half. Then he dips a piece of string into paint, lays it between the folds of his paper and, holding the paper firmly, wriggles out the string. The result, when the paper is opened, will be a symmetrical design. (As children become accomplished in string painting, they learn to plan and control effects.)

FELT PENS (MAGIC MARKERS)

Felt pens, a relatively new addition to the art scene, can be used for either drawing or painting, outlining or filling in. They are wonderfully versatile, easily controlled, rich-colored and nonmessy. I recommend them enthusiastically for any child who's old enough (1) to *put the cap back as soon as he's through with a color* and (2) to understand that felt pens are never, NEVER used on walls, clothing . . . or anything except the art materials provided. Beginner's sets of markers come in four to twelve colors with thick or thin tips. For an older child, serious about his work, there are studio markers in literally hundreds of subtle, thrilling shades.

Felt pens work well on paper, cloth, plastic, wood, egg shells, clay, rocks, porcelain, metal . . . a truly all-purpose medium.

Modeling

Modeling offers all the sensuous delights of fingerpaint with important new growing experiences: a fingertip knowledge of textures and the excitement of working with three-dimensional form.

CLAY

True potter's clay ("supermud") is the most satisfying of all materials. Unfortunately, it's sometimes the most difficult to procure for home use, and a nuisance to store. Where, in a small house or apartment, does one stash a twenty-five-pound bag of wet clay? If you happen to live in a good clay area, you may be able to dig your own—an enterprise specially pleasing to the young. Nearby users who order in large quantities—a potter, a nursery school, an art school—may be willing to sell clay. But generally parents have to depend on art supply stores, many of which stock only commercial play doughs. If you *can* manage to get real clay, cover it with a wet cloth and store in a container with tight-fitting lid. Clay that dries out can be restored to its original condition, but only by a pounding and mixing process few amateur potters care to undertake.

Introducing a three-year-old to clay requires nothing more than a work surface to which clay won't adhere (a cookie sheet, heavy shellac-coated cardboard, a piece of oilcloth with backing side up) and a ball of clay. Later on, you may want to offer modeling tools such as tongue depressors and knitting needles, and oddments for decorating finished pieces. In the beginning, though, the focus should be on simple manipulation. Don't suggest that the child "make something." Give him a lump of clay and let him find out what it's good for. Typically, he will roll, pat, punch and pound. Just as a scribbling child uses a pencil for pure pleasure, commenting occasionally when he spies resemblance to real objects, so a clay pummeler may keep up a running monologue. This is a snake . . . a waffle . . . a kitten . . . a thrillingly unmentionable bathroom production. Though he quite enjoys having something to show at the end of his labors, that's not the point.

Random exploration in time reveals to the child the properties of clay. It can be squeezed or pulled into new shapes. Pieces can be added on or pinched off; it can be hollowed out, made thick or thin by rolling. Its surface takes impressions from any hard object. A modeled form can be swiftly reduced to an inchoate mass.

Once a child has made these discoveries, he may be interested in producing a "real" thing. People and animals are favorite projects. With a little practice, a child can learn to make pots by one of three basic techniques: pinch, coil or slab. A pinch pot is really just a clay ball hollowed out, by finger or thumb, until it acquires sides of more or less even thickness and a flat bottom. A coil pot is made on a patted-clay base around which clay snakes are wound, built up higher and higher, coil upon coil, each pressed into the one below. A slab pot is made from rolled-out clay. (Use a rolling pin.) The flattened clay is then either bent upward at the edges into a bowl, or cut into pieces (bottom, sides) and the pieces joined to make a container. In any of these procedures, the child needs to be shown that moistening the clay gives a tighter join, and that finished surfaces can be decorated by scratching designs with a stick or pressing them on with shells, forks, coins, and so forth.

If an older child becomes sufficiently interested to want to carry a clay project over several days, the piece in process must be covered with a damp cloth; otherwise it dries out and becomes unworkable. A finished piece to be saved will dry, sometimes to rock hardness, if simply left on a shelf. A complete potting process involves firing in a kiln at high temperatures. That's a studio proposition. In any case, clay that's going to be fired has to be handled with great care about eliminating air bubbles and making joins. Few kitchen-made pots would survive a kiln firing.

BAKE-AND-PAINT CLAY

This mixture, to my knowledge never used in nursery schools or art classes, is a most satisfactory modeling material for children old enough to care about finished products. The original recipe, adapted from that employed for Peruvian bread-dough figures, was intended for making Christmas ornaments. It works very well that way, but its possibilities go far beyond the Christmas tree.

Mix together   4 c. flour
1 c. salt
1½ c. water (about)

As with pie crust, the amount of water needed varies a little according to humidity, so add water cautiously until you have a good manageable dough. Knead until smooth and not too sticky.

This soft, malleable dough lends itself beautifully to modeling animals, human figures, stars and butterflies and whatever catches the child's fancy. (If the dough dries out too much during working, add water cautiously.) The child can decorate his productions from the scrap box: a crown of colored beads for a fairy princess and sequins for her skirt; dried peas and beans for the spots on a fantastic animal; silver dragees for the heart of a flower . . . and wire, buttons, tacks or pins. If the figures are to be hung, a hairpin or a Christmas ornament hanger should be inserted in the dough before baking. Lay finished pieces on a cookie sheet and bake at 350 degrees until they are thoroughly dry but not browned. (Watch carefully.) Baking time will depend on the thickness of individual items: a flat butterfly will be ready in about twenty minutes, a plump kitten may take an hour. When the figures are dry, paint with felt pens, all colors; a coat of shellac gives added brilliance and is a nice touch if the child is old enough to brush it on delicately.

The advantages of this dough will be obvious once you've tried it. It keeps for several days (in plastic bags, in the refrigerator); it stimulates inventiveness of color and design; and it gives the satisfaction of completed pieces that are often truly dazzling.

HOMEMADE PLAY DOUGH

This is grainier than the preceding dough and needs no baking. Large objects made from it break and crumble easily, but it's good for making doll-house food items—apples, bananas, bread, hamburgers.

> Mix together 4 c. flour
> 3 c. salt
> 4 Tbsp. vegetable oil
> Few drops food coloring, or poster paint (liquid or powder)
> 1 c. water (about)

Knead thoroughly and store in plastic bags in refrigerator. If you want more than one color of dough, divide into three or four balls before adding poster paint, then knead in the color.

BIRTHDAY CANDLE WAX

When my younger daughter was seven or eight, she made a happy discovery. Tiny birthday candles left in the sun become soft and pliable; the resulting colored wax can be molded into charming dolls and animals. Half an hour on the sidewalk—or set out in a foil pan—on a hot summer's day and the candles are ready to work. I would guess the same amount of time in a pie pan on a warm radiator would produce similar results. Of course wax should *never* be placed over direct heat.

The heat of the fingers is sufficient to keep the candle wax in just-right condition while it's being worked; afterwards, it hardens again and figures made this way keep indefinitely.

Crayons

Most parents give a child a box of crayons and leave him to his own devices. Those devices consist, generally, of using crayons as if they were pencils. As the points wear down and the paper peels, stubs are gradually relegated to a jumbled can-of-last-resort. This is a great pity, because the humble crayon is a remarkably versatile medium, capable of effects both varied and original.

The best crayons for young children are sturdy fat hexagonals or crayons with one flat side. A wide range of colors is less important than good quality. To test, scrape a crayoned patch with your fingernail and see how much wax comes off. Cheap crayons flake easily off the paper, leaving only thin color behind, and they don't blend well. With good crayons (the kind carried by art supply stores, not in variety store stationery departments), a child can achieve rich subtle tones by overlaying colors directly on his paper.

Remember that peeled crayons have three usable surfaces: sharp point, flat end, and side. Furthermore, the side can be notched, incised or deeply grooved so that the crayon makes an interesting pattern for shading. Still greater textural variety will come from the use of different materials to crayon on—sandpaper, corrugated cardboard, wood, cotton, wallpaper, burlap.

Here are suggestions for young artists eager to experiment with crayons.

CRAYON RESIST

A technique based on the fact that wax and water, like oil and water, don't mix. Make a thick bright crayon drawing on paper. Then, using a wide brush, drag a light wash of transparent watercolor over the entire sheet. The crayoned areas will stand out vividly from the background.

Intriguing variation: place a sheet of wax paper over drawing paper and scratch a design firmly on the wax using a bobby pin or nail. Lift away the wax paper and brush the underneath sheet with clear watercolor. *Magic*.

CRAYON ETCHING

This involves scraping designs out of a richly built-up crayony surface. It can be done in several ways. The most effective technique is to mark off the paper into different-size areas, then use a different light-toned crayon on each, applying color thickly. Now cover the entire sheet with dark crayon—black, purple, brown or blue. Finally, with a sharp instrument (nut pick, fingernail file) scratch out a drawing, cutting through to the bright color crayon underneath. The result is a fascinating play of light and dark.

CRAYON CHIP BLENDING

This is a good use for crayon bits, particularly after they've picked up miscellaneous color flakes.

Scrape, chip or grate crayons into little piles of colored wax. Lay a sheet of wax paper on a newspaper padding and, using fingers or spoon, move the crayon chips about on the paper to make a design. The effect can be enriched with interesting scraps: confetti, ferns or seeds, yarn, torn bits of colored tissue paper scattered over the colored wax. Lay a second piece of wax paper carefully over the design and press gently with a warm iron. (Lift the iron up and down, not back and forth.) The wax melts and fuses the two sheets of paper with the pattern locked between them.

CRAYON RUBBING

Fun for children too young to use irons and scrapers. Arrange on a firm surface a pleasing pattern of hard, coarse-textured items. Buttons, coins, corrugated cardboard strips, pine needles, string, grained wood, seashells, hairpins, paper clips are all good. Lay over these a sheet of smooth, strong but lightweight paper and then crayon over the entire surface. Rub fairly hard, in one direction only, and the raised designs will appear.

CRAYON BATIK

This is most effective when used not with freehand drawing but with a repeated design motif—circles, triangles, wavy lines.

On sturdy paper, make a crayon design, then place paper in a pan of cold water to soak. Lift it out, crumple it into a ball, unfold onto a newspaper pad. Now brush over the entire surface with transparent watercolor; let dry.

On cloth (lightweight white or pale-colored cotton), tack the cotton to an easel or board and crayon with bright colors using firm, heavy strokes. Flower and leaf designs or abstract shapes are most appropriate if you want a Polynesian effect. Soak the cloth in cold water, then dip it in a dark dye solution (cold water) and dry. As in crayon resist, only the un-crayoned fabric changes color. Now place the batik between papers, and press with a hot iron.

Fabric treated in this way makes handsome pillow covers, wall hangings, place mats, bags. A child can also use the technique to decorate a plain white jersey or undershirt.

CRAYON ON CLOTH

A child not patient enough for batik can have the satisfaction of relatively permanent results by making his crayon picture on fabric which is then stamped with a hot iron. (Stamp on the wrong side over a newspaper or cotton pad.) My children used to make needle-book covers by this technique; it would also, like crayon batik, be effective on solid-color jerseys. Another possibility: a baby's first cloth book. (Baby might never recognize the apples and cars crayoned by big brother—but think what joy to the donor.)

CRAYON ON WOOD

A clean, well-sanded wood surface takes crayon beautifully. Any child would enjoy decorating a little wooden box. Oriental novelty stores frequently have a supply of neat little oblong balsawood boxes used to hold incense; somewhat more expensive are the plain wooden boxes carried by hobby stores for just such purposes. (A top coat of shellac gives a nice finish and makes crayon colors glow.)

Needlework

If needlework enters American art programs at all, it appears late, an activity for girls. But both boys and girls can find stitchery a satisfying outlet for creative impulse. Bright yarn is enticing as crayons to a three-year-old; he may not be ready for a needle, but he'll find interesting things to do with wire or plastic mesh (fruit baskets are good) and some thick rug yarn stiffened at the end with glue or tightly wrapped tape. (If you use a square of wire mesh, bind the edges with adhesive tape as a protection against cut fingers.) To begin with, he just pokes the yarn randomly in and out, "scribbling" in wool. Then—as with pencil scribbling or fingerpainting—he becomes aware of possibilities, making shapes. Quite without direction, he may discover an in-and-out weaving pattern.

The next step is stitching on cloth. Burlap, vegetable bags or rug canvas offer a continuation of the wire-mesh experience; a child particularly apt at fine movements can switch directly to sturdy cotton and a lighter weight yarn. Either way, the fabric should be stretched in an embroidery hoop to allow firm grip. For a child working on cotton, use a blunt tapestry needle at first. You will have to thread it and knot the end. To prevent the frustration of a needle that keeps slipping off, split the yarn a few inches from the end and slip the threaded needle through the split.

There are two schools of thought about beginning needle-craft. One is that the stitcher should dispense entirely with out-lines—just work freely on the fabric, thinking directly in terms of stitches rather than drawings translated into embroidery. The other favors a preliminary sketch. Jacqueline Enthoven, author of the delightful *Stitchery for Children*, suggests several varia-tions of this approach. One is to have the child make a crayon drawing on plastic shelf paper and stitch over that. The other is to staple a piece of crinoline over the drawing and let him stitch crinoline and drawing together, outlining his shape.

Preschoolers don't attempt representation with embroidery (though, as in paint and clay work, they may recognize and label what they've made: "Look at my fluffy kitten!"—a tangle of green stitches). Five-year-olds may make a serious attempt at "drawing" with yarn; by six or seven most children, if they're interested at all, can learn simple stitches. Leave French knots for later. Three basic stitches—running stitch, cross-stitch and blanket stitch—permit a good deal of variety. (Consult one of the embroidery books listed in the Bibliography for instruc-tions.) In fact, a child who knows only these three will be challenged to invent new combinations.

A child who develops real skill with a needle can achieve
stunning effects with yarn alone. (See Mrs. Enthoven's book for
enchanting examples of child embroidery.) A clumsy stitcher
may do better introducing collage elements—for example, instead of relying entirely on stitches to make a portrait, applying
button head, yarn hair, felt skirt and an umbrella made by top-
ping a drinking straw with a bit of bright ribbon. For a mixed-
media picture, burlap (edges glued or hemmed) makes a good
background. The child can draw directly on burlap with crayon
if he likes, then arrange scraps of felt, feathers, tinsel, lace or
whatever. Once the design suits his fancy, he stitches the elements in place; the charm of this way of working is variety and
surprise.

And of course: don't overlook the possibilities of the child's
adding gay personal touches to his own clothes. Embroidering
a design on the rear or the knees of blue jeans is a particularly
dashing, grown-up project.

Printing

This is one of the best possible art activities for the child with
a strong design sense but little aptitude for drawing.

Before introducing a child to printing, it's a good idea to make
him aware of patterns in the environment, and of the way a repeated shape creates satisfying rhythms. Look with him at
Langston Hughes's *First Book of Rhythms*. Point out the scales
of a fish, leaf veins, brick and tile patterns, bird tracks in sand
or snow . . . and the utilitarian grip patterns of bottle caps and
rubber tire treads. Once interested in the idea of repeated designs, he'll be eager to learn how these can be created by
stamping.

Printing is a simple procedure. You need only:

1. A color pad—absorbent material saturated with poster

paint, vegetable coloring or watercolor paint. Ink is good, but not for the very young.

2. A stamper, either a naturally interesting form (spool, sponge, cork, sliced carrot) or a personal design, glued to a block or cut out of suitable materials, such as a potato.

3. An absorbent surface, paper or cloth. Special effects are possible with colored paper, striped cloth, and material previously batiked (see CRAYON BATIK above).

ELEMENTARY TECHNIQUES

For preschoolers, use "natural" stampers. It's true that you can make a potato stamp for this age—by drawing a star, say, on a cut potato surface and then cutting it around the edges so you have a raised design. Nursery school teachers often do just that. I think it's best to introduce an art activity at a level that can be controlled by the child himself without adult assistance. For a start, show your child how a simple object like a wooden spool can be pressed onto a color-soaked pad and then used to make a double-circle impression. (I need hardly say that the artist's clothes should be well covered before he begins. Printing is messy work.) Let him press and stamp, press and stamp until he has the idea. Then ask him to think of other objects that might leave interesting marks. Button? Yes, but that would be hard to hold (though if you glued it onto a chunk of wood, you've got something). Toy car? Dear me no. Crayon? Try it and see. Doesn't work too well, does it? A hair roller now, works beautifully. So does a ball of string, or the end of a toilet-paper roll. He'll soon spot other printables. After the basic technique has been mastered, you might suggest that instead of random stamping the child try some controlled effects: a border; rows of different-shaped impressions; stamps superimposed over other stamps. And of course stamped cloth or paper can be further decorated by hand, with crayon squiggles or swirls of paint.

A fun game: let the child make prints with his thumb. When he has a page of thumbprints, offer him crayon or pencil and ask him to try converting the thumb blots into people, animals, food, household objects.

FOR SOMEWHAT OLDER CHILDREN

If a child can handle a nail, a nail file or blunt knife as a carving tool, he can gouge out a design on a cut potato surface. The potato must be carefully blotted before using (or left awhile so that the natural moisture evaporates). To print, stamp the prepared potato on a pad soaked with water-base paint.

Another printing technique: instead of cutting *into* a surface to obtain a relief design, the child builds the surface *up* and takes prints from the raised portions. Here again, a wooden spool makes a good beginning. Glue onto one end a coiled piece of pipe cleaner, an intriguing felt or sponge shape. (Felt gives a soft, fuzzy print.) Or, on a thick cardboard base, arrange a variety of shapes—made of other bits of cardboard, or sponge —in a pleasing pattern and glue in place. When the glue has dried, paint over the entire surface with a thin coat of shellac, so as to make it nonabsorbent, easy to print. This type of printer can't be used with a stamping pad; paint must be applied directly to the printing surface with a brayer, a small rubber paint roller (available in hardware and hobby stores). The child then lays his paper carefully over the prepared printer and, using the back of a wooden spoon or a stout tablespoon, presses the paper down so that it takes an impression. Both printing and lifting off the paper (in a single clean motion) is fairly tricky.

MONOPRINTING

So called because you get only one print per painting, it's another technique employing a brayer. The simplest form of monoprinting is really a variation of fingerpainting: a coat of slippery opaque paint is spread with a brayer on a sheet of formica (or any hard, smooth, nonabsorbent surface). The child swirls palms and fingers through the paint until he gets a design that pleases him. Then he lays a sheet of absorbent paper over the painted surface and presses it down firmly so it takes the paint at all points. Finally he lifts the paper (straight up, so as not to smudge) and hangs it up to dry.

Paper printed in this way makes striking gift wrapping. Sometimes the results are good enough to hang, matted, as pictures.

Chalk

Using chalk on blackboard is an activity familiar to most children. But chalk on paper offers a distinctive experience: a medium more manageable than paint and without the hard, tense character of crayons. Like crayons, chalk can be used for drawing (the tip) or shading (the full side). It blends well. Rubbing red chalk over blue, for instance, produces rich purple.

Chalk drawing is inevitably a dusty affair. You can minimize mess, though, by having the child roll up his sleeves, stand well back from the work table, and remember to keep his free hand clear of the drawing. An easel, with paper clipped in an upright position, is ideal for chalk work.

Chalk can be used on wet (sponge-moistened) or dry paper. By trying both techniques, the child makes discoveries: color is brighter on wet paper but must be applied more carefully, to prevent tearing; chalk on dry paper has a feathery, smoky effect.

Unless fixative is used, all chalk drawings are ephemeral. A particularly good effort can be preserved by spraying with hair spray or commercial fixative or—a homely old-fashioned technique—dipping the drawing in water to which a little glue has been added. Another way of "fixing" chalk is to coat the drawing paper before starting with a light buttermilk wash.

Collage

A collage (the root meaning is *glue*) is a two-dimensional composition made out of different materials pasted to a flat surface. A typical design may include bark, string, shells, newspaper, sacking . . . any substance, natural or manufactured, that lends itself to arrangement on paper or board. There are two kinds of collage. One is assorted junk pasted together; the other is a feeling-thinking organization of forms and textures that creates a single harmonious effect. The first kind is no more valuable than any other kind of busy work (and, beyond the early years, misleading if it gives rise to the notion that anything goes—and anything can be "art"). The second kind is a joyous synthesizing experience fundamentally creative, since it requires the artist to see all his materials in a new way. Not, *What is this used for* but *How can I use it?*

A good collage doesn't begin in the scrap box; it begins in the child's sensuous response to the world about him. What things are rough, slippery, smooth, gritty, soft? What things are shiny, dull, transparent? How many interesting shapes can be identified? Square, triangular, irregular, round. . . . Before you invite a child to make his own collage, show him some good examples, preferably not reproductions but originals he can touch. Then send him on a treasure hunt. What can he find to make pictures with? Once he gets the idea, seeing oddments in terms of texture, shape or color, he'll spot possibilities everywhere. Encourage him to start a collection of collage materials, not jumbled all together but separated into containers according to plan. For example:

A box of interesting surfaces
> Solid color: paper, shiny and dull; tissue and crepe paper; felt; cotton

Patterned: gift wrapping, wallpaper, newspaper, envelope linings, paper doilies, lace

Transparent: cellophane, X-ray film, plastic, netting

A box of interesting shapes

Irregular: seeds, pebbles, paper clips, sea glass

Round: bottle caps, confetti, buttons, beads, tacks

Linear: yarn, string, wire, bamboo, ribbon, tooth picks, straws, twigs, pipe cleaners, Q-tips

A box of interesting textures

Sandpaper, bark, wood shavings, leather, burlap, shells, corrugated cardboard, Styrofoam, cork, velvet, absorbent cotton, crushed washed egg shells

The only other requirements for collage are material for a base (cardboard, firm paper) and adhesive. Commercial library paste (with brush) is fine. Young children like making their own: a simple flour paste produced by stirring water *gradually* into a bowl of flour until it's just the right consistency. More effective is a wonderful old-fashioned concoction we used to call "missionary paste" (from its supposed origin in Chinese missions).

Stir in top of double boiler: ½ c. flour
½ c. white sugar
½ Tbsp. powdered alum
½ c. cold water

When these ingredients are well mixed, add

1½ c. boiling water

Cook over hot water, stirring constantly, until clear. Add 15 drops oil of clove (from drugstore) and beat with electric beater.

At three or four, a child won't do much meditating over collages; he just pastes away. A school-age child will take selection and arrangement more seriously. Whether he plans a representational picture (cutting materials into recognizable shapes) or an abstract design, it's advisable to work out ideas first on a piece of paper the same size as the final base. Encourage the child to move pieces about on his trial paper. Does that give a good balance? Would the sandpaper's grainy quality stand out better against velvet or metal foil? How about repeating the squash seeds in another part of the picture to create a rhythm? That bamboo strip gives a nice strong up-and-down feeling. Perhaps you'd get an interesting effect, a kind of drama, by having a piece of twine move *across* the picture. And so on. Perhaps you'd get a lively counterpoint by using coiled string in a horizontal movement? When the child finds an arrangement that pleases him, he transfers his design from trial paper to the final base, which he has carefully "buttered" with paste.

Photography

A five-year-old working with paint, clay—or words—may produce a genuine work of art. That level of achievement is not possible for a five-year-old with a camera: the technical problems of photography are too great. A very young child can, however, use a camera to produce results important to *him*. For the price of a toy truck, a simple Instamatic with flash-cube attachment offers a new way of seeing, understanding and communicating.

With a preschool child, photography instructions should be kept to an absolute minimum. He needs to know only a very few things:

▪If you want to take pictures outdoors, wait till the sun shines. For indoors, use a flash.

▪Hold the camera very steady, against your face if that helps.

▪ Look through the view-finder to locate your picture. If what you see isn't just what you want in your picture, move forward or back. If you've got mostly grass and Daddy looks too little, move forward. Back if you see Daddy's stomach but not his head. Keep your finger away from the lens.

▪ Press the button slowly and don't jerk the camera. (If you can hold your breath while you press, that helps.)

▪ Push the lever to advance the film.

Have the child work with an unloaded camera for about ten minutes. Then snap in a film cartridge and let him click away. Mother at the clothesline . . . the cat sleeping on a chair . . . the milkman's truck . . . the milkman . . . whatever strikes his fancy. If he chooses a stationary object (cat asleep) suggest that he try shots from different angles. Let him use the entire roll of film at one session; that way you can take it for developing at once and get pictures back while interest is high.

Whatever the results from an adult point of view, the young photographer will almost certainly be thrilled. *Real pictures.* This is the point at which you can begin to offer constructive suggestions. What a nice shot of baby in the sandpile. Pity you didn't get closer, we can't really see . . . Mother looks tippy here. Guess you didn't hold the camera straight. . . . Whoops —you cut off my head in that one. Remember, if you can't see the head in the finder before you press the button, it won't be in the picture either. . . . This one's all blurry. Grandpa must have moved—or maybe you moved the camera.

With the first picture results, limit your comments to purely mechanical matters. Later on, you can introduce suggestions about composition. Nothing fancy, just common-sense observations. It's better not to line people up like soldiers when you're taking pictures. Try not to have the background cluttered up with lots of things that aren't very interesting. A black poodle doesn't show up well on a black driveway, does he? Don't talk in terms of beautiful pictures; that's not a five-year-old goal. Talk about what's necessary to help other people see what he saw. "Working with a camera," says Don Brown, an Urbana photographer, "a kid can arrive at a very simple but profound understanding of what's involved in communicating. He sees something on the street that excites him, clicks the button. Then, when the picture comes back, he's disappointed. Maybe, in his picture, he can't even find the dog he thought he was photographing. He's got the cars and the stores and the telephone poles. So he learns that to get a record, show somebody else, you have to get up close and cut out the static, all those extras that become just noise on a flat two-dimensional surface."

As a child acquires experience with his camera, encourage him to take pictures in groups—trip to the zoo, birthday party, friends at the playground—and keep the best ones in an album. The easiest kind, for a young child, is the "magnetic" album which holds snapshots in place between sheets of semistick plastic. Have him write his own captions on oblongs of colored construction paper. ("This is Sammy being a pirate on Halloween.") The result is a kind of diary he'll look at often and add to proudly. And if he comes up with a really good shot, wouldn't it be nice to have that printed on a family greeting card? Or blown up, poster size, for his room?

Generally, a young child is more interested in getting pictures than in understanding how the camera works. If, however, your child is really curious, break open a cartridge to show him what film looks like; show him negatives and let him compare them with prints (light on the negative is dark on the print and vice versa). If he's still interested, explain what happens when he presses that button. A shutter opens, light comes into the camera's dark interior, carrying with it the image, the reflection, of whatever is in front of the shutter. When that image strikes the special material inside (film, made sensitive to light by chemical treatment), it's printed on the film.

To give this explanation real meaning, help the child make a primitive camera. All you need is a covered cardboard box about six inches long and somewhat less in width and height. In the center of one end cut a hole the size of a thumbtack head. Now, Scotch-tape a piece of aluminum foil over the hole; prick the exact center of the foil with a pin. In a totally dark room, "load" your box camera with a piece of sheet film. (Remember, any light striking film will ruin it.) To do this, Scotch-tape the film to the inside end of the box opposite the foil-covered opening. Keeping the pinhole covered with your finger, carry the box into bright sunshine and set it down on a chair opposite whatever scene you wish to photograph. Uncover the hole for about ten seconds, then cover it carefully and return the box to a dark room where you can safely unload the film. When the film is developed, you'll have a picture. Not a very sharp one, to be sure, because your box camera has no lens, but a picture nonetheless.

One final suggestion, to stimulate a child's interest in photography. Get from the library one of the many big, handsome collections of work by distinguished photographers. Three particularly good ones to look at and talk about with a child are Edward Steichen's *Family of Man*; *Family*, by Ken Heyman (with text by Margaret Mead) and David Duncan's *Self-Portrait: U.S.A.*

This by no means exhausts art activities for children. Other rich possibilities are puppetry, bookmaking, woodwork, stabiles and mobiles, weaving and papier-mâché. The Bibliography contains useful guides to all these.

"I Made It Myself!"—Paint, Crayons, Clay and So Forth

GENERAL WORKS ABOUT ART EDUCATION AND THE PLACE
OF ART IN THE CHILD'S LIFE

ASH, BERYL, and BARBARA RAPAPORT, *Creative Work in the Junior School*, Methuen, 1969. Written out of a faith that "the urge to create is universal, and all human beings need some means of doing so, as essentially as they need sleep and food and exercise," this book explores the creative possibilities of modeling, painting, music, movement, language and textile design.

BASSETT, RICHARD, ed., *The Open Eye in Learning*, M.I.T. Press, 1969. A provocative collection of essays on art.

BENSON, KENNETH, *Creative Crafts for Children*, Prentice-Hall, 1968.

BLAND, JANE COOPER, *Art of the Young Child*, Museum of Modern Art, 1968. A brisk, bright, compact little book on understanding and encouraging creative growth in children 3 to 5. Illustrations of children's work suggest admirably what can be expected (roughly) at different ages and stages.

BROWN, DORIS V., *Creative Art Activities for Home and School*, Lawrence, 1966.

COLE, NATALIE ROBINSON, *The Arts in the Classroom*, Day, 1940.

———, *Children's Arts from Deep Down Inside*, Day, 1966. In a book full of enthusiasm and understanding, a gifted teacher describes her techniques for releasing children from inhibition and giving them a sense of joy through art. Stunning examples of children's work.

CRAIG, JENNIE, *Elementary School Creative Art Activities*, International Textbook, 1967.

D'AMICO, VICTOR, *Art for the Family*, Museum of Modern Art, 1954.

——, *Experiments in Creative Art Teaching*, Doubleday, 1960.

DEAN, JOAN, *Art and Craft in the Primary School Today*, A. & C. Black, 1970. Intended primarily for teachers, this book provides a clear, common-sense guide to the standard arts and crafts—and some not-so-standard but extremely useful, like bookbinding.

DI LEO, JOSEPH, *Young Children and Their Drawings*, Mazel, 1970.

EISNER, ELLIOT W., and DAVID W. ECKER, *Readings in Art Education*, Blaisdell, 1966.

GAITSKILL, CHARLES D., *Children & Their Art*, Harcourt, 1958.

GREENBERG, PEARL, *Children's Experiences in Art*, Reinhold, 1966.

GROZINGER, WOLFGANG, *Scribbling, Drawing, Painting*, Praeger, 1955. Traces the evolution of a child's way of seeing and his muscular controls.

HAUPT, DOROTHY, and KEITH OSBORN, *Creative Activities*, Merrill Palmer, 1964.

HERBERHOLZ, DONALD and BARBARA, *A Child's Pursuit of Art*, William C. Brown, 1967. A book of concrete motivations for drawing, painting and modeling, so exciting that any reader (however untalented in the arts) will want to get out paints or clay and start work at once.

HOOVER, F. LOUIS, *Art Activities for the Very Young*, Davis, 1961.

JAMESON, KENNETH, *Art and the Young Child*, Viking, 1968. A sensitive exploration of what art means to the young child. With suggestions for parent guidance and many examples of children's work.

KELLOGG, RHODA, *Analyzing Children's Art*, National Press, 1969.

——, *What Children Scribble and Why*, National Press, 1959.

KNUDSEN, ESTELLE H., and ETHEL CHRISTENSEN, *Children's Art Education*, Charles A. Bennett, 1957.

KRANYIK, ROBERT, *Stimulating Creative Learning in the Elementary School*, Parker, 1969. A source book of activities.

LANSING, KENNETH M., *Art, Artists and Art Education*, McGraw, 1969.

LINDERMAN, EARL W., and DONALD W. HERBERHOLZ, *Developing Artistic and Perceptual Awareness*, William C. Brown, 1964.

LINDSTROM, MIRIAM, *Children's Art*, University of California Press, 1957. A study of normal development in children's ways of seeing.

LOWENFELD, VIKTOR, *Your Child and His Art*, Macmillan, 1954. A landmark in its recognition of the arts as central to a child's growth and happiness. Organized around typical parent questions ("When should children begin to draw or paint?" "Why does my child work sloppily—or scribble on the walls?"), Lowenfeld's book is illustrated with typical child art at different stages of development, and some lovely examples of experience happily realized in paint.

MARSHALL, SYBIL, *An Experiment in Education*, Cambridge, 1963. An English teacher's account—vivid, moving—of an extraordinary intellectual and artistic adventure. Working in a one-room village school, with 26 run-of-the-town children ranging from ages 5 to 11, she discovered how to make art the vital center of her curriculum and so elicit "the intelligence, integrity, creativity, and capacity for deep thought and hard work latent somewhere in every child." Any parent will find in it suggestions for assisting his children toward what Miss Marshall defines as the true end of education, "the knowledge of what it means really to live, and the wisdom to accept and make the most of what life offers each individual person."

MATTIL, EDWARD, *Meaning in Crafts*, Prentice-Hall, 1959.

MC FEE, JUNE K., *Preparation for Art*, Wadsworth Publishing, 1961.

MC ILVAIN, DOROTHY S., *Art for Primary Grades*, Putnam, 1961. A practical, well-illustrated book with chapters on every conceivable art and craft for children ages 5 to 10.

MENDELOWITZ, DANIEL M., *Children Are Artists*, Stanford University Press, 1953.

MONTGOMERY, CHANDLER, *Art for Teachers of Children*, Charles E. Merrill, 1968. The concluding chapter, on encouraging creativity, is particularly valuable.

READ, HERBERT, *Education Through Art*, Faber, 1964.

RICHARDSON, ELWYN S., *In The Early World*, Pantheon, 1964. A beautiful, original book about an art-centered program in a New Zealand country school. Full of extraordinary specimens of children's writing, drawing, wood and linoleum cuts, fabric designs and pottery—and of the teacher's respect for each child's individuality and integrity.

SNOW, AIDA C., *Growing with Children Through Art*, Reinhold, 1968.

TRUCKSESS, FRAN, *Creative Art, Elementary Grades*, Pruett Press, 1962.

TUCKER, DOROTHY G. with BARBARA-JEANNE SEABURY and NORMA CANNER, *Foundations for Learning with Creative Art and Creative Movement*, Massachusetts Department of Health, 1967.

WANKELMAN, WILLARD, *Arts and Crafts for Elementary Teachers*, William C. Brown, 1954.

GENERAL BOOKS ON ARTS AND CRAFTS

ABISCH, ROY, *Art Is for You*, McKay, 1967. Creative projects in papier-mâché, collage, mobiles and woodcuts.

CARLSON, BERNICE W., *Make It and Use It: Handicraft for Boys and Girls*, Abingdon, 1958. Over 100 easy projects using paper, cardboard, cloth, wood. Clear directions, helpful pictures.

DI VALENTIN, MARIA, *Practical Encyclopaedia of Crafts*, Sterling, 1972. Expensive but worth it, a book no family will ever outgrow. A guide to every conceivable craft from basketry to scrimshaw. Every level of simplicity and difficulty is represented; directions are admirably clear and supplemented with good photographs.

HAMILTON, EDWIN T., *Handicraft for Girls*, Harcourt, 1932. The costumes and party favors shown here are already museum pieces, but explanation of basic techniques is fine.

HUNT, BEN W., *The Golden Book of Crafts and Hobbies*, Golden Press, 1970. Not visually appealing (all dun browns and mustard yellows), but the projects are challenging and real. Heavy emphasis on Indian and Eskimo crafts, and Boy Scout type nature activities.

ICKIS, MARGUERITE, and REBA S. ESH, *The Book of Arts and Crafts*, Dover, 1965. Reprint of an old book: designs mostly dated and/or ugly, but clear and full instructions for every conceivable craft—including spinning and cement sculpture.

LEWIS, SHARI, *The Tell It—Make It Book*, Hawthorn, 1972. Combines stories to read or tell with how-to's for the crafts, games and activities featured in them. Shari Lewis has included more than 60 projects from her lucky Brownie troop (ages 6 to 9); says they were all immensely popular, and no wonder. Here are puppets, tepees, totem poles, masks, shadow plays, magic tricks and Latin American God's Eyes.

STEVENS, HAROLD, *Ways With Art: 50 techniques for teaching children*, Reinhold, 1963. Some quite unusual and attractive items: imitation stained-glass windows, butterfly transparencies, canvas-stretcher peg constructions.

TRITTEN, GOTTFRIED, *Art Techniques for Children*, Reinhold, 1964. Tritten's central concern is, How is the child's creative urge to be aroused, sustained, and developed? And his starting point is the conviction that without sound knowledge of techniques, spontaneous impulse is not likely to be either satisfying or productive. Careful, step-by-step explanation of all art techniques capable of being mastered by the young.

DRAWING, PAINTING, CRAYON WORK

ALKEMA, CHESTER, *The Complete Crayon Book*, Sterling, 1969.

BORTEN, HELEN, *A picture has a special look*, Abelard, 1961. Simple enough for beginning readers, the book explores the possibilities (in texture and mood) of various art media—crayons, ink, paint, collage.

CAMPBELL, ANN, *Start to Draw*, Watts, 1968. What to do with a box of crayons and a head full of ideas.

EMBERLEY, ED, *Ed Emberley's Drawing Book of Animals*, Little, 1970. A drawing book for children who can't draw. How to convert triangles, circles, rectangles and scratchy scribbles into appealing animals.

HAWKINSON, JOHN, *Pastels Are Great!*, Whitman, 1968. Easy, clear introduction to the use of pastel chalks.

HORN, GEORGE F., *The Crayon*, Davis Publications, 1969. An ingenious and suggestive exploration of the crayon's art possibilities, alone or in combination with paints and inks. Though some of the projects are highly sophisticated, most can be adapted for the very young. Attractively illustrated with both adult and child crayon work.

LALIBERTÉ, NORMAN, and ALEX MOGELON, *Painting with Crayons*, Reinhold, 1967. A historical and practical guide to the uses of wax and oil crayons, with illustrated step-by-step instructions for novel techniques. The book includes suggestions for games, murals, posters, and many examples of professional and child work.

MILLS, JOHN, *The Young Artist*, Sterling, 1968. Precise and practical guidance in watercolor, opaque and texture painting, oils, pastels, charcoal, pencil, ink. The treatment of perspective and shadow would be helpful to any beginner.

SEIDELMAN, JAMES E., and GRACE MINTONYE, *Creating with Paint*, Crowell-Collier, 1967. Basic information on paper, brushes, paints and techniques, and suggested projects.

SHAW, RUTH F., *Finger Painting*, Little, 1934.

SLOBODKIN, LOUIS, *The First Book of Drawing*, F. Watts, 1958. Beginning with a chapter on seeing, Slobodkin, himself a noted illustrator, progresses to a basic discussion of anatomy, movement, perspective, materials and tools for drawing. Pencil, pen and ink, charcoal, pastel, conte (dry crayon) and brush are all here.

SPILKA, ARNOLD, *Paint All Kinds of Pictures*, H. Z. Walck, 1963. For the very youngest (4 to 5 and up) an enlarging glimpse of what color and line can do.

WEISS, HARVEY, *Pencil, Pen and Brush*, W. R. Scott, 1961. Basic drawing techniques for beginners.

ZAIDENBERG, ARTHUR, *How to Draw with Pen and Brush*, Vanguard, 1965. For beginners.

CLAY, MODELING, CERAMICS

ARVOIS, EDMOND, *Making Mosaics*, Sterling, 1969. Tools, techniques, types of tile and projects.

LEE, RUTH, *Exploring the World of Pottery*, Children's Press, 1967. Addressed to children, but without talking down. Though it's not a how-to, the splendid variety of pots shown will send many children in quest of clay.

LEEMING, JOSEPH, *Fun with Clay*, Lippincott, 1944. A beginner's guide to working with all types of clay, both self-hardening and kiln-baked.

MAVROS, DONALD O., *Getting Started in Ceramics*, Bruce, 1971. It's a pity the author has chosen to illustrate with photographs of his own pots only: they are not likely to inspire all children to emulation. But the photos showing pot-forming (pinch, coil, slab) are clear. There is no attempt to demonstrate throwing on the wheel—an art not learned from books.

NUSSBAUMER, HANNY, *Lacquer & Crackle*, Sterling, 1972. A novel technique for decorating cardboard and wooden boxes, sheet metal and glass.

ROTTGER, ERNST, *Creative Clay Design*, Reinhold, 1963. Coil, pinch and slab pots, with over 250 pictures of children's and older students' work.

SCHILT, STEPHEN J., and DONNA J. WEIR, *Enamel Without Heat*, Sterling, 1971. The particular results shown here strike me as rather ugly, but the medium—a liquid polymer glaze with curing agent—has possibilities for an adventurous, able child.

SEIDELMAN, JAMES, and GRACE MINTONYE, *Creating with Clay*, Crowell-Collier, 1967. Tools, materials and basic techniques for clay modeling, and special section on firing, glazing, painting.

SLADE, RICHARD, *Modeling in Clay, Plaster and Papier-mâché*, Lothrop, 1968. Large print and elementary instruction adapted to a young reader. There are pots, tiles, blocks, masks, figures modeled on chicken wire and on wire armatures.

SOMMER, ELYSE, *The Bread Dough Craft Book*, Lothrop, 1972. The basic material used is white bread crumbled, mixed with glue and detergent to form a soft, malleable dough. Scissors, rolling pin, poster paints or food coloring, and the child's on his way.

TREVOR, HENRY, *Pottery Step-by-Step*, Ballantine, 1971. Much
space devoted to forming pots on the wheel; this is interesting, but probably not a practical help. The sections on
potting without a wheel, however, are well done. Children
will be especially intrigued by the instructions for making
clay beads.

FABRIC AND YARN

ALBAUM, CHARLET, *Ojo de Dios—Eye of God*, Grosset, 1972. Instructions for the old Indian folk art of wrapping yarn around
sticks to create ritual objects of striking beauty.

BEITLER, ETHEL J., *Create with Yarn*, Intext, 1964.

DAVIDSON, DELPHINE, *Soft Toys*, Charles T. Branford, 1971. Fish,
Lion, Hedgehog, Hippo, Owl . . . some to hold, some large
enough to sit on and climb over. With patterns.

DENDEL, ESTHER WARNER, *Needle Weaving—Easy as Embroidery*,
Countryside Press, 1969. Cardboard, a bent needle and
yarn, and a child's all set. Fascinating, manageable projects.

DEYRUP, ASTRITH, *Getting Started in Batik*, Bruce, 1971.

ENTHOVEN, JACQUELINE, *Stitchery for Children*, Reinhold, 1968.
Original in its range (preschool and up) and many of its
techniques. Over 200 stitch diagrams and 175 photographs,
mostly of children's work.

FISH, HARRIET U., *Creative Lace Making*, Sterling, 1972. An old-
fashioned craft (hairpin lace) brought up to date.

FRESSARD, M. J., *Creating with Burlap*, Sterling, 1970. Cut it,
paint it, embroider it for lamp shades, wall hangings, dolls,
unusual table linens.

IVES, SUZY, *Making and Dressing a Rag Doll*, Drake, 1972. Pattern
and instructions for a really sophisticated rag doll and many
nifty dresses, including period costumes (Victorian, medieval, Edwardian, Regency).

JOHNSON, JANN, *The Jeans Book*, Ballantine, 1972. Some of the techniques and projects here are for experts, but even the youngest will get ideas for painting (directly on denim), nailhead decoration, appliqué, patchwork and embroidery on a favorite pair of jeans.

KORNERUP, ANN-MARI, *Embroidery for Children*, trans. from the Danish by Gerde M. Andersen, Van Nostrand, 1969.

LIGHTBODY, DONNA M., *Let's Knot*, Lothrop, 1972. Simple macrame —history, techniques and directions for bookmarks, jewelry, belts and so forth from knotted string, yarn, ribbon.

MAILE, ANNE, *Tie and Dye*, Ballantine Books, 1963. Some of the simpler methods here are within the capabilities of elementary school children. The craft, of course, has great possibilities for charm and attractiveness.

MARTIN, BERYL, *Batik for Beginners*, Scribner, 1971. Enthusiastic and meticulous too—a lovely book that takes into account the problems of those too young to use hot-dye methods.

MEYER, CAROLINE, *Stitch by Stitch*, Harcourt, 1970. Very readable, very simple and clear: needlework for beginners, stitches and projects.

———, *Yarn: The Things It Makes and How to Make Them*, Harcourt, 1972. Beginning on the most elementary level, instruction to initiate the young into the skills of crochet, knitting, weaving and macrame. Organized to suggest possibilities rather than merely outline projects.

MILLER, IRENE PRESTON, and WINIFRED LUBELL, *The Stitchery Book*, Doubleday, 1965. This book combines instruction in basic embroidery materials and stitches with some captivating original projects—Christmas ornaments (embroidered felt-on-pellon), banners, book covers, highly sophisticated rag dolls and wall hangings in which decorative stitches are combined with natural grasses, pebbles and shells.

NEWSOME, ARDEN J., *Make it with Felt*, Lothrop, 1972. Some of these projects, since they use glue rather than needle and thread, are suitable for nursery-schoolers. Toys, decorations, party stuff.

RAINEY, SARITA R., *Weaving Without a Loom*, Sterling, 1972. A brilliant and original little book: weaving with paper, into burlap and scrim, on a pencil, into wire, with drinking straws and with such unlikely materials as felt bits, weeds, cattails, fabric strips. A liberating technique for the child who can't draw well but has ideas about texture, pattern and color.

ROBINSON, RENÉE and JULIAN, *Streamlined Sewing for Fun*, St. Martins, 1969. From simple soft toys to a garden hammock, and lots of gaieties along the way—for boys as well as girls. Many attractive, easy stuffed dolls.

ROBINSON, STUART and PATRICIA, *Exploring Fabric Printing*, Charles T. Branford, 1972. Tie and dye, batik, silk screen, block printing . . . with recipes for dyes, sources of material, full instructions.

SATTLER, HELEN RONEY, *Sock Craft*, Lothrop, 1972. Gay, easy projects that convert socks into potholders, alligator puppets, beanbags, dolls, stuffed animals.

SEYD, MARY, *Designing with String*, Watson-Guptill, 1972. String and rope used not only for weaving, but for glued-on-surfaces composition, a rich and striking technique.

SHILLINGLAW, PHYL, *Introducing Weaving*, Watson-Guptill, 1972. If you happen to have sheep, this book will tell you how to card, spin and dye the wool—and how to use the fleece, untreated, in wall hangings. And if you haven't any sheep—well, there are still all sorts of exciting possibilities here.

WILSON, ERICA, *Fun with Crewel Embroidery*, Scribner, 1965. Simple projects for age 8 and up.

WILSON, JEAN, *Weaving Is for Anyone*, Reinhold, 1967. Every possible type of loom, from cardboard to backstrap, and a great variety of weaving techniques. How to select yarns, prepare and use natural materials such as grasses and reeds —and directions for simple projects.

WISEMAN, ANN, *Rags, Rugs and Wool Pictures*, Scribner, 1968.

ZARBOCK, BARBARA J., *The Complete Book of Rug Hooking*, Van Nostrand, 1969. All the operations involved in rug hooking—cutting fabric strips, preparing burlap and pulling the wool through—are well within the capabilities of elementary school children (and some kindergarteners); it's a craft with which they can achieve satisfying, professional-looking results (in potholders if not full-size floor rugs). This book gives information on all types of hooks and frames, and on preparing a design.

PRINTING

ANDREW, LAYE, *Creative Rubbings*, Watson-Guptill, 1969. The novelty of this book is its proposed technique of rubbing, not just by placing paper over found objects, but by *creating* a special form to be printed by the rubbing process. A method that produces professional results even for amateurs.

KAFKA, FRANCIS J., *Linoleum Block Printing*, Dover, 1972. This reprint of an old book needs revision: suggested projects and designs are dreary. But techniques are clearly explained.

KATZ, MARJORIE P., *Fingerprint Owls and Other Fantasies*, Lippincott, 1972. An imaginative little book, witty and charming, with ideas for printing using nothing but ink pad, paper, felt-tipped pen (for elaboration) and the imprint of finger tips, sides, palms, heel-of-the-hand.

OTA, KOSHI, *Printing for Fun*, McDowell, Obolensky, 1960. An English adaptation of a splendid Japanese original: guide to rubbings, monoprints, stenciling. With full color illustration.

RICE, STANLEY, *Getting Started in Prints and Patterns*, Bruce, 1971. A good basic book on design and printing techniques.

SEIDELMAN, JAMES E., and GRACE MINTONYE, *The Rub Book*, Crowell-Collier, 1968. For the youngest artists—a simple way to capture texture and pattern by rubbing with crayon on paper over coins, keys, etc.

STROSE, SUSANNE, *Potato Printing*, Sterling, 1968. Since the technique is elementary, the child's attention is directed to pattern and design.

TOKURIKI, TOMIKICHIRO, *Woodblock Print Primer*, Japan Publications, 1970. Quite advanced—for the older, apter child.

WEISS, HARVEY, *Paper, Ink and Roller*, W. R. Scott, 1958. A handsomely designed volume with clear directions for potato, stencil, cardboard and linoleum printing.

PHOTOGRAPHY

AMPHOTO (915 Broadway, New York 10010), leading publisher of books on photography, issues a catalog listing 600 titles, free on request.

BRUCE, HELEN F., *Your Guide to Photography*, Barnes and Noble, 1971.

DAUGHERTY, CHARLES M., *Mirror with a Memory*, Harcourt, 1959.

DESCHIN, JACOB, *Say It with Your Camera: An Approach to Creative Photography*, Whittlesey House, 1950.

FENTON, D. X., *Better Photography for Amateurs*, Amphoto, 1970.

FOLDES, JOSEPH, *Everybody's Photo Course*, Amphoto, 1966.

FREEMAN, MAE and IRA, *Fun with Your Camera*, Random House, 1955.

JACOBS, LOU, *You and Your Camera*, Lothrop, 1971.

HOKE, JOHN, *The First Book of Photography*, F. Watts, 1965.

KOHN, EUGENE, *Photography: A Manual for Shutterbugs*, Prentice-Hall, 1965. Lively and enthusiastic.

RHODE, ROBERT B., *Introduction to Photography*, Macmillan, 1971.

SULLIVAN, GEORGE, *Understanding Photography*, Warne, 1972. One of the most useful books: basic, thorough, crystal clear: a nontechnical discussion of choosing camera and accessories, taking pictures, developing and printing, composition, lighting and careers with a camera.

WEISBORD, MARVIN, *Basic Photography*, Amphoto, 1966.

WEISS, HARVEY, *Lens and Shutter: An Introduction to Photography*, W. R. Scott, 1971. An attractive feature of this book —in addition to its lively and lucid text—is its inclusion of photographs by such masters as Ansel Adams, Dorothea Lange, Edward Weston.

PUPPETS

ADAIR, MARGARET W., *Do-it-in-a-day Puppets for Beginners*, Day, 1964. How to make your puppets, create your script and perform—all in one day. Full directions for producing "Three Billy Goats Gruff," "King Midas and the Golden Touch" and "The Three Little Pigs."

ALKEMA, CHESTER JAY, *Puppet-Making*, Sterling, 1971. Puppets from paper bags, construction paper, ice-cream sticks, paper cups, etc.

LEWIS, SHARI, *Making Easy Puppets*, Dutton, 1967. Brief history of puppetry, directions for constructing puppets from simple materials and for making puppet stages.

PELS, GERTRUDE, *Easy Puppets*, Crowell-Collier, 1951. Novel puppets from apples, bottle caps, clothespins, buttons, as well as more conventional papier-mâché heads.

ROSS, LAURA and FRANK, *Finger Puppets*, Lothrop, 1971. Clear step-by-step directions for nine different types (some painted directly on the fingers, some constructed with cardboard or cloth). Includes suggestions for stories and poems to be dramatized.

ROSS, LAURA, *Hand Puppets: How to Make and Use Them*, Lothrop, 1969. Simple enough for preschoolers.

PAPER

ANDERSON, MILDRED, *Papier-Mâché and How to Use It*, Sterling, 1970. A something-for-everybody (and especially for butterfingers) book.

BANK-JENSEN, THEA, *Play with Paper*, Macmillan, 1962. Doll furniture, mobiles, collages and table decorations. Good photographs and diagrams.

BETTS, VICTORIA, *Exploring Papier-Mâché*, Davis Press, 1955.

CUMMINGS, RICHARD, *101 Masks: False Faces and Make-up for All Ages, All Occasions*, McKay, 1968. From the simplest transformations of paper plates and grocery bags to more complex creations of plaster of Paris, papier-mâché. Also: brief history of masks, three plays and a pantomime.

GRANIT, INGA, *Cardboard Crafting*, Sterling, 1965. Ordinary shirt cardboard, corrugated paper and old gift wrapping used imaginatively.

GROL, LINI, *Scissorscraft*, Sterling, 1970. Old-fashioned fold-and-cut papercraft brought up to date.

JOHNSON, PAULINE, *Creating with Paper*, University of Washington Press, 1958. Cutting, folding and paper construction for all ages.

KRINSKY, NORMA, and BILL BERRY, *Paper Construction for Children*, Reinhold, 1966. Reassuringly illustrated with photographs of children's work.

KONIJNENBERG-DE GROOT, *Cellophane Creations*, Sterling, 1972. Collages, flowers, pseudostained glass and dramatic lanterns made by combining cellophane with chicken wire, iron wire, glass, metal.

LINSLEY, LESLIE, *Decoupage: A New Look at an Old Craft*, Doubleday, 1972. Tempting cut-and-paste projects, beautifully illustrated.

LEWIS, A. W., *Basic Bookbinding*, Dover, 1957. Intended for serious, advanced hobbyists, but the introductory chapters will help a child master a most satisfying and useful skill.

MARKS, MICKEY KLAR, *Collage*, Dial, 1968. A few beginning projects to copy, to get the child started and inspire confidence. But the basic message is: "Be your own junk collector and gather things that appeal to you. Be original and create your own compositions with the materials that will reflect what you want to say on canvas. You are you—there is no one else in the world that is."

MASSOGLIA, ELINOR T., *Fun-time Paper Folding*, Children's Press, 1959. Japanese methods of making sailboats, fish, swans, baskets and so forth without cutting or pasting.

MUNSON, DON, and ALLIANORA ROSSE, *The Paper Book*, Scribner, 1970. A truly marvelous volume, good for kindergarteners on up through grandparents. Doll houses and furniture, costumes and masks, lampshades, greeting cards, dolls, animals and mobiles: with lucid explanations and very precise diagrams.

PFLUG, BETSY, *Funny Bags*, Van Nostrand, 1968. An imaginative exploration of the possibilities of ordinary brown paper bags plus crayons, paint, scissors, glue and decorative junk. Kites, masks, piñatas, crowns, costumes.

SEIDELMAN, JAMES E., and GRACE MINTONYE, *Creating with Papier-Mâché*, Crowell-Collier, 1971. Easy-to-follow directions and lively drawings.

STROSE, SUSANNE, *Making Paper Flowers*, Sterling, 1970.

TEMKO, FLORENCE, and ELAINE SIMON, *Paper Folding To Begin With*, Bobbs, 1968. Easy enough for preschoolers, such classic productions as the paper fan, the paper airplane, the newspaper hat.

VAN VOORST, DICK, *Corrugated Carton Crafting*, Sterling, 1970. Exciting ideas for building things that move, like a marvelous biplane.

WOOD, LEATHER, WIRE

GOTTSHALL, FRANKLIN H., *Wood Carving and Whittling Made Easy*, Bruce, 1969.

HANAUER, ELSIE, *Creating with Leather*, A. S. Barnes, 1970. For techniques, not for producing the curious objects pictured.

HOPPE, H., *Whittling and Wood Carving*, Sterling, 1971. Includes basic information on tools, techniques, characteristics and varieties of woods.

MAGINLEY, C. J., *Make It and Ride It*, Harcourt, 1949. Careful directions and clear diagrams for making an intriguing collection of vehicles: wagons, scooters, bike trailers and racers for a Soap Box Derby.

PARKER, XENIA LEY, *Working with Leather*, Scribner, 1972. Crisply and pleasantly done.

SCHEGGER, T. M., *Make Your Own Mobiles*, Sterling, 1965. Ideas for mobiles large and small—what materials to use, how to shape, cut, arrange and mount.

SEIDELMAN, JAMES E. and GRACE MINTONYE, *Creating with Wood*, Crowell-Collier, 1969. Beginner's projects with toothpicks, balsa, bark, wood scraps.

VILLIARD, PAUL, *A First Book of Leatherworking*, Abelard, 1972. Emphasizes *the way to work in leather*, not particular projects.

WEISS, HARVEY, *Clay, Wood and Wire*, W. R. Scott, 1946.

WEISS, HARVEY, *Collage and Construction*, W. R. Scott, 1970. A book to encourage judgment and discrimination as well as ingenuity. Illustrations alternate examples of competent amateur work with serious professional achievement in the same medium (a chasuble with appliqué by Matisse, a Calder mobile, a Louise Nevelson construction).

WILLIAMS, GUY R., *Making Mobiles*, Emerson, 1969. Clear, basic handbook for projects of increasing difficulty (from paper to wire and metal). Good photographs of distinguished work.

BEADS AND SHELLS

CONROY, NORMA M., *Making Shell Flowers*, Sterling, 1972. A child may not warm to the ladylike arrangements proposed here, but the technique is suggestive.

CUTLER, KATHERINE M., *Creative Shellcraft*, Lothrop, 1971. Includes a guide to various types of shells and clear instructions for working. Though there are lots of projects, the writer urges that the child not copy, but use these as a springboard for personal creations. "Shells are so beautiful that it is too bad to see them distorted with paint, dye, artificial faces, pipe-cleaner appendages, and other mechanical aids. Besides, it is much more fun to accept the challenge of making something with shells in their natural state."

LA CROIX, GRETHE, *Creating with Beads*, Sterling, 1971. Revelation for a child who thinks the only thing you can do with beads is string them in a line. Stunning necklaces, brooches, earrings.

SEITZ, MARIANNE, *Creating Silver Jewelry with Beads*, Sterling, 1971. Good-looking constructions requiring only beads, silver wire or sheet silver, shears and pliers.

WHITE, MARY, *How to Do Bead Work*, Dover, 1972. Traditional methods and designs.

ODDS AND ENDS

ALKEMA, CHESTER JAY, *Crafting with Nature's Materials*, Sterling, 1972. As with many such books, particular designs and projects suggested are less valuable than the general approach. Bits of seaweed, driftwood, pebbles, fallen nuts, dried berries, pine cones, dried pods (opened and shut), cattails, twigs and grasses are used in new ways. The section on sandcasting opens up fascinating avenues to explore.

CLAPPER, EDNA and JOHN, *Pack-o-Fun Craft Projects*, Hawthorn, 1972. More ingenuity than taste here. Things to do with foil pans, coat hangers, notebook spirals, popsicle sticks, even old computer punched cards. . . .

CUTLER, KATHERINE, *From Petals to Pinecones*, Lothrop, 1969. A good accompaniment to nature walks, designed to develop a "seeing eye," a new way of viewing pods, cones and dried weeds. Some traditional uses of natural materials (corn husks for dolls), many novel.

D'AMICO, VICTOR, and ARLETTE BUCHMAN, *Assemblage: A new dimension in creative teaching in action*, Museum of Modern Art, 1972. Seventy-eight graded projects for children from 4 to 14 employ natural and man-made materials in original three-dimensional constructions. Sample: for a five-year-old, a collage, "my favorite color"—a pink feather, a strand of pink wool, a piece of pink net, a swatch of patterned fabric predominantly pink, arranged to express the child's feeling about quintessential pinkness. For eight- to ten-year-olds, an imaginative animal made from a clothes hanger bent and then coated with tissue-paper mâché, suitably adorned (feathers, sequins, yarn, buttons). A fascinating book.

DANK, MICHAEL CARLTON, *Scrap Craft*, Dover, 1969. One hundred and five hideous objects with instructions for making. But no doubt a child could get ideas about procedure.

DE BROWER, AB, *Creating with Flexible Foam*, Sterling, 1971. Judging from the photographs, one would have to conclude that the material precludes either beauty or elegance. But it might be fun.

ECKSTEIN, ARTIS AILEENE, *How to Make Treasures from Trash*, Hearthside Press, 1972. Bells (that really chime) from cans, animals from light bulbs, clowns from bleach bottles and a dragon emerging from an empty margarine tub. Lots of projects within the range of the blunt-nose scissors set.

HELFMAN, HARRY, *Fun with Your Fingers: working with sticks, paper and string*, Morrow, 1968. Attractive, easy to read. Typical projects: weaving on a cardboard loom, printing with ink pad and string-wrapped wood block, constructing a string design by wrapping string around random nails in a board.

KESSLER, LEONARD P., *Art Is Everywhere*, Dodd, 1958. An enthusiastic wake-up-and-create book.

LEE, TINA, *Things to Do*, Doubleday, 1965. Toys and decorative articles from throwaways (corks, stamps, window envelopes, etc.).

LOPSHIRE, ROBERT, *How to Make Flibbers, etc.*, Beginner Books, 1964. Things to make and do for the youngest.

MELL, HOWARD, and ERIC FISHER, *Making Things from Odds and Ends*, Drake, 1972. Dreadfully condescending text written in Dick-and-Jane prose, but the projects are good for the only moderately skilled.

NEWSOME, ARDEN, *Spoolcraft*, Lothrop, 1970. Good uses for the junk every sewing drawer provides. Mostly very easy.

PFLUG, BETSY, *You Can*, Van Nostrand, 1969. Step-by-step instructions for converting cans (coffee, fruit juice, tuna, pop-top) into useful items. Simple tools (can opener, hammer and nails, pliers, paper punch) and techniques that allow for independent work by children ages 6 and up.

PRIOLO, JOAN, *Ideas for Collage*, Sterling, 1972. Full of ideas for tissue paper, rice paper, newspaper, wallpaper, magazine cuttings, fabrics and found objects.

RAZZI, JAMES, *Simply Fun!*, Parents Magazine Press, 1968. Projects easy enough for nursery-schoolers: a comic strip show, a pussy cat mask, a castle.

SATTLER, HELEN RONEY, *Kitchen Carton Crafts*, Lothrop, 1970. Pigs out of cereal boxes and doll dressers from penny matchboxes. An approach to open a child's eyes.

SIMMS, GORDON and CARYLE, *Introducing Seed Collage*, Watson-Guptill, 1972. All you need is glue, a surface to glue on, and peas, beans, lentils . . . the contents of the kitchen cupboard.

WEISS, HARVEY, *Sticks, Spools and Feathers*, W. R. Scott, 1962. Original and provocative.

WHITE, ALICE, *More Performing Toys*, Taplinger, 1972. Charming and whimsical toys made with simple equipment and junk (egg cartons, bottle caps, plastic containers).

WILLIAMS, PETER, *Making Things That Move*, World, 1972. A British book that doesn't condescend: it assumes intelligence, skill and persistence—all of which can result (with older children) in some highly satisfying productions—helicopters, kaleidoscopes, cameras, periscopes—made from ordinary household materials.

WIRTENBERG, PATRICIA Z., *All-around-the-house art and craft book*, Houghton, 1968. Unusual in that it aims at not just gadgetry but genuinely artistic work in collage, painting, sculpture, printing. Emphasis on inducing children to look at familiar objects in new ways.

5

Rings on Their Fingers, Bells on Their Toes: Music in the Child's Life

"Childhood is a musical time," says dance critic Olga Maynard, "and children are a musical sort of people." An infant responds to his mother's voice before he recognizes her face; long before real speech, he vocalizes for the pure pleasure of trying out sounds. A nine-monther will hum and buzz as he plays; discovering the pleasing clash of spoon against plate, he tries it again and again. Even the toy dropping which drives mothers mad is partly a musical game, a listening for noises. The toddler, a natural percussionist, bangs pot lids as ardently as any cymbal player. On the school playground, older children fit traditional melodies to their rope and ball games ("One, two, three a-lairy, I saw Mistress Mary . . ."). They clatter sticks along picket fences, enjoying rhythmic vibration; they delight in squeaky door hinges—and for real music, the opening bars of a favorite piece, will stop the most boisterous play. Above all, when happy or merely absorbed, they sing.

And what, in the usual course of affairs, becomes of the child's instinctive feeling for rhythm and harmony? A parent may dismiss it, smiling. "She's no Tebaldi, that's for sure." "Heifetz has nothing to worry about." Or the child is given piano lessons. He begins eagerly, imagining the wonderful music to flow from his fingers. But scales are a drag, note-reading hard work. After three months, he can barely hammer out "Three Blind Mice." Discouragement affects his willingness to practice. Mother nags,

"Lessons cost money, you know," and Father wonders aloud where all this is leading. The upshot in most homes is that the venture dies and a door is permanently closed. Thirty years later, the adult says ruefully, "I don't know a thing about music."

This kind of experience, common in families anxious to "give the children everything," reveals fundamental misconceptions about musical talent and training. Lessons in piano (or violin, another popular choice) are not the only musical experience open to the young child. A failed piano player might have distinguished himself on the flute. A child with no talent for playing an instrument might develop an educated ear, a capacity for rich musical enjoyment and response. As for the question, "Is my child gifted enough to make any training worthwhile?"—are children with no head for figures kept out of mathematics classes? Do we reserve writing instruction for pupils whose talent is words? Music, a profession for the gifted few, is a universal human need and experience, and some musical training should be a part of every child's education. Such training may or may not lead to performing skills. (Certainly the ability to make music is a special joy.) But wherever it is seriously undertaken, it leads to a fuller and more abundant *life*.

When a child possesses a strong natural talent, there's usually no problem about what to do with it. The gift announces itself. For the first years of his life, Rubinstein used only "song language," refusing normal speech; at three, Paderewski sat at the piano, picking out melodies with one finger; at three too, Mozart entertained himself at the clavier by picking out thirds (and within a year, was playing minuets perfectly). Tschaikovsky as a child had often to be physically dragged from the keyboard, after which he drummed tunes on the windowpanes (on one occasion so rapt that he broke the glass and cut himself badly). Lesser gifts need care and nurturing. In a favoring environment, the spark may become, if not a great blaze, at least a small private fire that warms the whole of life.

How does a parent create an atmosphere in which the child's

native musical impulses find satisfying expression? Certainly not just by providing half-hour lessons once a week. Ideally, music should be part of his life from the very beginning. A child who has never been sung to is a deprived child. The quality of the parent's singing voice is not important. If Mother or Father sings really well, that's marvelous, of course. But young children respond to tone and rhythm and timbre and *feeling*; to a sleepy child, or an unhappy one, the most faltering rendition of Brahms's "Cradle Song" may be exquisite comfort. (My daughters, when they were little, enjoyed my peculiar weakness as a singer. Because I couldn't carry a tune, "Frère Jacques" was different every time.) If adults spontaneously sing or hum or whistle about the house, children learn early that music is one of the ways in which human beings communicate, express feeling—and that music is *pleasurable*.

Singing

All children love to sing, alone or in groups—until and unless they're reproved for being too loud or off tune. What a pity, then, not to teach them songs, and to have them share singing experiences with that most important of all groups, the family. In many households, the only singing occurs at Christmas. But singing at table, before or after eating, is an utterly natural, happy thing to do. (My children sang a grace—"For health and strength and daily food We praise Thy name, O Lord"—long after they stopped attending Sunday school, not as a religious act but as an expression of joy in living.) Singing in the car on long trips, around the fire on winter nights, at picnics and parties and on rainy days—this contributes to musical as well as personal growth. Burl Ives, asked how he learned to sing, replied, "I started singing about as soon as I could talk. It was just something that went on in our family." It's a suggestive example.

Even the adult who regards himself as totally unmusical will find, searching his memory, that he knows dozens of songs "Clementine," "Row, Row, Row Your Boat," "Yankee Doodle," "Coming Through the Rye," "My Bonnie Lies Over the Ocean," "Swing Low, Sweet Chariot," "Oh! Susanna." Children love these songs as well as those intended specifically for the young. What songs are best to sing with children? Any that give pleasure. A five-year-old will be as delighted by "What Shall We Do with the Drunken Sailor?" as by "Here Is Thumbkin." Ideally, though, songs for the very young are simple, direct, rhythmically strong and concerned with familiar things—animals, people, vehicles, holidays, daily activities.

Repeated words and nicely clinking rhymes are good, and swinging choruses. ("Jimmy crack corn and I don't care, Jimmy crack corn and I don't care, My master's gone away!") Children love songs with a strong pattern, regularly varied by small changes ("The farmer takes a wife . . . The wife takes a child . . . The child takes a nurse") and songs ornamented with delicious nonsense. ("To my wing wong waddle-O, Jack sing saddle-O, blowsey boys bubble-O Under the moon!") Onomatopoeia, imitative sound, provides rich dramatic opportunities: the animal noises in "Old Macdonald Had a Farm," the final explosion of "Pop Goes the Weasel" or the satisfying CHOO CHOO! of "Down by the Station, Early in the Morning." Some of the most popular songs for children carry their own vivid suggestions for accompanying action. ("I am a little teapot, short and stout; Here is my handle, here is my spout. Tip me over and pour me out.") Others, like "Oh Where, Oh Where Is My Little Dog Gone?" call on the child's natural dramatic inventiveness.

Songs are more meaningful when they're made personal. Wherever possible, introduce the child's own name ("To get a little rabbit skin To wrap our darling *Peggy* in") or events from his own experience. In "Oh, Dear, What Can the Matter Be?" forget about Johnny and the fair; it can be "Roger's so slow with his lunch!" Change "Paw Paw Patch" to wonderings more appropriate: "Where O where is sweet little Janet? Where O where is sweet little Janet? Where O where is sweet little Janet? Way down yonder swinging on the swing!" (Playing in the sand, Picking dandelions—whatever fits the rhythm and the child.) Action songs like "Here We Go Round the Mulberry Bush" can be adapted to any situation. ("This is the way we wash our hands . . . brush our teeth . . . eat our peas. . . .") Once children get the idea that a song is a live thing, they'll improvise on their own. The last time I watched five-year-olds playing "London Bridge," they progressed rapidly from the ritual "Build it up with bricks and stones" to a happy-loony "Build it up with bread and jam!"

Sometimes, try taking the tune of a traditional song and making a completely new song. "Scrub, scrub, scrub your arms Fresh and clean and white, Merrily, merrily, merrily, merrily in the bath tonight!": that's "Row, Row, Row Your Boat" made relevant. Take off "Yankee Doodle": "Little Harry went downtown to buy a bit of candy, He bought a great big lollipop And thought if fine and dandy."

A child not able to master a song's lyrics can still join in on the chorus, or with repeated phrases (*Fa la la la* or the *Ron, Ron, Ron Petit patapon* of "*Il était une bergère*")—an exercise which, incidentally, helps develop the sense of pitch. And don't forget that preschoolers love songs that grow by adding links to the chain. "Hush little baby, don't say a word, Mama's going to buy you a mocking bird. If that mocking bird don't sing, Mama's going to buy you a diamond ring. If that diamond ring turns to brass, Mama's going to buy you a looking glass" and so on to "If that horse and cart break down, YOU'LL BE THE SWEETEST BABY IN TOWN!" Others of this type are "There's a hole in the bottom of the sea," "Green Grow the Rushes O," and, of course, "The Twelve Days of Christmas." Finally, most joyfully, introduce children young to singing games—and don't just save them for birthday parties. "Looby Loo," "Hokey Pokey, "Pop Goes the

Weasel," "Go In and Out the Window"—these are as much a part of every child's rightful heritage as *Mother Goose*.

Every family should own a collection of recorded songs (folk, ethnic, traditional) and as many songbooks and hymnals as possible, from which children build up, over the years, their own repertoire of favorites. (Children who miss the experience of singing in their early years grow up knowing, for the most part, only singing commercials.) "I can't overemphasize the importance of singing with small children," says University of New Hampshire music professor Mary Rasmussen. "Twenty years later, you can pick out the kids who've had singing at home. They have a feeling for rhythm and pitch. Drop a comment, and they burst into song: it's like an extra language. You might say singing is the musical equivalent of hiking—something sociable and cheering you can do with friends and strangers."

Listening to Music

Hearing music played on radio or record player is another way children make music a part of their lives as natural as breathing. A necessary caution here, though. If the radio is snapped on mornings with the coffee percolator and kept going all day, so that everyone is constantly awash in a sea of sound, that's likely to have a reverse effect: the child grows up not sensitive to music but totally insensitive. Partly this is because the quality of so much commercial music is dreadful—cheap, banal, stupefying. But even the best music is misused if it's made mere background—music to iron by, eat with, talk across. Children learn active, truly responsive listening when listening is made a special activity—as it is, for instance, in a good nursery school, where toys are put away and the little ones comfortably settled before record time begins. The kind of music chosen, the occasion, the length of a listening period—all that depends on the individual. A dreamy, introverted youngster may enjoy a half-hour of "grown-up" music, Mozart or Vivaldi, before bedtime. An up-and-at-'em six-year-old may want only a single favorite song, "Brave Cowboy Bill," before he dashes out to play. Whatever the choice, the child should have some experience of music as special, a delight in itself.

In a household where adults regularly play music for their own enjoyment, children will want, sometimes, to listen too. This provides a happy opportunity for quiet sharing and perhaps some—*very* informal—instruction, if the child asks questions. It goes without saying that no child should ever be lectured about music. If, though, he's curious about the voice of a particular instrument—"What made that high tweety sound?"—a knowledgeable parent can provide answers. A less knowledgeable one can advance his own musical education along with the child's through such records as A *Child's Introduction to the Orchestra* (Golden). Sometimes a musically precocious youngster becomes interested in a particular composer. (I recall a four-year-old who was mad for Mozart and could identify his music infallibly.) That's a cue for a library trip to check the offerings in biographies of famous musicians.

Even where a family owns a first-rate stereo system, a child needs his own record player. The quality of sound reproduction will be inferior, certainly. But there's no substitute for the child's being able to control his own music time—play the same record over and over if he chooses—and to listen in absolute privacy. Besides, there's a special delight in squatting on the floor, beside the player, watching the disc spin around and around. I recall, from my older daughter's first years, her passion for a record called *Train to the* Zoo. "The train is in the station, It's going to the zoo, It's full of little boys and girls But there's still room for *you*. Choo-oo CHOO! Choo-oo CHOO!" The summer she was three, we spent several weeks with friends who owned a phonograph and a sizable collection of juvenile records. Rona listened with polite interest. But every afternoon, before nap time, she would sit on the floor by her bed and, crouched over an imaginary record player, would flip an imaginary switch. "Click! Wait until it warms up. . . ." A minute later, we'd hear singing, very soft. "The train is in the station, It's going to the zoo. . . ." Whatever it was that moved this three-year-old—images of animals, promise of friends, or simply a familiar melody —it had become an important part of her life rhythm.

Live Music

Listening to records and singing can do much to promote musical development. Good radio and TV programs (like Leonard Bernstein's brilliantly conceived children's concerts, or the Sunday "Camera Three" and "Wake Up and Live" offerings) enrich and extend musical knowledge. But there's no substitute for live music. An amateur folk singer accompanying himself on the guitar will probably mean more to a seven-year-old than a Pete Seeger recording (though he should certainly hear Pete Seeger too). Children want to see real instruments—touch them, if possible—and real people, ordinary people, playing them. Once past the wriggly stage, they enjoy grown-up concerts judiciously chosen. A full evening of symphony orchestra is too much for the average child, but most communities offer less concentrated musical experiences—an hour of choral singing, a chamber group or an operetta.

It's wise to prepare children in advance—not only with respect to the behavior expected of concert-goers, but also for the program's content. Before a child sees *The Magic Flute*, for example, he should know the story and its characters. Ideally, he should also have some familiarity with the music. Most libraries maintain a circulating record collection. If you procure the appropriate records and play them in the days preceding the concert, the child will enjoy the pleasure of recognition as well as discovery.

A special after-concert thrill is meeting a performer or talking to musicians in the pit.

Training the Ear

Before a child can respond to music, he must be able to *hear* it. That sounds obvious enough—but in a complex urban society, many "natural" skills cease to be natural and have consciously to be cultivated. Adults accustomed to constant, multifarious machine noises sometimes seem not to register anything. I've heard marijuana smokers say that until they got stoned, they had never really heard music, never been able to distinguish the separate voices of an orchestra. Yet ten-year-olds taught to listen do that very easily.

One of the best ways to train a child's ear is by the guessing games described in Chapter 7 (All Together: Family Activities). Begin with the simplest sit-very-quiet-and-tell-me-what-you-hear variety. You'll be surprised to discover how many noises an alert child will detect in a "quiet" house: the refrigerator hum, the clock tick, the *whoosh* of a car going by, footsteps in a distant room, a pot boiling, his own heartbeat. . . . Now reverse the procedure. Have the child shut his eyes while you produce noises for him to identify: a drawer closing, a light switch snapped on, the winding of a watch, knuckles tapped on the table, a shoe dropped, paper being crumpled. Or ask the child to make noises imitating common sounds, while you guess. Children are often startlingly adept at reproducing siren howls, the clop of horses galloping, the screech of brakes and the cork POP when a bottle's opened. Of the many special-sound-effects records which can be used in conjunction with these games, two are notably good: *Muffin in the City, Muffin in the Country* (Young People's Records), about a little dog who learns to listen when he can't see, and *The Lonesome House*, which reproduces lovely spooky empty-house noises.

Making Simple Musical Instruments

From such games, it's an easy step to the child's first systematic exploration of musical sound. When a preschooler bangs noisily on a pan, show him that different beaters evoke different sounds. A metal spoon produces a ring, a wooden one a dull bong. An old shoe tree (the kind with flexible stem and wooden ball tip) goes rat-tat-tat. Since the natural approach to music and rhythm is through tapping, hitting or shaking, show the child how simple percussion instruments can be made from household objects. A Band-Aid can half-filled with rice or pebbles makes a dandy shaker; empty, or holding water, it makes a good thing-to-beat. Beef rib bones, washed and dried, clatter against each other with wonderful resonance; walnut shells clapped together sound like castanets; pie plates or pot covers produce a muffled cymbal effect; a fork suspended by a string and struck with another fork gives out a delicate triangle-like note. A flat smooth stone, believe it or not, makes a bell: suspend it by a heavy cord or leather thong and strike with a stick, or with another stone. Ordinary drinking glasses offer an experience in music making that never fails to enchant a child. Line up your glasses according to the tone each gives off when struck, empty, with a spoon— lowest tone on the left, highest on the right. Pour increasing amounts of water into the glasses so that you get a series of ascending notes. (Using food color to make each note a different color adds to the fun.) Now, using a spoon or stick, try out your tunes.

Drum possibilities are endless. Use a wooden salad bowl with oilcloth tacked over the top, a coffee can with a heavy wrapping paper head secured by rubber bands (or partly filled with water and topped with rubber from an old inner tube).

From percussion, move on to primitive woodwinds, where

sound is produced by blowing. Blow through different-length paper or plastic straws; through a key; through a cornstalk or a hollow willow branch (to get a good note, cut a notch in the branch and use the notched bit to plug one end). Fold a piece of wax paper over the teeth of a comb and hold it to your lips, moving the paper-wrapped comb back and forth as you hum. Blow lightly across the top of an empty bottle pressing the top edge against your lower lip; pour in a little water and blow again.

Making a satisfactory stringed instrument takes some work, but ordinary rubber bands in combination with twigs and boxes will give some idea of sounds possible through plucking or strumming. The simplest possible stringed instrument is a rubber band held in the teeth and then looped over two fingers of one hand. Stretch the band—very gently—and pluck with the other hand. A wishbone or a slingshot with one or more rubber bands stretched across the Y makes a tiny harp. A cigar-box bottom, grooved to hold rubber bands of different widths, can be plucked or strummed. (Arrange the rubber bands in graduated sizes, thinnest to widest.)

Many of these home instruments can be profitably coordinated with art activities. A small child will enjoy painting his oatmeal box drum or pie pan tambourine. A child old enough to handle saw, hammer and drill can construct all sorts of ingenious instruments—marimba, recorder, clay maracas and so forth. (For a comprehensive guide to homemade instruments, see Chapter 9 of *Creative Rhythmic Movement for Children* by Gladys Andrews, or *Make Your Own Musical Instruments* by Muriel Mandell and Robert E. Wood.) In addition to the pleasure of making, the young musician can experiment with ways to use his instrument —composing little tunes, if he's set up toned glasses, or using his drum to beat the rhythm of a song.

Activity of this sort is diverting but more than diversion: it creates a basis for mature musical understanding. Playing about with reeds, glasses and coffee cans, the child discovers, for instance, that instruments need resonating chambers; if they are

held during playing, the sound is dulled. He will observe that a
drum with a skin head sounds different in dry and wet weather—
and that the sound changes according to where the head is struck
(a spot near the side being better, generally, than the center).
He discovers the relation between sound and vibration: on a big
drum, the vibration is both felt and *seen*. As the child's experience in music making grows, he sees that the larger an instrument is, the lower its sound; a long whistle makes a deep sound,
a short whistle makes a shrill one. If water is used to produce tone,
then the more water, the lower the tone. When rubber bands
are used as strings, the tone depends on the width and thickness
of the band (thicker = deeper). Short strings give a higher note
than long strings. On a primitive wood instrument—say, a whistle with holes—covering both holes gives a low note, opening
both gives a high note, and covering one gives a middle note. The
child who makes such discoveries *for himself* is developing a true
musical sense and an instinct for free, creative adventure in all
fields related to music.

Rhythm Instruments and Musical Games

In addition to devising his own music makers, the child should
have some experience with standard percussion instruments—
drums, bongos, rhythm sticks, wood blocks, maracas, gourd rattles, castanets, finger cymbals, sleigh bells and so forth. Many
can be purchased inexpensively. Don't go to a toy counter for
these; go to a music store.* Creative Playthings (Princeton, N.J.,
and representatives around the country) produces a seven-piece

* Good-quality, reasonably priced rhythm instruments can be ordered by mail
from the Children's Music Center, 5373 W. Pico Boulevard, Los Angeles, Cal.
90019. A set of plain rhythm sticks, for example, costs 25 cents, wrist bells and
jingle clogs are 50 cents, and a tambourine (5 pairs of jingles) is $3.00. For $19.95,
you can get a very complete rhythm instrument set (15 pieces), well balanced
for all kinds of rhythms and accompaniments, hitting and ringing activities.

set (including a skin-head tambourine) that sells for around ten dollars; it's not exactly professional quality, but quite adequate for a beginner.

The best use for such instruments is not, perish the thought, organizing children into a rhythm band. (Shades of elementary school teachers a generation ago, conducting troupes of glassy-eyed little robots.) Rather, show how they can be used to mark a beat or enrich familiar music. Begin by letting the child try out different instruments, observing the special "voice" of each. He'll discover that the triangle has a higher pitch than the tom-tom; that both drum and triangle resound longer than do rhythm sticks or jingle clogs. Direct his attention by questions. Which instruments can play fast? (Rattles, tambourines, shakers, maracas.) Which is louder, the big drum or the little one? Which is softer, the triangle or the finger cymbals? Which instruments produce metallic, ringing, high-pitched sounds? (Triangles, cymbals, bells.) Which produce sharp, staccato, hollow sounds? (Wood blocks, temple blocks, drums struck with a hard beater, tambourines struck with the hand. . . .) A scraping sound? (Wood blocks.) A crashing, roaring sound? (Cymbals struck with a hard beater or clashed together.)

Once the child knows what the various instruments can do, let him choose appropriate percussion accompaniment for familiar songs. Take "Old Macdonald Had a Farm." Rhythm sticks can beat the underlying pattern. For a MOO sound, drums, maybe? QUACK QUACK can be a rattle of maracas, OINK a scraping of sand blocks and BAA a high triangle note. Or elaborate the rhythms of any verse with a strong marked beat. Skipping rhymes are good for this:

> My *m*other *gave* me *fi*fty *cents*
> To *see* the *e*lephant *jump* the *fence.*
> He *jumped* so *high*
> He *skinned* his *eye*
> And *nev*er came *back* till the *fourth* of July.

So is almost any rhyme in *Mother Goose:*

> Hickory dickory dock   (rhythm sticks)
> The mouse ran up the clock.   (rattle)
> The clock struck one   (gong)
> The mouse ran down   (tambourine)
> Hickory dickory dock!   (drum)

Other Good Games

■ Ask the child to imitate common sounds by using percussion instruments. Which one can sound like a knock on the door? (Sticks, drum.) Like a horse galloping? (Wood blocks.) A telephone ringing? (Wrist bells.) Footsteps in the hall? (Sand blocks.) Marching soldiers? (Snare drums.) An alarm clock? (Triangle.)

■ Beat out on the drum (or by hand claps) a simple pattern:

Ask the child to repeat it on his instrument. Take turns making patterns for each other.

■ Beat out, with drums or rhythm sticks or hand claps, the rhythm of a *very* familiar tune and see if the child can identify it.

("London Bridge")

Then let him beat out a song for you.

■ Beat out names (his own, his friends, famous people) and see if he can guess. *Ben*-ja-min   *John* F. *Ken*-nedy

▪ Ask the child to go to the window and then try to describe, using a percussion instrument only, what he observes—rain, a car starting, a bird singing, the garbage truck banging cans. . . .

▪ Follow the drum. When you beat loud, he stomps in time; soft and fast, he tiptoe-runs. Take turns at this. (It's most fun if you have several children making a line.) A variation of this game is to use three rhythm instruments, each one calling for a different kind of moving. Drum, for instance, can mean marching, triangle is hopping or skipping, bells are running. As you shift from one instrument to the other, the child must change his gait.

Choosing an Instrument

Eventually—and with some children, eventually comes very early—the young musician wants a *real* instrument. Since any good musical instrument represents a substantial expense, choosing and buying should proceed with caution. Sometimes the child seems to know, in his blood and bones, the instrument he needs. There are children who want to *blow*, a longing satisfied by brasses and woodwinds, and children who want to feel the vibration of stringed instruments held close to the body. But most youthful choices are purely whimsical. A boy wants a drum because he admires the drummer of a rock group; a girl dreams of a harp over which she can bend with flushed cheek and streaming hair. Or the fourth-grade music teacher gives a demonstration in connection with the school's instrument rental program and the child runs home breathless. "Mom, I want a trumpet!" ("If the band needs three trumpets," says one conservatory teacher grimly, "you can be sure that three kids will choose trumpets.")

Choosing an instrument through the school instruction and rental program, where such an arrangement exists, has certain obvious practical advantages. The family rents an instrument for a modest monthly fee, rental costs being applied to purchase price if, ultimately, the student wishes to buy outright. This way, the child gets a chance to test his skill (and interest) before making a major commitment: that's tempting. The rented instrument is insured against loss or damage: that's useful. Less obvious are the disadvantages. Though many programs provide new instruments, some offer used ones discouraging both in their battered appearance and their worn, hard-to-work mechanisms. Don't underestimate the importance of *looks* as a beginning incentive. The child who has anticipated the gleaming brassy splendor of a French horn may get a sad shock on opening the case that has served dozens of horn players before him. In any case, for health reasons, no child should use a secondhand wind instrument; the dark, moist interior provides an ideal breeding ground for germs. The quality of rented strings—violins, violas, cellos—is particularly likely to be inferior. Most insidious of all, when instruments are rented through the school, there may be subtle pressure from the music teacher in favor of those instruments the orchestra happens to need. The fact that the school has a spot for an oboe player is no reason for a child to choose the oboe as his instrument.

Other typical wrong reasons for choosing are: the family already owns a clarinet (or can get one cheap from a friend); Father used to play the cello and has always regretted giving it up; trumpet players are said to be in demand; a piano would look marvelous by the bay window and so . . . A satisfying, creative musical experience is possible only if the child has a genuine desire to play his instrument—and if he's physically and temperamentally suited to it.

Physical considerations—size, strength, musculature and motor skills—come first. A tiny person would do well to steer clear of large, heavy, cumbersome instruments like the bass viol and the sousaphone. A cellist needs long fingers. A short fourth finger (a common condition) rules out any of the strings. A trombonist should have long arms (to push the slide all the way out). Sheer strength is a factor in playing the brasses. A trumpeter needs strong lips and good wind; he must also be able to hold his instrument straight out from the mouth without any other support.

Of trumpet playing generally, Mary Rasmussen, founder and editor of *The Brass Quarterly*, observes, "Many are called and few are chosen. It's the ultimate aspiration of 50% of small boys —and the attainable goal of about 2%." Physical characteristics are more important here than with any other instrument, with the possible exception of the French horn. With most instruments, gift and sheer determination may compensate for less than optimum physical equipment. But a trumpeter *must* have the right *embouchure*, set of mouth, teeth and lips ("a gift of God and heredity," says Miss Rasmussen). This is commoner among blacks who have a higher muscle tone in the face than whites; for Caucasians, a good trumpet-set involves very thin lips, a pronounced crease nose-to-mouth, and exceptionally flat, even teeth. If orthodonture is a possibility, the trumpet is out. If a child gets lots of colds and ear infections, trumpet should not be considered; blowing pressure drives mucus into the ears and may cause serious infection.

The oboist needs an *embouchure* similar to that of the trumpet player—thin lips and a well-muscled face, capable of holding a reed tightly in position for hours. Lung power, however, is less important with oboe than with trumpet, since air is expelled rather than blown. A clarinet player should have a natural overbite and flat front teeth. The bassoon calls for long fingers; it's a big instrument. And the French horn requires a very flexible face and mobile, even fairly full lips. ("If a kid has buck teeth and a receding chin," says Miss Rasmussen, "parents should not let him be pushed into playing a brass instrument. He can't possibly make the grade.")

With some instruments, coordination is more important than physical makeup. This is true of violin, viola, cello and bass;

each requires right and left hand and arm to do simultaneously different things. (Roberta Markel, head of the United Nations International School music department, compares aptitude for playing the strings with ability to pat the stomach with the right hand while rubbing the top of the head with the left.) Finger dexterity is essential for the flute but not, surprisingly, for the piano (which, according to some experienced teachers, is the best instrument for normally awkward children). "Handedness," however, good control of right and left, is important for piano, as is eye-hand and hand-foot coordination.

Natural musicality is the next consideration—a quality hard to define but not really hard to recognize. The musical child manifests early a strong feeling for rhythm; he responds to music with the passion other children bring to toys and treats; he recognizes a familiar piece after the first few bars, and can hum the melody; he can reproduce exactly a note or a musical phrase; he sings in tune (and knows when another voice, or an instrument, is out of tune). Such a child has the ear and sense of pitch for stringed instruments, which must be tuned before playing and which require a delicate awareness of the tone produced by movement of the bow. A good ear is also essential for the trombone, which offers a player no help in locating a note: if he can't hear it, he can't play it. That goes for the French horn too: its notes are so close together that a player needs the subtlest discrimination. As one junior orchestra conductor puts it, "for the French horn player, every entry is perilous. He has to pick his note out of nowhere. He hasn't the margin of error available to, say, a trumpet player."

In addition to having the right ear, a naturally musical child is likely to possess the stamina necessary for mastering those instruments with which no quick results are possible—violin, cello, French horn (the last fiendishly difficult to play). A musical child should also, probably, be guided toward those instruments for which the most interesting music has been written. Piano and violin have a rich, tremendous repertory. The range available for flute is extraordinarily wide—everything from easy duets through Mozart quartets to the most blazingly demanding contemporary music. The clarinet has the best nineteenth century repertory of any woodwind (lovely Brahms and Schubert) and much good contemporary music too. Oboe music, on the other hand, is not generally exciting; oboists learn a small repertory of études, have almost no solo repertory. As for the tuba—well, in spite of the determinedly upbeat message of the popular children's record, *Tubby the Tuba*, about a tuba who longed to play tunes, inspiring music has not been written for tuba players. Tuba and bass, natural "support" instruments that don't carry the melody, are frustrating for the passionately musical but generally satisfactory for children less gifted.

Temperament and emotional makeup should be considered in any instrument choice. Is the child persistent, serious about learning, willing to defer quick gratification for rich rewards later on? Then he might tackle violin or viola. A child not patient enough for the slow climb might be happy with clarinet ("perfect for unmusical kids who want to play," according to one school band director) if his physical makeup is right. Guitar offers rewards at every possible level. An indifferent musician can have a fine time just fooling around—and a good one can move on to serious achievement with lute or classical guitar. Recorder is ideal for the youngster who hasn't the stick-to-it-iveness for regular practice but who wants the occasional pleasure of tootling away. ("You can't get out of shape with a recorder," says Miss Rasmussen, "because you're never *in* shape. There's no *embouchure* involved, nothing to keep up. Recorder is easy to play badly, almost impossible to play well. It's like being a virtuoso on a tin whistle.")

Some instruments call for a special temperament. A bassoonist has to be content with undramatic supporting roles. A horn player needs flamboyance. And an oboist, because he can't purchase reeds commercially, should have a kind of watchmaker's mentality: a craftsman's willingness to sit quietly, meticulously scraping reeds. An oboe player will spend hours every week working with knives and wax. One slip of the knife and the reed's spoiled.

Another important question: what does the child want to do with his music? Is he a solitary individual or a joiner? Piano, violin and guitar can be completely satisfying to the introverted child (though of course they offer social possibilities too). The child eager for a group musical experience, on the other hand, should think of instruments used in parade and jazz bands, orchestras, chamber and rock groups. Tuba, French horn, oboe, bassoon, are always in demand. Bass viol is a good dance band instrument. An electric guitar player will have no trouble finding a rock group. (Special caution: if your child plays in a rock and roll band, see that he's fitted with ear plugs by a responsible physician. College health services report an alarming increase in cases of irreparable hearing loss caused by the decibel level of rock bands in small rooms. It's literally deafening.)

In considering what a child wishes to do with music, most parents naturally think in here-and-now terms. The difficult, necessary task is to project. What will he do with his music at age thirty-five? Saxophone, so thrilling to a fifteen-year-old, is a musical dead end unless a man wants to play in dance bands all his life. It's not a terribly expressive instrument; it's not used in symphony orchestras. Trumpet falls into the same category. What does a virtuoso trumpeter do at age thirty-five? Well, he can play with a civic orchestra—*maybe*, the catch being that there will be dozens of candidates for a single opening. If your child is hooked on trumpet or sax, let him play it by all means. But try also to persuade him to study another instrument (not one he blows) as a solidly practical alternative.

Viewed from the long-range perspective, many popular instruments look less good. Piano is fine for solitary pleasure, but it won't get you into a symphony orchestra, and no church choir needs more than one pianist. Flute is delicious, the ideal amateur's instrument, but so popular currently that there are always too many flutes. The high school's prize flautist finds, when he gets to college, that the orchestra has places for twenty-four violins—and two flutes. A good flute player, a good clarinetist, may find few opportunities, while even a ham-handed cellist is sought after. In fact, if you're thinking in terms of chances to play, there's nothing like the strings.

Finally, but by no means incidentally, the child's choice of instrument should be considered in relation to family expense and responsibility. Is music vitally important to this child, or should money available for his personal development be spent in other ways? Where music is a child's whole life, parents might properly consider some sacrifices for a costly instrument (English horn, oboe) that the child really longs to play. If, on the other hand, his chief talents and interest lie elsewhere, it would seem unwise to spend eight hundred dollars for a bassoon when a four-dollar recorder offers some elementary musical experience. Among orchestra instruments, flute and trumpet offer inexpensive choices (not much over a hundred dollars for student models). Used upright pianos can be acquired, often, for no more than the cost of moving; no instrument is more versatile, or more basic to musical understanding than the piano. And an outlay of seventy-five to a hundred dollars is sufficient for a guitar, a good choice for the child who loves to sing.

Another, related consideration: what about transporting instruments? A child who plays piccolo or violin can be independent (and for some children that's important), carrying his instrument wherever he plans to play. A drummer depends on the family car. As for the harpist—well, "A harpist should have lots of pluck, A long black formal—and a truck."

Music Lessons

How early should a child start? As soon as he asks for lessons. Four or five is not too young for beginning piano instruction.

Miss Rasmussen advises a year of piano for every child, because ability to visualize the keyboard—black and white notes, whole and half steps—is a valuable preliminary to mastering any instrument. Where possible, she feels, a child should also have at least one year with a stringed instrument, to train his ear.

Many teachers feel that before eight, a child is not mature enough, physically or emotionally, for serious instrumental study. One notable exception must be mentioned: the Suzuki method of learning violin. This system, originating in Japan, is based on the principle that children learn best by ear and by imitation. At three—or even younger—a Suzuki pupil is given a miniature violin, one-sixteenth normal size. He is shown how to hold it, how to finger and use the bow; he listens to a simple tune played by his teacher (or on a record) and then, before he can read a single note, he *plays*. By ear. Only after he has experienced the satisfaction of making music does he embark on the more tedious business of note-reading.

The success of the Suzuki method, here and in Japan, has been phenomenal. At an age when other young violinists are just starting out, Suzuki pupils perform difficult concertos. Two qualifications should be noted, though. Some musicians feel that Suzuki-trained violinists remain permanently deficient in sight-reading ability. And the method demands a high degree of parent participation. One parent must attend every lesson, learning how to tune the child's instrument and to supervise his home practice, checking position and bowing techniques.

In general, though, formal training won't begin until the child is in third or fourth grade—when he is physically well coordinated and has had some experience with simple music makers like the tonette (song flute) or one of the percussion instruments. Group instruction, a growing trend, offers distinct advantages to beginners—the pleasures of comradeship, friendly competition, and a first experience of ensemble playing. It is also less expensive than private lessons. Combining group instruction with some private work, say one half-hour lesson a week, is probably the best possible arrangement for a young child.

Choosing a teacher is a delicate, tricky, important matter. You can tell a lot by the students a teacher produces. Attend a recital. If all the students are playing pieces by composers you've never heard of, music contrived for pedagogical purposes, that's a bad sign. Do you want your child to play Mozart and Haydn? Then see what X's pupils do with Mozart and Haydn. If your child hopes to play popular music, then look for someone whose pupils play pop with style, taste and enthusiasm. Finding out which teachers are regarded as good musicians is easy; public school music departments, local orchestra leaders, musically knowledgeable friends, even music store employees can provide names. But an accomplished performer is not necessarily a good teacher. A good teacher for advanced students may be all wrong for beginners—too demanding, or too sophisticated in approach. And a teacher good for one child may be a discouraging or destructive one for another child. The "fit" between teacher and pupil is more important in music, probably, than in any other area.

Any parent can tell a good deal about a teacher's rightness, for though he may know little about music, he knows his child. If the teacher you're considering gives group lessons, ask to attend a session. If that's not possible, you can surely observe your child's first lesson. What is the teacher's attitude to his pupil? Some children wish to be treated with seriousness and a kind of adult dignity; they are offended by "talking down" ("Look, my fingers do a funny little dance on the piano keys") or by the teacher's talking over their heads to a parent. Other children need to be played with a bit. A scholarly youngster positively enjoys a bookish approach; he wants to study musical notation, have written-out assignments. Another child may be put off by theory until he's had a chance to coax some real notes out of his trumpet or pick out a simple piano tune. A good teacher understands the child's temperament and responds appropriately.

Other things to watch for in judging a music teacher. Does he begin by teaching the child how to hold his instrument? Does he appreciate not only the child's possibilities but also his limitations—of energy, motor controls, attention span? Does he take advantage of the child's natural curiosity and sometimes follow where that leads? Does he maintain discipline but still encourage spontaneous play with music (making up tunes, playing by ear, producing sound in unconventional ways)? Is he sensitive to the child's need for variety? Does he ensure some successful experiences at each lesson—for example, by ending with an exercise previously mastered rather than with a difficult new task? Is he teaching the child to *hear* music as well as to play it? Does he value the child's freedom and joy in music making above drill-induced perfection?

When a Child Loses Interest in His Music

However carefully chosen the teacher, there comes a moment in every child's musical experience when interest flags. Recurring moments, indeed. The boy who once couldn't wait to start lessons now inscribes, inside his carrying case, I HATE THE VIOLIN. (That's case history, not invention.) The girl who rushed to the keyboard when ecstatic or unhappy ("Piano is my special little friend") finds excuses not to practice or, pushed into putting in her time, bangs furiously. What makes children turn away from their music, and what can parents do to help?

The single commonest cause of failing enthusiasm is a tussle over practicing. The child misses a practice period, the parent reminds. He misses several periods (or cuts them short), the parent begins to nag. Ultimately the cycle of reluctance-reproof reaches a climax of recriminations in which, however high-minded the parent, money enters in. "Have you any idea what we've spent on your lessons—to say nothing of buying you that cello! If you don't practice, you don't get lessons and that's that!" At this point the little criminal may well decide to stop wasting the family substance. He gives up.

Perhaps the first thing to say of this familiar impasse is that no valuable experience should ever be made conditional on the child's behaving himself well, being "good." If your child didn't do his homework, would you threaten to withdraw him from school? Irregular practicing may mean that the family hasn't worked out a satisfactory routine (and music practice is inevitably a family matter). Particularly with a young child, it's vital that the best time for practice be carefully thought out and strictly adhered to. Otherwise, routine disintegrates. Mother remembers that this is her Women's Club afternoon, she needs the living room. Father has a television program and doesn't want distracting background noise. The young musician himself remembers a basketball game; he'll make up piano time another day. . . . And so on. Mornings, before school, is an ideal practice time if the family rises early. Seven-thirty A.M. is not likely to conflict with anything except a second piece of toast. Right after dinner often works magically, since it relieves the child of clean-up chores. Once the time is chosen, other activities should not be allowed to interfere. As for the duration of a practice period: that will vary according to the child's age, his physical and emotional maturity, and his stage of training. A young concert violinist may want to practice six hours a day; a five-year-old beginner can just last twenty minutes. Remember that daily playing is important. Half an hour every day is better than two three-hour sessions weekly.

Respecting practice period is one way of valuing a child's music and so sustaining his interest. Providing appropriate conditions is another. A pianist needs an adjustable stool; a chair is *not* right. An instrumentalist other than a pianist needs a proper music stand, a place to keep his instrument and his books. Good light, reasonable quiet, freedom from interruptions— these are minimum essentials. But I've seen young violinists with their music awkwardly propped on a windowsill, pianists trying to work out a difficult passage while the vacuum cleaner roars in an adjacent room.

The child who practices regularly but joylessly may be suffering from teacher trouble. If he drags himself to lessons and returns sullen and disconsolate, talk privately with his teacher. You may sense a temperamental clash. The teacher who was right for a beginning student may prove less good for one who's somewhat advanced. Whatever the source of difficulty, a parent should feel no embarrassment about making a change. A conscientious teacher, indeed, won't wish to continue with an unrewarding pupil-teacher relationship, and will probably have helpful suggestions. (Such as: this child might do better with a more easygoing instructor—or a stricter one. Or maybe just with the stimulation of a new person.)

A more agonizing situation, for most parents, is the child's deciding he wants a different instrument. (Money again. Here they've bought this expensive bass viol, and now . . .) When this happens, there's no use beating a kid over the head with, "We gave you a chance. You *chose* it.") How can an eight-year-old really understand what he's choosing? Since it's hard to distinguish between an instrument that's wrong and one that's merely discouraging (hard to master), the best way of dealing with a child's desire to switch is to provide him with a second instrument on a trial basis. He doesn't like violin anymore? All right. Let him rent a clarinet for six months—with the understanding that he continue violin practice, if not lessons, during that trial period. Or let him use his allowance for payments on a guitar.

Should parents use bribes to keep a child at his music? Purists say no. My own feeling is that here the end may justify the means. If my child were a natural string player and a responsible teacher had faith in his musicianship, I wouldn't hesitate to dangle a few carrots and maybe (*very* gently) wave a stick. Because string instruments are *hard*. They take concentration and willpower, qualities in short supply among the under-tens. A successful youth orchestra conductor once told me, "When I pick violinists, I don't pick kids, I pick parents. The worst dragon in town will produce the best fiddler, the kid who gets up at 6 A.M. to practice."

When a child seems to lose interest in his music, or goes into a period of decline, the best sort of "bribe," surely unexceptionable, is a musical treat. Give him some tempting new music books, solos or better yet duets. Locate an ensemble in which he can play, even if getting there involves considerable effort. Buy tickets to a very special concert. Get him an inspiriting book (biography of an admired composer, maybe) or record (performance by an admired musician). Have him polish one piece for recording and then make a tape to give as a present. Let him plan, with brothers and sisters if he has them, a family concert to which a few friends might be invited. Try doing more with family music. If you yourself play an instrument, now's the time to play with your child. If you don't—well, it's never too late to learn recorder, not a great instrument but one adults and children can enjoy fooling around with. Another incentive, particularly cheering when February doldrums hit, is a chance to go to summer music camp. Ask the school music director for recommendations and then let the child write away himself for catalogs. (State universities often have good, low-priced summer youth music programs. And some of the best music camps offer excellent scholarships.)

At least until your child enters high school (where demands on his time become conflicting and extreme), don't be afraid to push a little. Whether he continues to play or not, music can be, like reading, a profoundly personal joy throughout the whole of life. We've all known adults who say, "I'm grateful to my parents for making me keep at my music." Have you ever heard anyone say, "I'm glad I gave it up"?

Rings on Their Fingers, Bells on Their Toes:
Music in the Child's Life

BOOKS ABOUT MUSIC FOR CHILDREN

ARNOFF, FRANCES W., *Music and Young Children*, Holt, 1969.

BLOCKSIDGE, KATHLEEN, *Making Musical Apparatus and Instruments*, Nursery School Association of Great Britain and Northern Ireland, n.d.

COLEMAN, SATIS, *Creative Music in the Home*, Day, 1938.

———, *The Drum Book*, Day, 1931.

COLLIER, JAMES LINCOLN, *Which Musical Instrument Shall I Play?*, Norton, 1969.

COOK, CLIFFORD A., *Suzuki Education in Action*, Exposition Press, 1970.

DARAZS, ARPAD, and STEPHEN JAY, *Sight and Sound*, Boosey & Hawkes, 1965.

ELLIOT, RAYMOND, *Learning Music*, Charles E. Merrill, 1960.

ELLISON, ALFRED, *Music with Children*, McGraw, 1959.

FOX, LILLIAN M., and THOMAS L. HOPKINS, *Creative School Music*, Silver, 1936.

GARRETSON, ROBERT L., *Music in Childhood Education*, Appleton, 1966.

HOOD, MARGUERITE V., and E. J. SCHULTZ, *Learning Music Through Rhythm*, Ginn, 1949.

HORTON, JOHN, *Music*, Macmillan, 1972 (British Primary Schools Today series).

KINSCELLA, HAZEL G., and ELIZABETH TIERNEY, *The Child and His Music*, Lincoln, Nebraska, University Publishing Co., 1953.

LANDECK, BEATRICE, *Children and Music*, Sloane, 1952.

LANDECK, BEATRICE, *Time for Music—a Guide for Parents,* Public Affairs Pamphlet No. 260, 1958.

MANDELL, MURIEL, and ROBERT E. WOOD, *Make Your Own Musical Instruments,* Sterling, 1957.

MARKEL, ROBERTA, *Parents' and Teachers' Guide to Music Education,* Macmillan, 1972.

MASON, BERNARD S., *Drums, Tomtoms and Rattles,* A. S. Barnes, 1938.

MAYNARD, OLGA, *Children and Dance and Music,* Scribner, 1968.

MC CALL, ADELINE, *This Is Music for Kindergarten and Nursery School,* Allyn, 1966.

MC MILLAN, L. EILEEN, *Guiding Children's Growth Through Music,* Ginn, 1959.

MURSELL, JAMES L., *Education for Musical Growth,* Ginn, 1948.

——, *Music Education, Principles and Programs,* Silver, 1951.

MYERS, LOUISE K., *Music Fundamentals Through Song,* Prentice-Hall, 1954.

——, *Teaching Children Music in the Elementary School,* Prentice-Hall, 1961.

NYE, ROBERT and VERNICE, with NEVA AUBIN and GEORGE KYME, *Singing with Children,* Wadsworth, 1962.

PAPE, MARY, *Growing Up with Music,* OUP, 1970.

PAYNTER, JOHN, and PETER ASTON, *Sound and Silence,* Cambridge University Press, 1970.

RAEBECK, LOIS, and LAWRENCE WHEELER, *New Approaches to Music in the Elementary School,* W. C. Brown, 1969.

RICHARDS, MARY H., *Threshold to Music,* Fearon, 1964.

RUNKLE, ALETA, and MARY L. ERIKSEN, *Music for Today's Boys and Girls,* Allyn, 1966.

SHEEHY, EMMA, *Children Discover Music and Dance,* Holt, 1959.

SLIND, LLOYD, and D. EVAN DAVIS, *Bringing Music to Children*, Harper, 1964.

SNYDER, ALICE M., *Creating Music with Children*, Mills, 1957.

STRINGHAM, EDWIN J., *Listening to Music Creatively*, Prentice-Hall, 1946.

SWANSON, BESSIE, *Music in the Education of Children*, Wadsworth, 1961.

TAUBMAN, HYMAN H., *How to Bring Up Your Child to Enjoy Music*, Hanover House, 1958.

THACKRAY, R. M., *Creative Music Education*, Bellwyn Mills, 1965.

TIMMERMAN, MAURINE, *Let's Make Music*, Summy-Birchard, 1958.

WEILAND, ADELL MARIE, *Music, Rhythms, and Games*, Follett, 1953.

SONG BOOKS, COLLECTIONS OF GAME AND ACTION SONGS

BAILEY, CHARITY, *Sing a Song*, Plymouth Music, n.d.

BENTLEY, BERNICE, *Music in Playtime*, Clayton F. Summy, 1948.

BERTAIL, INEZ, *Complete Nursery Song Book*, Lothrop, 1947.

BONI, MARGARET, *Fireside Book of Folk Songs*, Simon & Schuster, 1947.

BURCHENAL, ELIZABETH, *Folk Dances and Singing Games*, Schirmer, 1938.

CHANIAN, PHYLLIS, *Favorite Nursery Songs*, Random House, 1957.

CHASE, RICHARD, *Hullabaloo and Other Singing Games*, Houghton, 1949.

COLEMAN, SATIS N., and ALICE G. THORN, *Singing Time*, Day, 1929.

CROWNINSHIELD, ETHEL, *Mother Goose Songs* (1948), *Sing and Play Book* (1938), *Stories That Sing* (1945), *Songs and Stories About Animals* (1947), *Walk the World Together* (1951), Boston Music Co.

DALTON, ARLENE, and MYRIEL ASHTON, ERLA YOUNG, *My Picture Book of Songs*, M. A. Donohue, 1947.

GLAZER, TOM, *A New Treasury of Folk Songs*, Bantam, 1961.

HAMLIN, ALICE P., and MARGARET G. GUESSFORD, *Singing Games for Children*, Willis Music, 1941.

HUGHES, DOROTHY, *Rhythmic Games and Dances*, American Book Co., 1942.

KENAGY, NINA M., *Musical Experiences for Little Children*, Willis Music, 1932.

LANDECK, BEATRICE, *Songs to Grow On* (1950), *More Songs to Grow On* (1954), Marks Music, recorded by Alan Mills for Folkways Records.

LOMAX, JOHN and ALAN, *Folk Songs: U.S.A.*, Duell, 1948.

LUNT, LOIS, *Hop, Skip & Sing*, T. S. Denison, 1959.

MAC CARTENEY, LAURA P., *Songs for the Nursery School*, Willis Music, n.d.

MC CONATHY, OSBOURNE, *et al.*, *Music for Early Childhood*, Silver, 1952.

NORMAN, RUTH, *Sing a Song of Action*, Mills Music, 1950.

PITCHER, GLADYS, *Playtime in Song*, Witmark, 1960.

POSTON, ELIZABETH, *The Baby's Song Book*, Crowell, 1971.

SANDBURG, CARL, *The American Songbag*, Harcourt, 1927.

SEEGER, RUTH, *American Folk Songs for Children* (1948), *American Folk Songs for Christmas* (1953), *Animal Folk Songs for Children* (1950), Doubleday, recorded by Pete Seeger for Folkways.

WILSON, HARRY R., and BEATRICE A. HUNT, *Sing and Dance*, Schmitt, Hall and McCreary, 1945.

WOOD, LUCILLE F., and LOUISE B. SCOTT, *Singing Fun* (1954), *More Singing Fun* (1961), Webster, recorded by Bowmar Records.

WINN, MARIE, *Fireside Book of Children's Songs*, Simon & Schuster, 1966.

RECORDS FOR CHILDREN

Children don't *need* special records; they'll enjoy the Beatles at least as much as *Little Brass Band*, may prefer classical music to the music composed especially for the young. But if you're buying children's records, I recommend the following.

Folk Songs, Game and Action Songs, and Just Plain LISTEN! *Songs for Children, Abiyoyo and Other Story Songs for Children* (Pete Seeger; Folkways). Includes "The Green Grass Grows All Around." Particularly nice for rest or bedtime.

American Folk Songs for Children (Pete Seeger; Folkways). "She'll Be Coming Round the Mountain," "Jim Crack Corn," "This Old Man" and other lusty selections.

American Game and Activity Songs for Children (Pete Seeger; Folkways). These are the standard, traditional play songs: "Skip to My Lou," "Ring Around a Rosy," "London Bridge," "Shoo Fly."

Animal Folk Songs (Pete Seeger; Folkways). Alligators, hedgehogs, the teensy-weensy spider and the old gray goose.

Ballads of Black America (Pete Seeger; Folkways). Modern ballads about black heroes: Harriet Tubman, Martin Luther King, "Satchel" Paige.

Building a City (Tom Glazer; YPR). Sounds of the carpenter, bricklayer, painter, cement mixer. . . . Available separately or with *What the Lighthouse Sees, Rainy Day* (YPR).

Burl Ives Sings (Decca). A winning voice and manner, appealing selections.

All Aboard ("Train to the Farm" and "Train to the Zoo")
(CRG). Both sure-fire for imaginative travelers.

Chantons en Français: French Folk Songs for Learning French
(Alan Mills, with guitar; Folkways).

Children's Folk Songs of Germany, with guitar (Folkways).

Children's Marching Songs (Simon Says).

Children's Songs of Shakespeare's Time (Counterpoint/Eso-
teric).

Children's Songs from Spain, with guitar (Folkways).

Circus Comes to Town (YPR). Songs about the fat man, the
tumblers, the jugglers and clowns.

Creepy Crawly Caterpillar (CRG). A musical story about the
plain little caterpillar who becomes . . . guess what. Also
available with *Visit to My Little Friend* and *Merry Toy
Shop* (YPR).

Do This, Do That (CRG). Authentic American melodies,
good for games, dancing or free rhythmic movements.

Drummer Boy (CRG). Strong marching rhythm and a sing-
along song. Also available with *Let's Play Together* and
I Wish I Were (YPR).

Eensie-Beensie Spider (CRG). Traditional finger play. Also
available with *Skittery Skattery* and *Sleepy Farm* (YPR).

Folk Songs for Young People (Pete Seeger; Folkways). "Skip
to My Lou," "John Henry," "Joshua Fought the Battle of
Jericho." . . .

Folk Songs for Little Singers, with guitar (Bowmar). A very
delicate and artistic presentation. "Frog Went A-Courting,"
"Animal Fair," "Man on the Flying Trapeze."

German Children's Folk Songs (Folkways).

Golden Slumbers (Pete Seeger and others; Caedmon). Sixteen
enchanting lullabies.

Hooray! Today Is Your Birthday (Tom Glazer; YPR).

I Am a Circus (CRG). Also available with *Castles in the Sand, Out-of-Doors* (YPR).

I Wish I Were (CRG). An imagination song.

Jewish Children's Songs and Games, with guitar accompaniment (Folkways).

Jingle Bells (YPR). Songs for winter activities—snow shoveling, walking in the snow. . . .

Kindergarten Playtime Songs (Golden).

Latin American Children's Game Songs (Folkways). From Puerto Rico and Mexico—with suggested movement and hand clapping.

Let's Play Zoo (YPR). Animal songs with characteristic rhythms.

Little Cowboy (YPR). Hank and Tex ride the range, singing. Also available with *Little Fireman* and *The Little Hero* (YPR).

Little White Duck and Other Children's Favorites (Burl Ives; Harmony). This one also has lots of Mother Goose, and "The Little Engine That Could."

Look at Michie Banjo (YPR). Activity songs, two in Creole patois. Children who had this record as nursery-schoolers will be singing it twenty years later.

Lord Invader: There's a Brown Boy in the Ring, and Other Calypso Songs (Folkways). Creative improvisational singing that will suggest to children how they can make their own songs out of daily happenings.

Me, Myself and I (CRG). Things a sick child can do in bed. Also available with *My Playful Scarf* and *Nothing to Do.*

Mother Goose Songs (Frank Luther; Decca). Warm and gay.

Music Time with Charity Bailey (Folkways). "Brass Wagon" (learning and activity song), "Missie Mouse" (clapping song), "Toodala" (a makeup song). Fun.

Nature Songs; More Nature Songs (Marais and Miranda; Motivation). Two very fine South African folk singers.

Negro Folk Songs for Young People (Folkways). The great Huddie Ledbetter (Leadbelly).

Noisy and Quiet, Big and Little (Tom Glazer; Camden). Musical fun with sounds and sizes.

Nursery Rhymes and Singing Games, Album 7 (Ruth Evans). For the littlest: "Baa Baa Black Sheep," "Humpty Dumpty," "Hey Diddle Diddle" and other favorites.

1, 2, 3 and a zing, zing, zing: Street Games and Songs of the Children of New York City (Tony Schwartz; Folkways). Jump rope, ball, clapping—all sorts of pavement diversions.

Sesame Street Songs (Golden) and *Muppet ABC Album* (Columbia).

Sing Along (YPR). Also available with *Another Sing Along* and *Let's Join In* (YPR).

Singing Games (2 albums; Bowmar). All the familiar ones— "Did You Ever See A Lassie?", "Go Round and Round the Village," "Farmer in the Dell," "Looby Loo"—and some interesting offbeat additions: "Marusaki," "Chimes of Dunkirk."

Skittery Skattery (CRG). Three nonsense songs for singing, games, dramatic play and rhythm instruments.

Sleepy Family (YPR). Integrates a mother's lullaby with folk tunes and familiar household sounds.

Songs for the Wee Folk (Susan Reed; Elektra).

Songs to Grow On, Vol. 2: School Days (Pete Seeger, Charity Bailey, Leadbelly and others; Folkways). Lively, distinctive renderings of "Go Tell Aunt Rhody," "Mary Wore A Red Dress." . . .

Songs to Grow On For Mother and Child (Woody Guthrie; Folkways). Just right for preschoolers to sing with, move to.

Stories and Songs (Ed McCurdy; Folkways). An unusually winning voice and presentation.

Three Little Trains (YPR). Fun to dramatize.

You'll Sing a Song and I'll Sing a Song (Ella Jenkins; Folkways). A participation record—call and response.

When I Grow Up (YPR). I'm going to be . . . a railroad engineer, a farmer girl, a ballet dancer. . . . Song and story material.

When the Sun Shines (YPR). Activity songs about summer fun—bicycling, running, jumping.

Where Do Songs Begin? (CRG). Opportunity for children to make up their own songs.

Who Wants a Ride? (YPR). Songs about rides on a pony, a tugboat, a red wagon.

The Sesame Street Book and Record (Columbia).

NOTE: Single titles YPR (Young People's Records) and CRG (Children's Record Guild) are 78 or 45 rpm only—good for a child's own phonograph. Since YPR and CRG have merged, many of these listings are now available in combination on 33⅓ rpm records.

INTRODUCTION TO SOUNDS, SERIOUS MUSIC, AND
THE INSTRUMENTS OF THE ORCHESTRA

Adventures in Music, RCA. A complete listening series, planned to give children of school age a familiarity with different periods and styles of music. Six albums (with a heavy emphasis on moderns—Vaughan Williams, Debussy, Britten, Copland, Bartok).

Billy Rings the Bell (CRG). The theme uses favorite toys and leads up to real symphonic music.

Child's Introduction to Gilbert and Sullivan (Golden). Thirty-one of the best songs.

Child's Introduction to the Orchestra (Golden).

Conduct Your Own Orchestra (Golden).

Golden Goose (CRG). Introduction to melody and orchestration. Also available with "Hot Cross Buns" and "Where Do Songs Begin?" (YPR).

Goofing Off Suite (Pete Seeger; Folkways). The joy of creative improvisation: Seeger uses his banjo, sings, whistles, hums, makes throat sounds as he suggests to a child how to take a tune and then—take off.

Great Composers (CMS Records). Vol. 1—Liszt, Mozart, Schubert, Beethoven, Mendelssohn, Haydn. Vol. 2—Tchaikovsky, Bach, Chopin, Brahms, Schumann, Debussy.

Hansel and Gretel (Humperdinck; Camden).

His Story and Music series (Vox). Titles available: Bach, Beethoven, Brahms, Chopin, Handel, Haydn, Liszt, Mendelssohn, Mozart, Schubert, Schumann, Verdi, Wagner.

Instruments of the Orchestra (with book; Cabot).

Introduction to Musical Instruments (Golden).

Introduction to Strings, Reeds, Brass, Percussion (Golden).

Little Brass Band (YPR). The instruments are heard both separately and together.

Licorice Stick (YPR). A charming introduction to the clarinet.

Listening Program, RCA, 3 vols. Brahms, Debussy, MacDowell, Grieg, Haydn, Schubert, Mendelssohn, Beethoven, Mozart.

Little Indian Drum (YPR). Introduction to rhythmic use of drum. Also available with *Hiawatha, Pony Express* (YPR).

Lonesome House (CRG). Story and music built around the sounds of an empty house. Also available with *Billy Rings the Bell* and *By Rocket to the Moon* (YPR).

Mr. Grump and the Dingle School Band (CRG). Introduction to the woodwinds and brass.

Muffin in the City, Muffin in the Country (YPR). Based on Margaret Wise Brown's *Noisy Books*, about the blindfolded little dog who learns to listen more acutely when he can't see. With *Mother Goose* and *Musical Mother Goose*.

Music Listening Game (YPR). Teaches child to identify variations in pitch, and to elaborate songs and melodies independently. Available with *Fog Boat Story, Do This, Do That*.

Music for Children (Angel). Carl Orff leads children in chants, songs, choral speaking and playing rhythm instruments.

Play Your Instruments and Make A Pretty Sound (Ella Jenkins; Folkways). Children first hear a full jazz band, then each instrument separately. The tune is improvised on each instrument, and by the group as a whole; it's played as a march, a waltz, as jazz. Trumpet, banjo, clarinet, trombone and drums—Ella Jenkins uses harmonica and ukelele. Lots of opportunity for children to identify instruments, conduct, move, improvise, elaborate with rhythm instruments.

Rhythms of the World (Langston Hughes; Folkways). Based on Hughes's *First Book of Rhythms* (F. Watts), the record reproduces a variety of natural rhythms, from the heartbeat to animal and bird sounds, mechanical sounds, etc.

Sounds of My City: the Stories, Music and Sounds of the People of New York (Tony Schwartz; Folkways). People of varied ethnic backgrounds dance, sing and pray; children play and sing—and the street has its own sounds.

Tubby the Tuba (Golden). Musical story about the tuba who wanted to carry a melody.

Walk in the Forest (YPR). A small boy meets imaginary animals represented by the different instrument combinations.

Wonderful Violin (YPR).

SOURCES OF RECORDS FOR YOUNG CHILDREN

Bowmar Records, 622 Rodier Drive, Glendale, Cal. 91201.

Caedmon, 505 Eighth Ave., New York, N.Y. 10018.

Children's Music Center, 5373 W. Pico Blvd., Los Angeles, Cal. 90019. (In addition to records, carries a good supply of books and sturdy, inexpensive rhythm instruments.)

Folkways Records, 701 Seventh Ave., New York, N.Y. 10036.

Young People's Records, Children's Record Guild, 225 Park Ave. South, New York, N.Y. 10003

Lyons, 430 Wrightwood Ave., Elmhurst, Ill. 60126. (In addition to a very extensive variety of records—Bowmar, CRG, YPR, Childhood Rhythms, Rhythms Production, Golden —carries educational games, school equipment, rhythm instruments.)

6

Let's Dance

Watch a six-year-old's progress down the street on any bright, brisk day. He starts off running. At the curb he jumps and finding that diverting, he covers the next hundred yards with an off-again on-again curb-to-street movement. Any marked-off area, like lines in cement, tempts him to hop. He spins around a telephone pole, splashes through a puddle. All this while his arms move freely—swinging, reaching out for balance, performing throwing gestures with real or imaginary objects. In the radical sense of the word, this child is *dancing*: employing rhythmical body motions not for purely functional purposes (getting from *here* to *there*) but to express feeling and experience the pure joy of movement.

All children love to dance. All children *will* dance, unless severely handicapped or restrained by others. An infant joggles rhythmically to music and—once he's discovered his arms and legs—creates steady rhythms of his own. Slap, *slap*, hands on thighs. (Never a single slap.) Slap, slap, *slap*. Some observers suggest that the infant's feeling for regular beat comes from prenatal conditioning, the mother's heartbeat. Whatever its origins, the feeling is there, easily observed. An experiment at City Hospital in Elmhurst, New York, demonstrated that newborn babies kept in a nursery where they heard, all day long, the amplified rhythms of a human heartbeat ate better and gained more weight than babies kept in conventional silence.

Rudolph Laban, pioneer of modern educational dance, points out that the baby's first activity—pushing the legs away from the body, hitting with the arms, loosening the ball-like fetal position—is essentially a dance movement (very like the dancing jump which characterizes many primitive adult dances). Long before the toddler commands the vocabulary to *say* what he feels, he can express through movement a complicated range of emotions. Furious, he flails and kicks; happy, he runs, jumps, claps; sad or frightened, he curls up small, hands to head. At this age and much later, a child's body, dance teacher Blanche Evans asserts, is "the most mature expressive medium he possesses."

If it is true, as experts claim, that human beings are natural musicians and dancers, how does it happen that so many adolescents—and adults—move awkwardly and self-consciously, embarrassed by their own arms and legs? One reason, surely, is that the conditions of modern life steadily erode native impulse. Compare the experience of a ten-year-old New Yorker with that of a child in, say, a Mexican village. The young Mexican goes barefoot; his feet know and respond to the feel of sand, water, asphalt, rock. Living in the sun, he wears few clothes— and those are loose, hanging free from the body. He may spend a few hours daily in school; the rest of the time, he actively uses his whole body. He plants corn, he harvests, he gathers cactus leaves, drives a burro, pounds corn in a stone *metate*, hauls wood and charcoal. Because life in Mexico is an unbroken series of festivals, he's accustomed to seeing adults dance in the streets. He joins in himself. He knows all the traditional dances, and even when he's performing menial chores his gestures and body control suggest, often, the strength and grace of the *Quetzales* or the *huapango*.

And the young American? He's worn shoes since he could walk. Also underwear and belts and tucked-in shirts and ties. He spends approximately seven hours a day in school. His range of physical activity is limited and repetitive: he rides a bike, maybe, plays baseball. The only dance he sees is on the TV screen and that, mechanical-perfect or highly charged sexually, bears no understandable relation to his life. Dance is not something he does, but something he watches with detachment or envy. (How could he possibly move like Sammy Davis?)

Of course many American children beg for, and get, dance lessons. Most of those children are girls. In this country, male dancers are unreasonably viewed with suspicion as effeminate, *queer*. Partly, no doubt, the association of dance and homosexuality is a reaction to the male dancer's typical costume—the same tights as worn by women, but more erotically suggestive on men. Partly it occurs because male homosexual performers are more conspicuous than homosexuals in other occupations. The truth is that there are probably as many "gay" people in the army, or in General Motors, as on the stage—and that dance, far from being effeminate, is an activity requiring great strength and energy. The New York *Times*'s music critic, Clive Barnes, thinks dancing more "natural" for men than for women, since "there's a great deal of pure athleticism in dance and men are better athletes. They jump higher, move faster, and generally cut the air with more excitement." But few little boys are given dance lessons—and often, those who secretly long to learn would be ashamed to ask, because that stuff is supposed to be for girls.

And what do the girls get? Ballet. Around the age of five or six, little girls often become infatuated with ballet. Not with the art itself—how could they realize what's involved?—but with its romantic trappings. Toe shoes, gauzy tutu, lovely dreamy music, feathers and crowns. . . . The child who has barely mastered first position already sees herself in *Swan Lake*.

Now ballet is a high and serious art. Many children profit by ballet lessons, and some few, after years of training, may make it a lifework. But cautions are in order. The first has to do with the choice of teacher. In ballet more than any other form of dance, it's important that the teacher be herself thoroughly trained and *responsible*. Otherwise, there's a danger that little children will be encouraged to perform physical feats for which their bodies are not ready. The turnout, for instance, is harmful if attempted too early. As for dancing on toe—it should *never* be permitted unless a child has studied ballet for several years, practices daily and takes several lessons a week with a qualified teacher. (One professional dancer I spoke to insists that unless a child is seriously considering a career in ballet, dancing *en pointe* makes no sense whatever. It's a terrific strain on the spine, and contributes to grace or poise nothing that can't be gained from less arduous exercises.)

Unfortunately, many less-than-professional teachers succumb to pressure from child or parents and put into toe slippers a youngster who belongs in flats. This is particularly likely if the teacher is not a ballet specialist but someone offering a salamagundi of dance lessons—tap, jazz, acrobatic, ballroom, ballet.

With a properly qualified teacher, of course, lessons in ballet can be a great experience, imaginative as well as physical. It should be borne in mind, though, that the first requirement for serious ballet dancing is a particular type of body build. When Balanchine auditions, he makes his initial selections on the basis of looks alone. If a girl is heavyset and short in the leg, she will never make a ballerina, no matter how hard she tries, and it is surely a mistake to encourage her hopes with years of ballet lessons when she might instead become a competent modern dancer.

As common as the toe-shoes-in-six-months trap is the Big Recital gambit. Here you find the teacher whose whole efforts are geared to a superspectacular end-of-year concert with all her charges expensively costumed and prizes to those selling the most tickets. Though children love an audience—who doesn't?—it's questionable whether public performance serves any useful function for the young, whether indeed it doesn't foster a self-conscious imitation of grown-ups that is the opposite of creative. If children are to be given dance lessons, the aim should be not showing off accomplishments but acquiring those profoundly joyful and enriching experiences that only dance can give.

A major value of dance or creative movement for the young is that it makes possible the most direct and personal kind of communication—communication with the whole self. All other arts require some intermediary or instrument—brush, clay, flute, pen. In creative movement, the body is the instrument; the dancer and the dance are one. As a child discovers his body and learns to control it, he increases his "movement vocabulary," his range of expressiveness. He learns what individual body parts can do: heads can nod, swivel, droop, lift, turn. He becomes conscious of different ways of moving: he can walk, run, hop, skip, shuffle, gallop, slide.

With awareness and control comes a liberation that's imaginative as well as physical. Children will "say" in movement what they couldn't express any other way; they dance out their repressed emotions and secret dreams. The result may be a startling release of aggressive impulses. Blanche Evans describes preteen girls improvising a dance consisting of beating and stabbing motions. When the music stopped, one notably gentle child protested, "But I still had three more people to kill!" Dance may calm the hyperactive child or stimulate the normally withdrawn—as in Miss Evans' account of a four-year-old's response to her request for a "big strong dance." By way of suggesting appropriate movements, she asked, "Who do you know that's big and strong?" (Thinking of giants, policemen, daddies and so forth.) At this point the timidest child in the class, one who habitually sat apart sucking her thumb, came forward with "ME!" and dazzled them all with a strong improvisation full of energy and panache.

The child who enjoys what Rudolph Laban calls "a rich movement life" acquires a special sort of confidence. Conversely, the child who never learns to manage his body well suffers a special disability and unease. All children long for physical mastery and admire those who possess it. (The pecking order on any playground is established by body-management skills.) Certainly the way a child moves tells us a great deal and affects our attitude toward him. Does he toe in, slump, manage his arms as though they were attached with safety pins? Or does he walk gracefully and confidently?

If children don't learn to dance early, they may never learn. Ideally, some kind of dance experience should be available to boys as well as girls before the second or third grade. Most nursery schools and kindergartens provide at least minimal opportunities for creative movement. As for dance lessons, what's available varies enormously according to community size. A large city offers the full range from classical ballet to folk and square dance groups (the latter particularly helpful to shy children). A small town may have a single teacher whose real specialty is baton twirling.

If you decide to give your child dance lessons, the integrity of the teacher (or the school) should be your first consideration. Judith Jacobs, a New York dancer and choreographer, suggests the following questions as an aid to evaluating a prospective teacher. What is her background and training? Has she studied at reputable schools, or performed professionally with well-known companies? Is she a member of a dance teaching association? What are her tastes in dance? Does she occasionally invite guest teachers? What students has she produced? Have any gone on to professional careers in dance? Do you admire anyone who has studied with this teacher for a number of years? What kind of music does she play for her dance classes? Does she live for the annual recital? Does she encourage her pupils to see good, professional dance companies when they come to town? Does she not only encourage spontaneity but also instill a sense of discipline? Are children in her classes tense, straining to do things beyond their physical capacity? *Is the dance lesson a happy, satisfying experience?*

When dance lessons are not available, there's still a good deal you can do, at home, to introduce a child to the possibilities of creative movement.

The way to begin is *not* by playing a record and asking your five-year-old to dance a snowflake or a fairy. That poses a double problem: be something, and make it fit this music. Furthermore, unless a child has first been made aware of what his body can do, it's likely to produce a limited and monotonous series of motions. Norma Canner, a Boston creative dance teacher, begins her classes with a procedure that can be easily adapted to a parent-child situation. First, there's a ceremonial removing of shoes and socks. Then the children, sitting on the floor, are encouraged to become conscious of individual body parts and the sensations connected with them. What does it feel like when you wiggle your toes on the floor? On the rug? What different things can you do with your hands? ("We go in, we go out. Our hands are high, our hands are low.") Make circles with your thumbs. Bend the fingers, separate them. Curl and stretch. What about finger noises? Snap, tap, pound, slap. Arms can push and pull and stretch. They can swing, separately and together. Feet do different things, depending on whether you're sitting, lying on your back or flat on your stomach: they can stamp, shuffle, slide, scrape, tap. Eyes can open, shut, blink, look up and down. Even the tongue has movement possibilities: it can curl, wiggle, stick out; can click, hum, buzz, and so on. Any part of the body can do its own dance. "Make a head dance," Mrs. Canner tells her pupils. Or an arm dance, a foot dance.

After this basic exploration of body movement, Mrs. Canner suggests, the child is ready to consider movement in space. How many different ways can he figure out of getting across a room? (If you're doing this at home, you'll want a good-sized cleared area.) He can walk, skip, leap, slide, run, gallop, hop, crawl. When he's run out of ideas, propose others. Can he prance? Whirl? Move on his stomach? Move on his back? Ask him to walk feeling big all over—then feeling very, very small. Have him hop first on one foot, then on two, forward and back. Can he walk on tiptoe? Stamp? Kick? How would he move in a heavy way? A light, floaty way? Ask him to make up his own special walk.

Vera Gray, producer of the BBC's highly respected "Music and Movement" program series, points out that every movement has a time element, occurs in space, and uses weight. So children should become separately conscious of these three elements. Some sample exercises (more fully developed in Miss Gray's *Music, Movement and Mime for Children*):

To become aware of time

Run very fast.
Walk very slowly.
Jump all over the floor quickly.
Sit down on the floor slowly.
Slowly grow up as tall as you can.
Slowly curl up on the floor as small as possible.

To become aware of space

Since so much of a child's life (particularly at school) involves forward looking and movement, he needs encouragement to use *all* the space around him—backwards, sideways, up and down. Miss Gray suggests asking him:

Lift your leg up in front of you.
Lift it up backwards, sideways.
Lift your leg and step forwards, backwards, sideways and around and around.
Reach up to the ceiling.
Stretch out to touch the walls.
Punch down to the floor.

To become aware of weight

To *feel* the difference between heavy and light, the child should experiment with his own body force.

Punch down to the floor hard.

Lift your arms up slowly and gently.

Stamp on the floor.

Walk on tiptoe.

Kick out one leg as hard as you can.

Very smoothly and lightly, glide one foot along the floor.

Combining these three areas of awareness, the child learns to organize movement into dance.

Walk a circle on the floor, fast.

Tiptoe around your circle, slowly.

Jump around your circle, hard and strong.

Draw a circle in the air with your arm, above your head.

Draw a circle right around yourself with your head or your elbow or your foot.

Now draw circles everywhere. Make up a circle dance.

With a three- or four-year-old, this kind of predance activity may occupy many brief sessions. (Make the occasion special, if possible, with a dance "costume," leotard and tights or shorts.) You might want to develop some particular body awareness—feet, for instance, by having the child walk barefoot on grass, cement, sand, blacktop, vinyl, jute or rubber. Afterwards, talk about the different feelings, from cold-wet to gritty and warm. If he has several different kinds of footwear—sneakers, sandals, oxfords, party shoes, boots—let him move in ways suggested by each kind (a sneaker tippy-toe, a boot stomp).

Once a child commands a basic movement vocabulary, he's ready for something like formal dance. Ask him to combine several movements: creep-hop-pounce; leap-twirl-run-collapse. At this point, you may want to introduce simple accompaniment. You can clap your hands in time, or use a percussion instrument. Very young children move most easily to percussion instruments because they produce a clear, definite rhythm uncomplicated by harmony or change of pitch.

Accompaniment

A child's first exploration of movement and dance needs none. In fact, any kind of accompaniment at this stage is likely to restrict inventiveness by prematurely imposing a structure and a beat. Sometimes children make up their own accompaniment as they move—humming, clapping, slapping, making lip-popping noises. Fine. Once a dance has been worked out, though, the young dancer may feel he wants a final flourish—music, or rhythmical beating of some sort. As far as possible, he should choose his own accompaniment. Percussion instruments are extremely versatile. Is he dancing a hurricane? Gongs or cymbals will make crashing, roaring sounds. A light rain? Finger cymbals, triangles lightly tapped, jingle bells. For a "frightened" dance, he might use drums struck with different beaters, hard and soft, or wood blocks and tambourines. Talking with a child about his dance may help him choose just the right record. If the feeling is grave and sad, a Chopin nocturne, perhaps? If sprightly and gay, what about Mendelssohn's *Spring Song?* Or you might use one of the splendid recordings specially designed for creative movement (see Bibliography).

Remember that time beaters can be used in two ways. The parent—or another child—can work the drums, rhythm sticks, shakers, whatever's been chosen. Or the dancer can carry a small percussion instrument and shake it to emphasize movement. Tambourines and clappers work well that way; small bells can be either carried or tied to ankles and wrists.

Dance Games and Exercises

All of these are designed to stimulate a child's imagination, increase his joy and competence in movement and his sense of himself.

▪ Dance your name. HAR-ri-et JONES. ROY HOL-lins-worth. The child moves to the rhythm of his name, chanting and clapping the beat.

▪ Read aloud a poem that carries a strong action suggestion and let the child move to it. *Mother Goose* is wonderful for this. Try "Hey Diddle Diddle," "Hippety Hop to the Barber Shop," "Ride a Cock Horse." A. A. Milne's *When We Were Very Young* is full of irresistible cues for dancing.

> John had
> Great Big
> Waterproof
> Boots on.
> John had a
> Great Big
> Waterproof
> Hat.
> John had a
> Great Big
> Waterproof
> Mackintosh
> And that,
> (Said John)
> Is
> That.

I remember watching a four-year-old girl dance that one. She seemed, as she clomped in her invisible boots, to have gained twenty pounds. Other good poems-to-move-to here are "Lines and Squares," "At the Zoo," "Sand-Between-the-Toes" and "Busy."

▪ Read aloud a poem that suggests a strong feeling or definite mood. After the child has listened to the poem, let him dance what he felt. Carl Sandburg's "Fog," Walter de la Mare's "Silver," R. L. Stevenson's "My Shadow," Vachel Lindsay's "The Little Turtle" are good for this—and Japanese *haiku*, if they're not too subtle:

> Butterfly asleep folded soft on temple bell . . .
> Then bronze gong rang!

> (Buson)

▪ The child stands, eyes closed, hands behind back as you pass through his fingers different-textured materials: velvet, thick yarn, canvas, a length of flowing silk. After each texture has been experienced, ask him to express through movement what he felt.

▪ Suggest imaginary activities to be danced. Let's

> Jump over a puddle
> Swing on a rope
> Reach up and get an apple from the tree
> Run into the waves
> Fly kites
> Plunge through deep snow
> Walk on hot tar
> Bicycle fast down a hill

▪ Dance out the complete life cycle of a flower from seed to bursting roots to sprout to stem and leaves reaching sunward and so on to the last dropped petal. Children are fascinated by life cycles. They'll enjoy too dancing egg-tadpole-frog and chrysalis-caterpillar-butterfly.

■ Walk like different animals: a cat stalking a bird, puppy chasing a ball, galloping horse, kangaroo, robin pecking for a worm, a worm wriggling away from a robin, an old dog, a crab.

■ Walk like a storybook character: the Little Lame Prince, a giant in seven-league boots, Cinderella at the ball, Red Riding Hood skipping through the forest, the raging dwarf in "Rumpelstiltskin," the Tin Woodman of Oz.

■ Make up a dance that gives the feeling of

> A gentle soft rain; a hard driving rain
> A wild October wind blowing the leaves
> A clock ticking
> Snowflakes falling on a white bright morning

■ Dance out the morning sounds in your house: alarm ringing, Father walking downstairs, bacon sputtering in the pan, toast popping in the toaster, coffee perking, door slamming.

■ Start to move, and change to the new movement suggested each time the bell rings.
Be a seesaw. Now be a goose flying . . . a snake . . . a marching soldier . . . a skater . . . an airplane . . . a rabbit in a lettuce patch . . . an astronaut walking on the moon . . . a bowl of Jello shaking . . . the Little Engine That Could (first, I-think-I-can puff puff and then I-thought-I-could!). Be a spinning top, a bouncing ball. . . .

■ Dance a color. Before you do this, ask the child how a particular color makes him feel. Red? Red is strong, happy, jumpy, exciting, angry. . . . OK, dance *red*. Blue? Soft, calm, gentle, floaty, sleepy, sad. . . . Afterwards, get out crayons and paper; ask the child to make a picture of the color he's danced, using that color only.

▪ Dance objects and materials from your own home. Dance out the action of a can opener, a typewriter, a washing machine, a vacuum cleaner, a record player, a pencil sharpener. Dance out the pattern of the wallpaper, the curtains, the bedspread. Dance the feel of the living room rug, the bathroom tile. Choose one picture and dance that. (Preliminary questions here, to stimulate expressive movement, might be: Which color is most important? Can you walk the pattern of the picture? How do you feel when you look at this picture?) Chagall's *I and the Village*, Wyeth's *Christina's World*, a Jackson Pollock drip painting—these are full of strong movement cues. If the child is old enough—that is, has listened to records and has a collection he knows well—ask him to choose music that seems right for the picture and his dance.

▪ Choose some household article—a basket, a stool, a candle, a box—and make up a dance around it. The child can *use* the object chosen (swing the basket, sit or climb on the stool), perform movements that suggest its shape, dance the *feeling* of the object or incorporate it into a story-dance.

▪ Dance out images from common speech: snug as a bug in a rug, slow as molasses in January, straight as an arrow, quick as a flash, sharp as a tack, happy as a clam, flat as a pancake, smooth as silk, tall as a beanpole, bold as a lion, shy as a violet.

▪ Ask the child to think of things that turn or spin, and dance those (clock hands, tape recorder spools, merry-go-round, Ferris wheel, airplane propellers). Then:

Things that go up and down—elevator, umbrella, jack-in-the-box, balloon.

Things that are light and soft—feather, dandelion seeds, kite, summer clouds, soap bubbles.

Things that are hard and heavy—hammer pounding, bell clanging, wrecking ball swinging, tree falling in a storm.

▪ Walk like different kinds of people: a proud king, a wicked witch, a sleepy child, a baby learning to walk, a funny happy person, a sad person, a show-off, a person blindfolded, an old lady with a cane.

Props and Accessories for Dancing

Strictly speaking, children need nothing more than their own bodies in order to dance well. Often, though, a skillfully chosen prop will inspire exciting new movement possibilities. To vary the range and quality of a child's dance explorations, try:

▪ An old hula hoop. To spin, wave about, pass through, to be lifted and swung.

▪ Bright-colored crepe paper streamers, either twisted together or tacked to a stick.

▪ Bells, tied to wrist and ankles or held and shaken.

▪ Ropes. To grasp and stretch, coil and spin, snake along the floor.

▪ Bean bags. To balance on the head, swing from hand to hand, toss.

▪ Large beach ball. To toss, bounce, balance.

▪ Parasol, fan, balloon on a string, pinwheel . . . any small, light object that suggests a movement or mood.

Dance Activities Related to Other Arts
(Painting, Drawing, Sculpture, Drama)

Johanna Hatch, a New Hampshire related-arts teacher, proposes these activities to cultivate a whole-self expressiveness in children ages six to twelve. The special virtue of these exercises is that they offer the child many different ways of saying what he feels—with paint, clay, paper or pure movement.

■ Ask the child to make any vowel sound and experiment with it, seeing what kind of noise it will produce. (Ooooooo-OOOO. A-a-a-a-a-a-ah! EEEEEEE!) Then have him compose a single-sound dance, providing his own "accompaniment" as he moves by saying his vowel over and over—high, low, staccato or long-drawn-out. Try the same exercise with consonants. K-K-K-K-K or a well-trilled R.

After a breathing space, get out crayons or pencils and paper. Have the child draw his favorite letter, A to Z (or the letter he danced to) so large it fills the entire sheet of paper. Now he's to use the letter shape as the basis of a drawing. (Does the A suggest a house? The O or S a human figure?)

■ For two children, or child and parent. Partners sit on the floor, eyes shut, holding hands. Without speaking, they move each other's hands about, taking care never to lose contact. After this experience, the child may want to talk a bit. ("It felt funny—like flying." "We made a windmill.") With paint or crayon, let him try to get the feeling on paper. Now have him trace his hands in different positions on the paper, cut out these shapes and form people, animals or objects from them.

■ Play the mirror game. First use a real mirror to show how it copies movements. Now, two children or parent and child sit on the floor. Each takes a turn at being the mirror, copying exactly the other's movements with head, arms, hands. You might want to talk about the feeling created by related or balanced impressions—that is, by symmetry (though you wouldn't use the word with a very young child). If you own a book of good art reproductions, let the child browse through looking for examples of repeated forms. (For example, in Botticelli's *Birth of Venus*, see how the central fluted-shell motif is repeated in the waves, the flowing draperies and flying hair.) Now ask the child to create his own symmetrical design, using crayons and paper—or to fold paper, cut a design, and then open it out to see the repeated pattern.

■ After active exercising, have the child lie on the floor and close his eyes. Ask him to move only his fingers, very slowly; then only his wrists. Continue separating each body part until the child has explored moving every body joint individually. Then let him move as many parts of his arms and legs together as possible—fingers, feet, elbows, knees, all moving. Have him open his eyes and give him a small mirror, some paper and pencils. Tell him to explore his body by observing it through a mirror. Have him pick an area such as eyes, nose, or finger and draw it.

■ Have the child close his eyes and respond physically to words evoking facial expressions: happy, sad, ugly, itchy, gay, cross, tired, amazed, worried, cold, angry, hot. Then give him paper and poster paint and have him represent himself with one of these facial expressions.

■ Let the child experiment with the physical differences involved in various occupations. He decides on one activity and mimes it. (This is like the game Charades. His audience—the parent or another child—tries to copy the movements and then guess the occupation represented. (Bus driver, steelworker, orchestra conductor, storekeeper, cook. . . .) Then take out paints and let him paint the activity he would himself enjoy.

▪ Body sculpture: the child plays sculptor while another child, or the parent, acts as his clay, relaxed and mobile. The "sculptor" moves his partner's limbs about until he achieves a pleasing position. Then, while the "clay" holds the position, the child models it in real clay.

▪ Play the record *Sounds of My City* (Folkways) and then talk about city noises. Ask the child to think of all the different ways people can get around a city—by car, bus, subway, trolley, bicycle, helicopter, plane. What sounds do these vehicles make? How do they move? Ask the child to suggest, by movement, some mode of city transportation; you have to guess what it is. Now, with materials from his "useful junk" collection (boxes, fabric, pipe cleaners, spools, tacks, wire, corks) have him construct a vehicle.

Let's Dance

BOOKS ABOUT DANCE, RHYTHM, CREATIVE MOVEMENT

ANDREWS, GLADYS, *Creating Rhythmic Movement for Children*, Prentice-Hall, 1954. This lively book includes a thoughtful discussion of the growing child's developmental needs and relates these to creative experiences in music, movement and dance. Particularly good on the place of percussion in early music and dance training.

ASSOCIATION FOR ARTS IN CHILDHOOD, INC., *Creative Movement and Music*, Hemphill Press, 1952.

BAUER, LOIS M., and BARBARA A. REED, *Dance and Play Activities for the Elementary Grades*, 2 vols., Chartwell House, 1951.

BEEBY, IDA, *Dance, Child, Dance!* W. A. Paterson Press, 1947.

BOORMAN, JOYCE, *Creative Dance in the First Three Grades*, McKay, 1969.

BROWN, LILLIAN W., *Studies in Basic Rhythms for Young Children*, Willis Music, 1956.

CANNER, NORMA, . . . *and a time to dance*, Beacon, 1968. A loving and sensitive account of the possibilities of creative movement in teaching retarded children—but full of suggestions appropriate to any child.

CHITTY, A. W. I., *The Play Way to Rhythmics*, Paxton, 1939.

CLEMENS, JAMES R., *Invitation to Rhythm*, William C. Brown, 1962.

CRAWFORD, CAROLINE, *Dramatic Games and Dances for Little Ones*, A. S. Barnes, 1936.

CRAWHALL-WILSON, PHYLLIS, *Rhythmic Movement for Nursery School or Kindergarten*, Paxton, 1942.

DEPARTMENT OF EDUCATION AND SCIENCE AND THE CENTRAL OFFICE OF INFORMATION (British), *Moving and Growing*, Her

Majesty's Stationery Office, 1952. A study of factors affecting motor skills (genetic and environmental), modes of movement and creative ways of expanding movement possibilities.

DOLL, EDNA, and MARY J. NELSON, *Rhythms Today!*, Silver, 1965. Two artist-teachers present exercises, games, music and dances designed to help children express through movement their innermost feelings and ideas.

DRIVER, ANN, *Music and Movement*, Oxford, 1936.

EVANS, BLANCHE, *The Child's World: Its Relation to Dance Pedagogy* (Articles reprinted from *Dance* magazine), St. Mark's Editions, 1964. An imaginative approach to movement as the language of feeling.

GRAY, VERA, and RACHEL PERCIVAL, *Music, Movement and Mime for Children*, Oxford, 1964. Based on a splendid BBC radio program series on music and movement, this little volume is full of stimulating ideas for enriching the child's body awareness and control.

HARRIS, JANE A., ANNE PITTMAN, and MARLYS SWENSON, *Dance Awhile*, Burgess, 1955.

H'DOUBLER, MARGARET N., *Dance: A Creative Art Experience*, University of Wisconsin, 1959.

HUMPHREYS, LOUISE, and JERROLD ROSS, *Interpreting Music Through Movement*, Prentice-Hall, 1964.

LATCHAW, MARJORIE, and JEAN PYATT, *A Pocket Guide of Dance Activities*, Prentice-Hall, 1958.

LEE, MARJORIE, *Dance With Me!*, Ryerson Press, 1949.

METTLER, BARBARA, *Materials of Dance as a Creative Art Activity*, Mettler, 1960.

MURRAY, RUTH LOVELL, *Dance in Elementary Education*, Harper, 1963. A comprehensive guide to children's experiences in creative movement, with chapters on basic locomotor skills, responding to rhythm, making up dances, group dancing, dance games and so on. Full of splendid concrete suggestions for working with young children.

NORTH, MARIAN, A *Simple Guide to Movement Teaching*, Werner Studios, 40 Hazlewood Rd., London S.W., England, 1959.

RENSTROM, MOISELLE, *Rhythm Fun*, Pioneer Music, 1957.

RILEY, ALICE C. and JESSIE L. GAYNOR, *Thirty Rhythmic Pantomimes*, John Church, 1937.

ROWEN, BETTY, *Learning Through Movement*, Columbia University Press, 1963.

RUSSELL, JOAN, *Modern Dance in Education*, Macdonald and Evans, 1958.

SAFFRAN, ROSANNA B., *First Book of Creative Rhythms*, Holt, 1963.

SEHON, ELIZABETH L. and EMMA L. O'BRIEN, *Rhythms in Elementary Education*, Ronald, 1951.

SHEPPARD, LILA, *Dancing on the Desk Tops*, Harper, 1960.

WATERMAN, ELIZABETH, *The Rhythm Book*, A. S. Barnes, 1936.

RECORDS FOR DANCE AND RHYTHMIC MOVEMENT

You don't have to buy special records for a child to dance to. If you have ballet classics like *Swan Lake, Coppelia, Giselle*, those are ideal. So is Stravinsky, Villa-Lobos, much of Bartók. Electronic music, African drums, Negro spirituals will all inspire dances. Here, however, is a list of records specially designed for creative movement. Records marked * can be ordered from Lyons, 430 Wrightwood Ave., Elmhurst, Ill. 60126.

Adventures in Rhythm (Folkways).

*Basic Rhythms** (Ruth Evans). Specially for teaching rhythms and music listening. Begins with music for clapping, swaying, etc. and progresses to "Skaters' Waltz" and "Pop Goes the Weasel."

Childhood Rhythms* (Ruth Evans). Album 1 Fundamental rhythms—walk, run, skip, march, jump, gallop, skip again. Animal and toy rhythms—ducks, camels, trains, soldiers, etc. Play and character—seesaws, bicycles, fairies, giants. Album 2 Rhythm combinations (up and down, around and around, fast and slow, etc.). Bouncing balls, jumping rope. Interpretive and dance rhythms—elevators, clocks, jumping jacks.

Circus in Town! (Decca). Thirteen selections used for circus acts and parades, including the ringmaster's voice and appropriate animal sounds.

Come Dance with Me (Anne Landry; James H. Heineman).

Come and See the Peppermint Tree.* A unique and wonderful record, a stimulus to free imaginative expression.

Dance-a-Story series (Ann Barlin; RCA Victor). One side of each record is narration, the other music to move to. 1—At the Beach; 2—Brave Hunter; 3—Flappy and Floppy; 4—Toy tree.

Dance Along (Folkways). Dance and rhythm improvisations.

Dance, Sing and Listen (Esther Nelson and Bruce Haack; Dimensions Five)*, 3 vols. A stimulus for children 3 to 12 to think, move, dance, create. Music ranges from medieval to modern electronic: invitations to be a seed growing, to discover one's own bones and make them dance, to be a sailboat, a kitten, a train.

Garden Varieties (Phoebe James).* Be bees, butterflies, small and large birds, wind, rain, sun and growing plants.

I Love a Marching Band (Golden). Best loved marches of John Philip Sousa.

Little Puppet (Children's Record Guild). For stiff puppet movements to the music of "La Petite Marionette."

Music for Contemporary Dance (Ruth White; Rhythms Productions).

Marching Across the Green Grass and Other American Children's Game Songs (Jean Ritchie; Folkways). With guitar and three-stringed Appalachian dulcimer.

Listen, Move and Dance (Vera Gray; Capitol).

Music for Dance Rhythms (Folkways). Piano—for creative rhythms and movement.

Nothing to Do (Children's Record Guild). Rhythmic patterns for marching, tiptoeing, spinning, clapping hands.

Rhythm Activities, Album 9 (Ruth Evans).* Giraffes, kangaroos, clowns, dolls; music for climbing motions, swinging, jigging, etc.

Rhythm Band and All-purpose Music (Mary Jane Le Crone; Rhythm Record Co.).

Rhythm Time (Bowmar). 2 albums. 1—Basic Rhythms, Mechanical Rhythms, Circus. 2—Basic and Combination Rhythms; Interpretive Rhythms (Baby Bear, Mother Bear, Father Bear, Goldilocks, windmills and scarecrows and soaring hawks).

RCA Victor Record Library for Elementary Schools, The Rhythm Program, 3 vols. Schubert, Gluck, Corelli, Schumann, Dvořák, Brahms, Tchaikovsky, Gounod, etc. Music to suggest horses (high stepping, running, galloping), tin soldiers, dancing peasants, ticking clock. . . .

Sound, Rhythm, Rhyme and Mime for Children (Folkways).

This Is Rhythm (Ella Jenkins; Folkways).

All Together: Family Activities

When my children were very young, their favorite game was called Animal Farm. Animal Farm was a family invention; we played it on a Candyland board redecorated with pasted-on pictures, so that prizes, forfeits and goal corresponded to events in our daily life. Landing on a good square meant "Package from Grandmother; advance three," "Birthday party invitation; take another turn," "School picnic" and so forth. Bad squares were labeled "Take out garbage" (go back five), "Forgot to make your bed" and "You lost the shopping list" (go back home). Goal was Animal Farm, a kind of circus-zoo to which for years we made semiannual outings.

We played that game, updating the board decorations, even after the girls had mastered more sophisticated diversions. And I remember that when, at age ten, Rona protested, "This is babyish," Joyce defended it with, "I love Animal Farm. It gives me W.F.F.—Warm Family Feeling."

Because W.F.F. is so necessary to a child's sense of security and identity, it seems to me specially important that families discover activities in which every member can participate. What a child does with his family has special meaning and value. Often it becomes the foundation for a lifelong interest, something he returns to, years later, with *his* children. In any case, the serious pursuit of butterflies, opera or mountain climbing in company with parents and siblings contributes something vital to individual development—a sense of family style, the family way of doing things. Behind the cliché of "togetherness" lies a real human truth: the child grows strong, finds his own direction, by first following in his parents' steps.

Just where those steps lead doesn't greatly matter. The shared activity can be birdwatching, charades, baking bread, building electric motors, learning macrame or Spanish or chess. It can even be watching TV together, if talk and questioning is made part of the total experience. The critical tests for a creative family activity are these:

▪ Do the parents really enjoy it? No use faking a passion for shell collecting if you hate beaches. Adult boredom, sure to reveal itself ultimately, spoils a child's pleasure.

▪ Can it fruitfully occupy participants of widely different ages? Ceramics, for example, offers scope for all. Small children can help prepare clay, make coil and pinch pots, while older potters work on the wheel.

▪ Does it allow room for growth? A family interested in wild flowers can collect seeds and specimens, study plant families, make illustrated books of flowers seen, plan trips with rare specimens in mind, start a wild flower garden.

Ideally, family activities would cover a wide range. In actual fact, though, most families have clearly marked abilities and interests. Some are outdoorsy, athletic; others are bookish; some are music mad. Fine. From the strong center of family pleasures, the healthy child moves out to an expanding universe.

Family Activities That Develop Language

"To teach a child to speak well," says the Russian poet Kornei Chukovsky, "means also to teach him to think well. One is inseparable from the other." Language is a uniquely human gift. Porpoises can be trained to produce recognizable sounds, chimps can learn sign language—but such skills are utterly remote from the rich possibilities of human speech. Through language the child comes to understand himself and the world around him—and to reach out to others. If his language is impoverished, his range of thought and feeling, his whole development, is circumscribed.

Part of a parent's job, then, is to refine and enrich the child's language skills. This involves not "vocabulary building" in any crude mechanical sense, but a gradual and natural communication of what words are for, what they can do. Chukovsky points to the "tremendous speech-giftedness of the preschool child": the two-and-a-half-year-old who, seeing a ship in the distance, cries out, "Mommy, Mommy, the ship is taking a bath!"; the little boy who announces, "I sing so much that the room gets big and beautiful." Young children often reveal a natural feeling for metaphor ("Snowdrops are umbrellas for flies"); simile ("a wet hedge smells like bread and cheese"); imitative sound ("buzzing bees busy in nests"); for words that are strange and suggestive and exciting. "My pretend friend is named Isabel," a four-year-old told me, "because she's *invisabel.*" Richard Lewis' *Journeys*, a collection of prose by children of the English-speaking world, is full of moments that make one shiver with the sheer delight of a child's way with language. Of creation, an eight-year-old writes, "the earth voomed out like a baseball." A seven-year-old watches cars "slippin' around just like tails swishin' on cats"; a ten-year-old sees a fire hydrant "like a strange plant bursting with its juice. Like a city's waterfall. I wouldn't be surprised if a whale came out today." How does daytime change to nighttime? "Daytime melts" (age five). How does a seven-year-old feel as she drops off to sleep? "I snuggled in my bed like a rose closing." An Irish child, writing of spring, sets the page on fire: "The rhododendron, flowers of a great cluster, single petal, crimson flame, living burning, growing till the yellow, golden brown leaf-falling autumn. The Dandelion clock, time in the tight, clamped hand. One, three, five or thirteen o'clock. The Daffodil in its prime, yellow, bright golden yellow."

As the last selection suggests, children can be extraordinarily sensitive to the *sound* of words. Rhyme is universally delighted in. Children playing will hit upon a rhyme and joyfully convert it into a taunt—or a song. I remember a group of little girls linking arms and chanting, "He *shook* her and he *shook* her and he *shook* her and he *shook* her, Just because she wouldn't use the other fellow's *hook*er." No need to ask what the song meant. The sound was the meaning.

The best way to excite children's feeling for language is by talking and reading to them from infancy. Babies respond very early to rhythmic sound (a ticking clock by the crib has a notably soothing effect) and they begin early their own experiments with it. These first vocalizings—the oo's and ee's and k-k-k-k's—have nothing to do with the urge to communicate; like the baby's kicks and thrusts, they're purely muscular. For the first few years of life, indeed, children continue at times to use sound as they use paint and clay and blocks and body movement, for sheer pleasure, not to "say" anything. Playing with sound, they make patterns (as they do with colors and block shapes). Here is a twenty-four-month-old boy climbing the slide: "Giddy, giddy, giddy. Demme, Dem-me, dem-me. Dub-dee, dub-dee, dub-dee. Wuh, wuh, wuh; Duh, duh, duh. Bee, bee, bee; lee, lee, lee; dub, dub, dub." And here is a nursery-schooler responding to an adult's "Soon we'll go bumpety bump to your house." The child, who had been drinking milk, set down her mug, eyed the adult solemnly and announced,

> Bumpety bump to *my* house,
> To *my* mamma,
> To *my* daddy,
> To *my* ba-lamb,
> To *my* table,
> To *my* chair.

These examples, reported by Harriet M. Johnson in *Children in the Nursery School,* are not unusual. Most children play with language in this way. So reading to a child in the prespeech period satisfies an already existent interest and need. A year-old child will listen rapturously to poems that have a strongly marked beat:

> A farmer went riding upon his grey mare,
>> Bumpety, bumpety, bump!
> With his daughter beside him so rosy and fair,
>> Lumpety, lumpety, lump!
> A raven cried "Croak!" and they all tumbled down,
>> Bumpety, bumpety, bump!
> The mare broke her knees, and the farmer his crown,
>> Lumpety, lumpety, lump!

Will a baby understand what that's all about? Of course not. But he'll respond to the rhythm, the modulated voice, adult attention—and the sense that this large person is doing something *interesting*. One of Dylan Thomas' biographers, Constantine Fitzgibbon, reports that Thomas' father started his son out on Shakespeare. "Oh, Daddy," practical Mrs. Thomas used to protest, "don't read Shakespeare to a child only four years of age." And Thomas senior would say, "He'll understand it. It'll be just the same as if I were reading him ordinary things." But it wasn't the same; how could it be? Thomas himself writes that because of that early dip into poetry, he fell in love with words. "What the words stood for, symbolized or meant, was of very secondary importance; what mattered was the *sound* of them . . . And these words were, to me, as the notes of bells, the sounds of musical instruments, the noises of wind, sea and rain, the rattle of milk-carts, the clopping of hooves on cobbles, the fingering of branches on a window pane, might be to someone, deaf from birth, who has miraculously found his hearing."

Speech and understanding come earlier if a child is constantly spoken to. P. M. Pickard, of Britain's Maria Grey College of Education, reports the case of a five-year-old brought to a Child Guidance Clinic because she had not begun to speak. It turned out that her mother, an educated woman, had never talked to the little girl because she "felt like a fool" addressing someone who couldn't understand. This is an extreme instance, and freakish; but many children talk late, and talk badly, for this simplest of all possible reasons: nobody talked to *them*.

When a child begins to talk, parents should not unnaturally restrict their vocabulary in an attempt to bring things down to a two-year-old level. Naturally you won't discuss politics or philosophy with a toddler; but you can certainly, in the course of daily life, give him the right words for things. "This is a *vacuum cleaner*." (Not a boom-boom.) "It sucks up the dirt. Look—you can feel the *suction*." "Don't put your mouth on a water fountain. It's not *sanitary*." Children enjoy learning and using "big" words. "This ice cream is *delicious*." "I'm stirring my cake very *vigorously*." Sybil Marshall, a gifted English schoolteacher, says of exposing pupils to "showers of English used for its true purpose": "if you stand out in the rain long enough, you are bound to get wet, and may even get soaked to the skin."

Though talking and reading are the best ways to soak a child in language, word games provide another kind of pleasurable language experience.

(Games marked * are suitable for young children.)

Rhyme Games

*SIMPLE RHYME CATCH

You "throw" a rhyme: CAT. The child returns BAT, you—or the next player—offer MAT, and so on until someone gets stuck for a rhyme and is out.

*RHYME JACKPOT

Propose a rhyme word. See who can make the longest list of rhymes in, say, five minutes. (Use a bell timer for excitement.) Children too young to write their words can move away from the group and dictate to an adult scribe.

*SPINNO

Mark a paper plate into sections and let the youngest child crayon each section a different color. Now label each section with a simple end rhyme (AN, ING, UN, OAT, etc.). Attach to the center of the plate the spinner from an old board game. Each player spins; then he provides as many rhymes as he can for the ending the pointer lands on (PAN, CAN, MAN, RAN, TAN: SING, RING, WING, BRING, FLING. . . .) Keep a count of the number of rhymes each player produces on his turn. The top scorer wins—a colored star, a jelly bean, a bead for a string, or whatever method of scorekeeping you've chosen. Punching numbered holes in a card is a method young children particularly enjoy.

I'M THINKING OF A WORD

"It" begins, "I'm thinking of a word that rhymes with BUG" (for example). Next player asks, "Is it something you walk on?" and "It," if he guesses what the other is thinking of, says, "No, it's not a RUG." This might go on—

> "Can you carry water in it?"
> "No, it's not a JUG."
>
> "Can you give it to someone you love?"
> "No, it's not a HUG."

If "It" can't correctly guess what rhyme word is being offered, he's out.

INKY PINKY

This, the best rhyme game I know, has the advantage of being genuinely challenging to all ages. (When a family has had some experience with it, it's a great game for long car trips.) "It" thinks of a rhymed description for any object, creature or activity. If only one-syllable words are involved, he says, for example, "A bright-colored sleeping place, Ink Pink" (A RED BED).

> "An angry father, Ink Pink"   (A MAD DAD).
> "What you get if you sing all the verses of 'The Twelve Days of Christmas'"   (A LONG SONG).

Two-syllable puzzlers might be:

> "A comical rabbit, Inky Pinky"   (A FUNNY BUNNY).
> "What you get around the neck when a shirt shrinks in the wash, Inky Pinky"   (A SMALLER COLLAR).
> "A Hitchcock thriller where lots of people die, Inky Pinky"   (A GORY STORY).

And for three-syllable Inkily Pinkily superchallenges . . . well, you can invent your own. (On these, you have to be fairly lenient. FRIGHTENING LIGHTNING, for example, is not a perfect triple rhyme definition of "something scary you get in a summer storm," but good triple rhymes are hard to find.)

*PUZZLE RHYMES

On cards, compose a set of simple rhyme definitions with the last word left blank. For example,

> On a hot sunny day you can come to me
> And sit in my shade; I'm a tall green ———
>
> I have bright glass eyes and stiff brown hair,
> I squeak when you press; I'm a teddy ———

Older children will enjoy making up these puzzles for younger siblings. For those who find rhyming difficult, an easy technique goes like this:

> I'm an animal that rhymes with HAT.
> I love to drink milk; I'm a soft furry ———

(An inexpensive rhyming dictionary is a good investment for this and many other word games.) Jot down puzzle rhymes as they occur to you, and you'll soon have a sizable collection. To play the game, make a pool of puzzle cards and let children take turns drawing. No matter if they draw familiar cards; knowing the answer right off is one kind of pleasure. (Playing with a single preschooler, you read off the puzzles one by one and let him guess.)

*RHYME CONVERSATION

The model for this game is that nonsense question-and-answer verse children love:

> What's your name?
> Puddle-in-tane.
> Where do you live?
> In a sieve.
> What's your number?
> Cucumber.

Children experienced in rhyme games (and children who have heard a lot of poetry) will have a marvelous loony time batting absurdities back and forth:

> What do you see?
> A pig in a tree.
> Where's your cat?
> Under my hat.
> How do you know?
> He licked my toe.

And so on. (The same technique can be used in a group for rhymed story telling, with players taking turns adding to the action:

First player	There once was a queen
Second	Whose face was green
Third	She ate her milk and drank her bread
Fourth	And got up in the morning to go to bed. . . .

Word Games

Some of the best are old-fashioned word games popular before radio and TV took over family entertainment. For some reason, they seem to surface now only at birthday parties; but they're ideal for families sitting by the fire, around the table, traveling. . . .

*ALPHABET SOUP

In its commonest form, this is a take-turns-around-the-circle game called I Love My Love ("I love my love with an A because she is amiable, affectionate, adorable, ancient, apple-cheeked, ambitious, agile . . . I love my love with a B because she is bossy, beautiful, brainless, buxom, bewitching, boring . . . and so on through the alphabet.)

For very young children, just learning to read (and more comfortable with nouns than with adjectives), a simple variation goes:

"I went to the circus and I saw—" (an antelope, a bear, a clown, a deer, an elephant . . . all the way to zebra).

"I walked down the street and I saw—" (an ambulance, a billboard, a car, a dachshund, an envelope, a fruit stand, a grocery . . .).

"I went to the store and I bought—" (apples, barley, corn, detergent . . .).

*RAINBOW

Mark off a paper plate into eight sections and have the child paint or crayon each section a different color: red, orange, yellow, green, blue, purple, black, white. Attach the spinner of an old board game to the plate's center. Players take turns spinning, must call off, in a given amount of time, as many objects as possible that are the color of the section he's landed on. (A clock timer is useful here.)

This game helps young children with colors as well as with language.

*BLOCKBUSTER

Take an ordinary child's block and paste on each side a gummed label or picture representing a category like: flowers, cities, famous names, vegetables, actors, book titles. For first- or second-graders, categories should be kept very simple (*animals* is sure-fire). For older children, introduce categories that will draw on special interests and knowledges (birds, scientists). Roll the block like dice and call out the category that comes face up. First player to provide an acceptable example gets the next roll.

*TELL-A-TALE

Have children cut from magazines and paste on cards (3 by 5 index cards work well) pictures of objects, people, vehicles, animals, foods. The more unusual the pictures, the more fun you'll have. To play, make two pools of cards face down—one for people cards, one for all other kinds. Let each player draw a set number of cards—two people cards and four nonpeople is about right. Allow a few minutes for everyone to arrange materials and think; then each player gets a turn to tell a story involving all the cards in his hand. It's not easy to connect, say, a grandmother, a pair of skis, a red-throated blackbird, a motorcyclist and an elephant. Often a five-year-old does better than his parents.

IN THE MANNER OF THE WORD

This is the game Noel Coward used in *Hay Fever*. "It" leaves the room and the group chooses a strong, colorful adverb (wildly, lovingly, furiously, awkwardly, indignantly, mournfully). When "It" returns, he directs different members of the group to perform particular actions *in the manner of the word*. Dance that way—or talk, eat, pick flowers, swim, sing, weep, smile that way. When "It" guesses the right adverb, the player whose action gave the clue becomes "It."

THE GAME

You need at least six people for this—two teams. One team goes into a huddle and chooses the title of a movie, book, play or song. Titles chosen must lend themselves to dramatization (*Great Expectations, Tale of Two Cities, Gone With the Wind, Sleeping Beauty,* "I Wanna Hold Your Hand," "Row Row Row Your Boat." They whisper their title to the leader of the other group. He then tries, by action and gesture only, to communicate the title to his group. If they guess correctly, it's their turn to assign a title.

Family Activities That Develop Observation and Sensory Awareness

An eminent science educator, Lazer Goldberg, reminds us that in primitive societies where awareness of environment may be a matter of life and death, the youngest child learns to watch and interpret signs. A tiger passed that way; this is the kind of terrain where edible berries thrive; that sky means rain. In a complex technological society, however, the young often don't look closely because they don't have to. It becomes important, then, for parents to help children develop their observing skills.

Now, there are a number of simple games that stimulate perceptual awareness. You can blindfold children and let them try to identify by smell such substances as mothballs, vanilla, wet wool, rubber, lemon extract, turpentine, cinnamon; by taste, licorice, gingersnap, peppermint, apple, lemon, salt, onion. You can ask them to identify the sounds made by knocking on the floor, crumpling paper, tapping a spoon on a glass, pouring water, tearing cloth, blowing bubbles through a straw into a glass of water. You can play Mystery Objects, asking a child to put his hand into a paper bag and identify objects by texture or felt shape alone (fur, rock, sandpaper, velvet). A preschooler will enjoy just sitting under a tree and playing, "I see" or "I hear." All these games are fun—and instructive. In the last analysis, though, the only way to make a child aware of his environment is to explore it with him. Take walks in all seasons, and see what you can find.

Outdoor Excursions

Because I have lived all my life in the country, a walk to me is a country walk, and I can't help feeling it's the best kind. But of course cities are rich not only in fascinating human activity—cranes, planes, factories, shops—but in natural history too. John Kieran, exploring New York City, found 230 species of birds, a great variety of rocks and minerals, a profusion of flowers, lichen, fungi, ferns. On a 75 by 100 foot lot in New Jersey, one investigator collected 1,402 insect species. So living in a high-rise apartment doesn't rule out the possibility of field trips. If you're not within reach of a pond or a wood, isn't there a park nearby? An arboretum?

In spring, you can show a child all the myriad, thrilling signs of life stirring—birds carrying bits of nesting straw, the first sharp crocus tips, tadpole movement below the water's surface, muddy puddles with snails in them, swelling lilac buds. Have him listen for peepers and mourning doves, smell the spring wind—and fly a kite in it. Help him plant a little garden—something to smell good (thyme, dill), something to eat (radishes come early, look lovely washed on his plate), something to look pretty (nasturtiums, maybe, or petunias—foolproof flowers). Also something, like everlasting flowers or Chinese lanterns, that can be dried in fall and kept for winter.

If you live in a city and can't garden, try for a window box. Failing that, show the child how to start a plant from an avocado seed, a pineapple top, an orange pip. One way or another, grow something to celebrate spring and, in the growing, let him discover how sun and moisture and soil together produce "the force that through the green fuse drives the flower." Children need to know these things. (Once I showed a visiting city child, four years old, a corn field. "Corn?" he said, puzzled. "Does it come from corn flakes?")

To make excursions more meaningful, get a pair of field glasses and a microscope, for different ways of seeing. Invest in a good field guide to minerals, or birds, or wild flowers; it can become a focus of every outing. "Look, here's a columbine just about to open." . . . "Did you hear that note? I think it's an oriole. Let's watch." "This looks like mica chips in the rock. Shall we take a piece home?" Help the child start a collection. Shells, maybe, if the ocean is within reach . . . or rocks, or pressed leaves. Reflecting on the number of scientists who were passionate collectors as children, Lazer Goldberg observes that collecting is really—and meaningfully—"a way of playing with the world."

Sometimes it's fun, on a walk, to organize a special activity like a nature scavenger hunt. Each child gets a list of things to find: a twig shaped like an animal, three different kinds of leaves, two kinds of bark, a flower gone to seed, an acorn. . . . But just walking and looking can be a rich experience. Here's an ant struggling through the grass with a dead fly. Here are the tracks of a sandpiper, sharp little V's at the water's edge. There's a bee, throbbing in a bluebell cup; a meadowlark's nest; a suffocating gypsy moth's web choking the living tree. . . . Children are fascinated by these marvels. Once trained to look, they easily discover "a world in a grain of sand and heaven in a wild flower."

To deepen your child's experience of the natural world, give him a chance, occasionally, to explore one particular phenomenon that catches his eye. He notices an earthworm, perhaps. Let him collect a few worms in a glass jar with handfuls of loose soil. (A good moment to show him the different kinds of soil—clay, spongy dark humus, sandy earth—and let him figure out which kind his worms would prefer.) Back home, he can hammer air holes in the jar lid and dampen the soil to keep his worms comfortable. With a strong magnifying glass, he can examine one closely, observing the two rows of stiff hairs that act as legs. If he keeps the earthworms for several weeks he'll find castings, small piles of coiled dirt excreted on the soil's surface. He may even—what joy!—find wiggly baby worms.

A family interested in exploring the outdoors together will be enthralled by Katherine Wensberg's introduction to ecology for five-to-eight-year-olds, *Experiences with Living Things*. To illustrate her theme, the interdependence of all living things, Miss Wensberg considers such creatures as robins, ants, spiders, cats, outlining in each case projects that will tempt the young to observe, question, reason and remember. A chapter on trees, for instance, suggests that children choose an individual tree as *their* tree. They can study the bark under a magnifying glass, observe its bloom (all trees flower, however inconspicuously), watch formation of seeds and plant some. They can study its leaves, comparing them with leaves of other trees; they can use leaves to make spatter prints. They may be able to get from a lumber yard specimens of *their* wood (maple, oak or whatever) which they can sand smoothly—always a pleasure for children—and use for block printing. They can observe the way roots draw water by observing what happens when a flower (preferably white) is set in colored ink. They can make tree poems and tree-in-the-wind dances and, if sufficiently inspired, can browse through the tree books suggested in Miss Wensberg's tempting lists.

Though cold weather restricts the range of living things to see, it needn't limit the pleasures of exploring in field or park. Show children how to watch for winter patterns: squiggly field mouse tracks, the fan-shaped prints of birds, the signs that deer or rabbits have passed by. (Deer tear off twigs, rabbits make a clean cut into branches.) Stand still and listen; sounds are different in a snow world. Collect snowflakes on freezer-chilled black construction paper and examine them under a magnifying glass— icicles too, snapped open so you can see a cross section. Small children will want to make snow angels. Remember how? Lie down carefully in the snow, arms at your sides, legs straight. Then, move arms gently up and down to make wings, open and close legs to create an angel robe in the snow. Get up cautiously so as not to spoil the print.

Children will also enjoy making up a snow song. Take any familiar tune that lends itself to improvisation and start them off:

To the tune of "Here We Go Round the Mulberry Bush"

> Here we go running down the hill,
>> Down the hill, down the hill,
> Here we go running down the hill,
>> Upon a snowy morning.
>
> This is the way we slip and slide . . .
>
> This is the way we throw the snow . . .
>
> This is the way we jump and fall . . . etc.

Or, to "Old Macdonald Had a Farm"

Joan and Martin had some snow, [Fill in appropriate names]
    Ee-i, ee-i, O.
And on this snow they rode their sled,
    Ee-i, ee-i, O.
With a swish swish here and a swoosh swoosh there,
    Here a swish, there a swoosh,
Everywhere a swish swoosh,
Joan and Martin had some snow,
    Ee-i, ee-i, O.

Continue with, "And in this snow they made a man . . . With a pat pat here and a pat pat there"—or whatever the players dream up.

Children of elementary school age may be stimulated to explore all kinds of intriguing questions concerning the changes from water to snow to ice. (Does snow melt faster on a dark or a light surface? When snow or ice melts, how does the volume of liquid compare with the volume of the original solid?) Back home, they might like to try an imaginative experiment devised for the Newton, Massachusetts, schools. Place a thermometer in a paper cup of water, then put into the freezer. When the water has frozen solid, peel off the paper cup so that you have a kind of thermometer-popsicle. Now hold this over a candle flame—and watch the reading of the thermometer as the ice melts. The surprising result will set young minds stirring.

Special Excursions

Until children move into the teens (a period when going about with parents becomes embarrassing), few pleasures match the joy of a special family excursion. To be special, an outing needn't be exotic. I remember with some chagrin a massive effort we made to show our three-year-old daughter a real circus. We drove

sixty miles that hot summer afternoon, describing along the way
the delights of calliopes, elephants, pink cotton candy. When
we entered the big tent, though, Rona seemed dazed. The
clowns frightened her. Our seats, backless benches high above
the ring, she clearly thought precarious. Shortly after the main
action began—a noisy confusion of roaring lions, trapeze artists
and bicycling chimpanzees—she leaned against my arm in weary
boredom. Watching the man who, a hundred feet in the air,
balanced a chair on a wire and then sat on the chair, Rona
yawned. She'd seen people sit on chairs before. Just as I was about
to suggest leaving, our drooping child came ecstatically to life.
"Oh, Mummy, look! There's a man *feeding a horse!*"

Our circus fiasco points up a not-really-so-obvious fact: to a
child, the most ordinary things can be remarkable. (As I once
heard a book editor say, "We forget that children are new and we
are not.") Certainly the young enjoy extra-special treats like a trip
to Disneyland. They also enjoy playing train with the kitchen
chairs or traveling to China by way of the coat closet. Sights
adults take for granted, like window washers on a high perch or
a road repair truck spreading tar, they find endlessly interesting.
And often the most fascinating excursion possible involves no
more than a walk down the street. Here are suggestions suitable
for families with children between the ages of, roughly, three to
ten.

FIRE STATION

Telephone first to find out a good visiting hour. If the firemen
aren't busy, they may let children climb up on the truck, polish
a bit of chrome, try on a jacket and hat. Older children will be
interested in the fire alarm system, the sleeping and eating arrangements, firemen's stories of memorable fires.

GREENHOUSE

If you go about two weeks before Easter or Memorial Day, you'll find a lush variety of plants—and workers won't be too busy to show you around. Children will enjoy smelling flowers, observing plants in different stages of growth (a just-started spider plant, a mature one dropping dozens of "babies"), watching soil preparation and potting activities. A friendly proprietor may offer a cutting which the child can take home and root in water. Or the child can purchase a small plant to tend at home. (He may want to reset it in a pot he decorates himself.)

A greenhouse trip is very likely to send an older child to the library in pursuit of a new interest. (How can orchids grow on bark only, with their roots in the air?)

LIBRARY

If you've ever taken a four-year-old on his first library trip, you'll remember his amazement at the privilege adults take for granted. "Can I take out any book I want? I don't have to pay?" The children's room will naturally be the highlight of the visit (though an older child may want to explore the card catalog, the reference and magazine reading rooms). If you're lucky, you'll find a children's room with tempting climb-or-stretch-out-on-it furniture, displays of children's work and a friendly librarian who can tell you when the next story hour will be held. Most librarians welcome young borrowers' contributions to their room: drawings, paintings inspired by favorite books, hand-printed book reviews, clay sculptures.

If the library has a Xerox machine, let the child make a copy of something that interests him.

AIRPORT

Try to go by bus or car, rather than subway, so children can get a sense of the total area as you drive up. Show them the ticket counters, the baggage handling system, the insurance machines. Let them watch security men checking passengers and baggage for concealed metal: that will have special meaning to a child who has experimented with a magnet at home. Go up to the observation deck to see planes landing and taking off; point out the way control tower and ground crews work to insure safe landing. Finish up with ice cream at the airport restaurant; maybe there's a special flight-motif menu the youngest can take home.

POST OFFICE

A good preliminary to this trip is a letter-writing or picture-making session at home. Children can then mail their letters at the Post Office—being sure to include one item addressed to their very own house. If you visit at a time when employees are not too busy, you may find someone willing to show just what happens after an envelope drops through the slot—the sorting and canceling, the trundling away of mail into trucks.

A FACTORY

The absolutely ideal place would be something like a chocolate factory, full of delicious smells, fascinating operations—and a free sample at the end of the tour. (Samples are terribly important. When I was a child, I went almost every Saturday to a local Coca-Cola plant—to collect yet another miniature Coke bottle.) But all *processes* are fascinating to children. Seeing how leather hides become shoes, how yarn becomes cloth, and milk turns into ice cream: this is mind-expanding and, for many, an inspiration to try new things at home.

A MUSEUM

Many children grow up imagining that museums are collections of dusty old treasures interesting only to dusty old people. That's a pity. There are museums for every taste—science museums, children's museums, marine museums, museums of natural history. Every child should have, periodically, the experience of visiting a first-rate comprehensive art museum like the National Gallery (Washington), the Metropolitan (New York City) or Boston's Museum of Fine Arts.

If you want your child to grow up responsive to the arts, don't try to give him massive doses of culture. A museum visit should be carefully scaled to the child's attention span and to his particular interests. If he's been working with clay, show him some Ming vases, some contemporary sculpture. (I think of an awkward-graceful Degas ballerina, bronze with real net skirt; Picasso's lively goat and his monkey with a toy-car mouth; a Henry Moore family group.) If he's just heard about mummies, there's the Egyptian room; if he's been reading King Arthur, he can inspect medieval weapons and armor (discovering, incidentally, how much smaller men must have been five centuries ago). Help him find paintings he specially likes—you can return to those on future visits—and don't spoil his pleasure by "arty" comments. ("This is the impressionist style" or "Notice the use of light and dark. It's called *chiaroscuro*.") You may find a child's taste is more catholic than yours: that he responds equally to a de Staël abstraction and to a Rembrandt portrait. Though you want children to make their own discoveries, share with them occasionally one of *your* favorites. (If I were escorting a six-year-old, I'd want to show him one of those Flemish paintings that reveal worlds within worlds as you live into the picture. Breughel's *The Numbering at Bethlehem*, for instance, its canvas so crowded with life—children tussling, hens pecking, peasants gathering firewood, skaters and carpenters—that you have to look long before you find the picture's mysterious heart, a shrouded woman on a donkey. A child could return to it again and again, each time seeing a new, suggestive detail.)

Before you leave, let the child buy a few postcard reproductions to start his own art collection.

Other good excursions, some country, some city:

> A bakery
> A children's theater performance
> An apple orchard
> A dairy farm
> A police station
> An arboretum
> A lumber yard
> A train station
> An aquarium
> An auto body repair shop
> A zoo
> A boat, train or bus ride
> An outdoor market
> A newspaper or printing office
> The studio of any artist or craftsman

And to make any excursion more meaningful, bear in mind that

▪ Preparation helps. Before a zoo trip, get from the library an illustrated book of animals that you can go through together. You might pursue one particular theme or question to be explored at the zoo—animals belonging to the same group as the family cat, for example, or the relationship between animals and their native habitat. If you're going to a children's play, you might give the younger ones an advance idea of what they're going to see.

▪ Children like to get some souvenir they can carry home and keep—even if it's only a collection of railway timetables. Best of all are mementos with play possibilities: scraps of wood from the lumber yard, to be sanded and used for building; a moist ball of potter's clay from a studio; pieces of newsprint to make a book with.

▪ The excursion can become a basis for all kinds of play and learning activity. A trip to a farm will inspire farmer games; a theatrical performance will set children to making their own plays. Encourage children to draw pictures of what they've seen, make books, write or dictate a letter telling Grandmother all about the adventure.

Family Activities That Promote Free Expression

All children love to pretend. At two, they hold animated conversations on the toy telephone; at three, they play house, joyously or passionately imitating family activities; at five, they act out favorite fairy tales with friends; at ten or eleven, they want to put on a *real* play for an adult audience. Dramatic experiences of this sort play an important part in the child's development. They provide emotional outlets. (Oh, the joy of roaring like a troll, stamping and complaining like the proud princess, threatening like a wicked witch!) They inspire expressive movement. (How do fairies walk? And giants in seven-league boots?) They increase verbal facility, give poise to the awkward and confidence to the shy. They provide the beginnings of an interest in drama and the arts. And they promote not only realization of the self but also understanding of others. Playing angry father or ugly duckling, a child learns how other people must feel.

For the most part, children enjoy acting out independent of adults. But some dramatic games and activities provide whole-family fun.

Drama for the Playpen

With babies and toddlers, finger plays are great sport. A nine-month-old baby will love "Cree-eep mouse, cree-eep mouse, from the barn up to the house!" with your fingers creeping up bare legs and arms to an under-chin tickle. Then there's

Two little blackbirds
Sitting on a hill,   Your fingers make birds, first
One named Jack,   perching on his shoulders and
The other named Jill.   then fluttering about him
Fly away, Jack!
Fly away, Jill!
Come back Jack!
Come back Jill!

Other old favorites will occur to you from your own childhood. Remember

Here's a ball for baby,   Shape ball with first finger
Big and soft and round.   and thumb
Here is baby's hammer,   Bang fist in palm of your hand
Oh, how he can pound!
Here is an umbrella,   Index finger for handle, other
To keep the baby dry.   hand over it for umbrella top
Here is baby's cradle,   Hug arms into cradle shape and
Rock-a-baby-bye!   rock

(In all of these, substitute the child's own name for *baby*.)

If dignifying these diversions with the label "dramatic" seems absurd, let me assure you that to a two-year-old, "Ring the bell" is thrilling as a performance of *Othello* to an adult playgoer:

Ring the bell,   Tweak a central lock of child's hair
Knock at the door,   Knock gently on forehead

PEEP IN!	Circle your own eyes with index finger and thumb, then look straight into his, very close
Wipe your shoes,	Index finger "wipes" over his upper lip
Lift the latch	Pretend lifting up of nose
And WALK IN!	Index finger pops into child's mouth (sure to be open by now, in happy astonishment)

Pantomime Games

MOTHER GOOSE

For this game, players act out a nursery rhyme which the others must guess. It can be done as solo performance (Jack nimbly leaping over his candlestick, the Duke of York followed by an invisible army) or in pairs (Miss Muffet and the Spider, the mouse and the Hickory Dickory clock, Jack Sprat and his wife picking over their joint dinner and then licking the platter clean). No words may be spoken.

WHAT AM I DOING?

Players take turns silently miming a familiar action: baking a cake, opening a stuck window, sewing on a button, hammering a nail. First one to guess correctly gets his chance at stumping the family.

HOCUS-POCUS

Start with a simple prop: a stool, a basket, a trash-can lid. Each family member performs a magical hocus-pocus pass over the prop, converting it into something else. Then, by his behavior or use of the "transformed" object, others guess what it has turned into. (Is the stool now a car? a tree? a cradle? a sandpile?)

NAME THE ANIMAL

Cards bearing names of domestic and wild animals are mixed in a pile. Each player draws a card, then acts out his animal—without sound—for the others to identify. This is fun for very young children (use pictures rather than printed names). Steer clear of creatures like the anteater; how does an anteater move? Sure-fire suggestions: frog, caterpillar, rabbit, alligator, kangaroo, mouse, bear, pony, kitten.

Making Plays

Learning parts, in the early years, is confining—and not much fun. But children love to act out familiar stories—"Cinderella," "Sleeping Beauty"—inventing dialogue as they go along. Though occasionally they may enjoy having parents join in, the greatest pleasure is a grown-up audience. Set aside an evening when you will be free to attend a performance, and encourage the children (or child) to make professional-type preparations: advertising posters put up around the house, programs, tickets (to be punched at the living room door), cookies or popcorn and lemonade to be sold at intermission. Treat their work seriously. Coming in apron or work clothes, announcing that you have a TV show to watch at eight so would they just hurry a bit—that is *not* treating children's offerings with the respect they deserve.

Sometimes, for a change of pace, children will enjoy staging a variety night, a sort of showcase for assorted talents: magic tricks, dances, songs, some guitar strumming or flute tootling and—why not?—a commercial or two. (If children get hung up on merely reproducing standard TV commercials, ask them to invent a sales pitch for some family treasure—a shabby rug, an ashtray, the baby or the cat.)

Dramatic Reading

Reading poems aloud is a natural family activity. If some children are too young to read, they can provide refrains, the delicious recurring nonsense in Edward Lear's verse narratives, for example:

> Far and few, far and few,
> Are the lands where the Jumblies live;
> Their heads are green, and their hands are blue,
> And they went to sea in a Sieve.
>   (from "The Jumblies")

or

> And there in a wood a Piggy-wig stood,
> With a ring at the end of his nose,
> His nose,
> His nose
> With a ring at the end of his nose.
>   (from "The Owl and the Pussy Cat")

Narrative poems—with one person carrying the story line, and others taking different voices—are specially good. Try some old English or Scottish ballads, "Sir Patrick Spens":

> The king sits in Dunfermline town,
>   Drinking the blood-red wine:
> "O where will I get a skeely skipper
>   To sail this new ship of mine?"

If you think the blood and heartbreak of medieval ballads strong fare for your children, look at nineteenth-century ballads, where these elements are muted. "Lochinvar" swings along with a beat the young find irresistible:

O, Young Lochinvar is come out of the West—
Through all the wide Border his steed was the best . . .
So faithful in love, and so dauntless in war,
There never was knight like the young Lochinvar.

It also has individual speaking parts with great theatrical possibilities: the bride's father, steel hand in velvet glove ("O come
ye in peace here, or come ye in war, Or to dance at our bridal,
young Lord Lochinvar?"); the whispering bridesmaids; and the
hero himself, so obviously the best man in Netherby Hall:

I long wooed your daughter—my suit you denied;
Love swells like the Solway, but ebbs like its tide;
And now I am come, with this lost love of mine,
To lead but one measure, drink one cup of wine.

Just as children love stories in which the young outwit their el-
ders, they show, often, a precocious interest in the theme of romantic love triumphing over parental opposition. My daughters
at six and ten respectively—an age when suitors, welcome or un-
welcome, seemed a remote possibility—were mad for "Lord
Ullin's Daughter," a sentimental but gloriously swinging tale of
a Highland chief who abducts his bonnie bride and drowns with
her while her father weeps on shore:

"Come back! come back!" he cried in grief,
    "Across this stormy water;
And I'll forgive your Highland chief—
    My daughter—O my daughter!"

For very young children, the best dramatic reading material
I know is found in A. A. Milne's pure-delight re-creations of the
child world: *When We Were Very Young, Now We Are Six,
Winnie-the-Pooh* and *The House at Pooh Corner*. For a nonreader, there are lots of poems with choruses and repeated lines—
the recurring "What *is* the matter with Mary Jane" (a line to be

enunciated smugly by self-consciously model children who know *they* never behave so badly at table) or the deliciously silly spinning

> Perhaps I am a Postman. No, I think I am a Tram.
> I'm feeling rather funny and I don't know *what* I am—

BUT

> *Round* about
> And *round* about
> And *round* about I go—

Milne's verse sings itself so effortlessly that four-year-olds will find, after a few family reading sessions, they *know* their favorite parts and can join in with "Whenever a good nor' wester blows, Christopher is certain of Sand-between-the-toes" or "But *I* give buns to the elephant when *I* go down to the Zoo!" In any case, they can act out the verses while a parent reads: the illustrations, and the rhythm, are sufficient cues. "Whenever I walk on a London street, I'm ever so careful to watch my feet"—a high-stepping wise child avoiding the pavement lines (where bears lurk). Certainly you needn't give directions for this sort of kinetic response; a three-year-old will be off his chair after the first few lines of

> Christopher Robin goes
> Hoppity, hoppity,
> Hoppity, hoppity, hop.
> Whenever I tell him
> Politely to stop it, he
> Says he can't possibly stop.

And of course you will want to read aloud, taking parts, "The King's Breakfast" ("The King asked The Queen, and The Queen asked The Dairymaid: 'Could we have some butter for The Royal slice of bread?'") and "Disobedience," with its glorious, triumphantly nervy inversion of the usual state of affairs in a child's world:

> James James
> Morrison Morrison
> Weatherby George Dupree
> Took great
> Care of his Mother,
> Though he was only three.
> James James
> Said to his Mother,
> "Mother," he said, said he:
>> "You must never go down to the end of the town,
>> if you don't go down with me."

Many parts of *Winnie-the-Pooh* and *The House at Pooh Corner* read splendidly: assign one voice to the narrator, while other family members read Piglet, Tigger, Eeyore. A nonreader can play Roo, who mostly squeaks, or Rabbit, whose part is so brief that an adult can whisper-feed lines at the right moments.

Any dramatic reading gains in concentration and pleasure if you tape it. Playing the tape back is almost as much fun as the original reading.

W.F.F. (Warm Family Feeling) Activities

This large loose category includes all sorts of activities that bring parents and children together in the joy of creating. Most families, as the years go by, develop such special shared experiences on their own. I know families where the special sharing is baking bread on Sunday morning; others where it's tying flies all winter and going fishing together in summer. Here are activities that worked particularly well for us.

FAMILY SCRAPBOOK

This is simply a book, or series of books, to which every member contributes things that matter to him. When children are small, parents will do most of the choosing and pasting. There'll be snapshots, of course—preferably not posed family-at-the-front-door but candids: Mother raking leaves, Baby with her first ice-cream cone, Father helping with dishes or fallen asleep by the TV. There may be scraps of fabric (from a security blanket, a birthday party dress), a pressed four-leaf clover from a picnic, a nursery school report, a newspaper clipping mentioning one of the children, a letter to or from camp that first summer, a hand-printed Father's Day card, a ticket from a performance of *Sleeping Beauty*. . . . Part of the fun is pasting in entries and writing captions, and part is in taking the book out evenings and remembering together.

"FLOSFY"

What my youngest child called "flosfy" (for *philosophy*) is really just talking together, but talking to a special point or purpose. Parents sometimes forget how much the young enjoy conversation with adults—about real things and in a setting where their ideas are respectfully listened to. I think it's important to set aside special times for serious family talk. Sitting around a fire—or, if you have no fireplace, in a circle on the floor, with pillows—gives a good feeling. Children of different ages can take part, each on his own level, in considering those large questions that help each one discover who he is and where he wants to go. For example:

▪ What was the last thing that happened to make you feel really good—about another person or about yourself?

▪ What was the last thing you did that made you feel disappointed in yourself or in someone else—and why?

■ If you could spend a day with any person in the whole wide world, who would you choose?

■ What do you like *best* about each member of the family?

■ If you could have three wishes, what would they be?

■ What was the best present you ever got?

■ What frightens you most? What makes you feel excited? Worried? Unhappy?

■ What place do you like best of all? What do you like to do there?

■ What toy—any that you've ever had—would you like to give to *your* children?

In a family where talking and sharing of this sort are natural, children will often take the opportunity—the *risk*—of raising spontaneously a problem that's been bothering them.

FAMILY NEWSPAPER

You don't have to wait until children can read and write to start your own family bulletin (*The Jones Journal, The Smith Scuttlebutt,* or whatever). For a three-year-old, you might start with a large piece of colored paper, suitably titled and Scotch-taped to the side of the refrigerator. Print out a few "news" items. Keep them very simple, like:

> JOE HAS SHINY NEW SHOES.
> DADDY IS GOING ON AN AIRPLANE.
> JOE AND MUMMY WILL DRIVE HIM TO THE AIRPORT.
> FLOSSIE IS GOING TO HAVE KITTENS VERY SOON.
> SHE IS MAKING A SOFT PLACE FOR THEM IN THE CLOSET.

Illustrations are a happy addition—simple line drawings or, if any line is beyond you, pasted-on pictures. Joe will want to hear these items read over and over—and point to the word that says

JOE. He'll also, from time to time, volunteer items of his own for the paper, like "I fell off the jungle gym but I didn't cry."

Once a child starts school, he'll take a hand in the printing and drawing. Gradually, over the years, the newspaper becomes a true family venture, changing format (typed or mimeographed; sheets stapled together) and reflecting the full range of family interests. So a typical issue might contain plans for a birthday party, a report on the Grade Four science fair, a joke, a riddle, an article on the fascinating demolition project down the street, an interview with a dinner guest just back from Japan, the funny thing Sandy said about her nursery school teacher, a report on a new TV show or a rock concert.

A newspaper like this constitutes a priceless record of a family's growth and change. And individual copies, xeroxed, make welcome gifts for relatives and distant friends.

THINKING CAP

This is a catchall label for any activity in which the family sharpens its collective wits, either "brainstorming" to generate ideas on a given topic or working out puzzles. Major choices confronting the family ("Shall we take a trip, or use the money to convert the basement into a playroom?") can be more sharply defined in this way—and solutions more easily seen. Puzzles—mathematical, detective-style, or trick-answer—make a wonderful group diversion; where children are too young to work on their own, you can make parent-child teams. You might start with material from Donald J. Sobol's Encyclopedia Brown books. In this series, a boy detective solves, by common sense and close attention, mysteries that baffle older heads: whether it's missing roller skates or a diamond necklace, Encyclopedia goes straight to the heart of the dilemma. The format of these books lends itself to family think sessions: a brief, simply written story which presents the mystery and, at the back of the book, a solution to check after everybody's presented *his* theory.

Trick problems, many of them of folk origin, provide another kind of challenge. Like the story of the wicked old moneylender who wants to marry the merchant's beautiful daughter. The merchant owes money which he can't pay. Desperate, he accepts a gamble offered by his creditor: all three principals will meet on a pebble path before the moneylender's house. The moneylender will put into a bag one white pebble and one black; the daughter is to reach in and, without looking, select a stone. If she picks a black one, she marries the moneylender, and her father's debt is canceled. (If she picks a white one, the debt is canceled too—and she's free.)

At the appointed time, the three meet. The girl sees the moneylender bend down and pick up *two black pebbles* for the fatal bag. How can she avoid angering him by exposing his treachery—and yet save herself and her father?

That one should occupy any group for some time. Solution? Why, without revealing her knowledge that there's no white pebble in the bag, the girl reaches in, chooses a stone—and drops it instantly on the pebble-covered path. Then she has only to smile and say, "Goodness, how clumsy! But I must have picked the white one—because see, the pebble that's left in the bag is black."

Puzzles for Pleasure and Leisure, by Thomas L. Hirsch, is a good source of story puzzles for school-age children—the kind of problems that stimulate creativity because they force the problem solver to approach his task with a freshly cleared vision. A nice example is Hirsch's story of the general who notices a one-armed soldier at a review parade. "Did you get a medal when you lost your arm in battle?" the general asks. "No, sir," says the soldier. Promptly, the general removes one of his own medals and pins it on the soldier's uniform. "My," says the soldier, "what would I have got if I'd lost both arms?" "A commission," says the general. Hearing this, the soldier draws his bayonet and with one swift stroke cuts off his other arm.

Problem: Should the soldier have been awarded the commission or declared insane?

Answer: How can a one-armed man cut off his only arm?

Problem solving with one's family is fun. It's also an important kind of learning and, regularly practiced, is likely to develop a creative approach to real-life situations. I think—with some mortification—of a problem I *didn't* meet successfully. I was rushing to catch a bus one morning when I spied, on an affluent neighbor's trash barrel, a beautiful rope hammock in good repair. It was just what my girls had been asking for—and I'd had to tell them rope hammocks were too expensive, about forty dollars. Well. I looked at my watch, I looked at the hammock. If I didn't take it at that moment, the trash collectors would sweep it off to the dump. But if I took time to carry it back home, I would miss my bus and an important appointment. I walked on.

That evening, I told my children about the agonizing decision. "You didn't take it?" howled the ten-year-old. "I couldn't," I said. "I had no time to go back."

"Mummy," said the child, patient but exasperated too, an experienced problem solver. "You wouldn't have had to go *back*. You could have gone *forward*—picked up the hammock and checked it at the bus station!"

All Together: Family Activities

MOSTLY FOR INDOORS

ABRAHAM, R. M., *Easy-to-do Entertainments and Diversions with Coins, Cards, String, Paper and Matches*, Dover, 1961. Over 300 games, card tricks, puzzles and pastimes, ranging from simple to very advanced.

BANCROFT, JESSIE H., *Games*, Macmillan, 1937. An old book revised, enlarged and still useful. Divided into active games, quiet games, singing, bean bag, ball games, etc.

BOIKO, CLAIRE, *Children's Plays for Creative Actors*, Plays, Inc., 1967. Very short plays with seasonal and holiday motifs; a number of historical playlets, some science fiction material and some lively comedy (like the story of Cinder-Riley, an Irish heroine whose wicked stepmother has betrothed her to the King of West Muffinland: "He has turned-up toes and a wart on his nose, and he's fat as a tub of butter!")

CARLSON, BERNICE W., *Act It Out*, Abingdon, 1956. Simple drama for the young: puppet performances, acting games and pantomimes, dramatic stunts, tableaux, pageants.

——, *Do It Yourself! Tricks, Stunts and Skits*, Abingdon, 1952. Abingdon, 1952.

CASSELL, SYLVIA S., *Indoor Games and Activities*, Harper, 1960. Arts and crafts, puzzles, games, experiments to entertain a solitary child or groups of children.

CHUKOVSKY, KORNEI, *From Two to Five*, trans. and ed. Miriam Morton, University of California Press, 1965.

CROSSCUP, RICHARD, *Children and Dramatics*, Scribner, 1966.

EISENBERG, HELEN and HARRY, *The Family Fun Book*, Association Press, 1953. A little of everything.

ELLISON, VIRGINIA H., *The Pooh Party Book*, Dutton, 1971. Inspired by the Pooh books, ideas for such typical undertakings as an Eeyore birthday party, a honey-tasting party, an expotition and a wozzle-wizzle snow party. With the appropriate, original Shepard illustrations.

HARBIN, O. E., *Games for Boys and Girls*, Abingdon, 1971. Indoor and outdoor, all ages and group sizes.

HENRY, MABEL WRIGHT, *Creative Experiences in Oral Language*, National Council of Teachers of English, 1967.

HIRSCH, THOMAS L., *Puzzles for Pleasure and Leisure*, Abelard, 1966.

HOAGA, AGNES, and PATRICIA RANDLES, *Supplementary Materials for Use in Creative Dramatics for Younger Children*, University of Washington Press, 1952.

JOHNSON, HARRIET M., *Children in the Nursery School*, Reprint of 1928 ed., Agathon.

KRISVOY, JUEL, *New Games to Play*, Follett, 1968. Sixty-two group games for indoors or out, preschool and grade one, all emphasizing verse chants and rhythmic movement.

LEEMING, JOSEPH, *Fun with Pencil and Paper*, Lippincott, 1955. Games, stunts and puzzles for one person or the whole family.

LEWIS, RICHARD, *Journeys*, Simon & Schuster, 1969. Vigorous, imaginative prose by children of the English-speaking world.

LOPSHIRE, ROBERT, *It's Magic?*, Macmillan, 1969. A first reading book in which Boris the bear demonstrates 14 easy tricks any little reader can emulate.

MEYER, JEROME, *The Big Book of Family Games*, Hawthorn, 1967. One of the most complete and inexpensive collections of fun things to do.

——, *Puzzle, Quiz and Stunt Fun*, Dover, 1956. A wonderful winter-night book for families—everything from tongue

twisters and quizzes to simple stunts (how to dip your bare
finger into a glass of water without getting it wet, how to
draw a perfect circle composed entirely of long, straight
lines).

MILGROM, HARRY, *Adventures with a Cardboard Tube*, Dutton,
1972. Also in this series, *Adventures with a Ball, a Paper
Cup, a Party Plate, a Plastic Bag, a Straw, a String*—all describing simple experiments which demonstrate the fundamental laws of matter. In this book, for example, Milgrom
shows the young scientist how a cardboard tube can block
light, collect sound, move objects from one place to another, act as a balance scale. . . . Designed to set the
reader thinking.

MULHOLLAND, JOHN, *Book of Magic*, Scribner, 1963. A professional magician's tricks of the trade. Intriguing for a whole
family to explore.

POSSEIN, WILMA M., *They All Need to Talk*, Appleton, 1969.
Creative dramatics, poetry and reading in a language arts
program.

RAWSON, CLAYTON, *The Golden Book of Magic: Amazing Tricks
for Young Magicians*, Golden Press, 1964. Magic with
household objects; mind-reading tricks.

RAZZI, JAMES, *Easy Does It!*, Parents Magazine Press, 1969.
Games, magical tricks, optical puzzles, simple craft projects. A good rainy-day book.

SCHWARTZ, ALVIN, *The Rainy Day Book*, Trident, 1968. Crafts,
games, nature and science projects, dramatic skits.

SEVERN, BILL and SUE, *Let's Give a Show*, Knopf, 1956. Lots of
ideas for living room and backyard entertainment, as well
as for more ambitious projects.

SEVERN, BILL, *Magic Across the Table*, McKay, 1972. Everything the young magician will need—with easy-to-follow
diagrams. Others in this series: *Magic Wherever You Are,*

Shadow Magic, Magic with Paper, Magic in Your Pockets, Magic Shows You Can Give, Packs of Fun, Magic Comedy.

SIKS, GERALDINE, *Creative Dramatics: An Art for Children,* Harper, 1958.

SLADE, PETER, *Child Drama,* University of London Press, 1952.

SOBOL, DONALD J., *Encyclopedia Brown,* Nelson, 1963. Three-minute mysteries for amateur detectives to solve.

THANE, ADELE, *Plays from Famous Stories and Fairy Tales,* Plays, Inc., 1967. Lively and charming modern dramatizations of "Rapunzel," "Sleeping Beauty," "Cinderella," "Puss in Boots" . . . all admirably suited to family readings or living room production.

WARD, WINIFRED, *Playmaking with Children,* Appleton, 1957.

———, *Stories to Dramatize,* Children's Theatre Press, 1952.

WEBB, MARIAN A., *Games for Younger Children,* Morrow, 1947. Over 150 group games for parties or for just plain fun. With lists of good stories, poems, songs and suggestions for party favors and decorations.

WEATHERBY, JOAN C., *100 Hours of Fun!,* Doubleday, 1962. Puzzles, jokes, quizzes, word games, simple things to make and scientific experiments (like how to get a hard-boiled egg into a narrow-mouthed bottle).

WINN, MARIE, ed., *What Shall We Do and Allee galloo!,* Harper, 1970. Play songs and singing games, briskly and cheerfully done.

WYLER, ROSE, and GERALD AMES, *Magic Secrets,* Harper, 1967. An I Can Read Book—how to eat a live goldfish, make objects appear and disappear. . . .

———, *Spooky Tricks,* Harper, 1968. An I Can Read Book. How to see through paper with X-ray eyes, stick pins into your thumb without feeling pain—to say nothing of making your friends disappear or float on air.

WYLER, ROSE, and EVA-LEE BAIRD, *Science Teasers*, Harper, 1966. Basic science imaginatively explored through diverting puzzles, tricks, experiments.

The Zoom Catalog, Random House, 1972. Jokes, riddles, stories, songs, games, plays, crafts and art by the lively kids who produce WGBH's weekly TV shows for the young of all ages. Fresh, funny, inventive, buzzing with life and high spirits. The book introduces its own secret language, Ubbi Dubbi (better than Pig Latin), its own mythology (Franny Dooley who likes feeling but hates touching, loves sleeping but hates naps), has instructions for making relief sculpture, Jewish holiday bread, stuffed animals and bottle cap tambourines.

MOSTLY FOR OUTDOORS

BROWN, VINSON, *How to Explore the Secret Worlds of Nature*, Little, 1962. The wonders that await the imaginative explorer in his own house, backyard, city parks and in the countryside.

BUSCH, PHYLLIS S., *Exploring as You Walk in the Meadow*, Lippincott, 1972. Carry a magnifier, compass, thermometer, pencil and paper, and there are all sorts of fascinating discoveries at hand. In the same series, *Exploring as You Walk in the City*, *A Walk in the Snow*.

CASSELL, SYLVIA, *Nature Games and Activities*, Harper, 1956. One hundred and one games, experiments and crafts.

CRAIG, M. JEAN, *Spring Is Like the Morning*, Random House, 1968. An invitation to explore sights, sounds and smells, and to observe the changes in growing things as the season advances.

GOLDBERG, LAZER, *Children and Science*, Scribner, 1970. Readable and mind-expanding.

HUNTINGTON, HARRIET E., *Let's Go to the Woods,* Doubleday, 1968. A simple science picture book that takes children through a deciduous forest, looking at plants and animals.

KANE, HENRY B., *Four Seasons in the Woods,* Knopf, 1968. Splendid introduction to changes in animal and plant life through the year's cycle. Also: *The Tale of a Meadow* (1959)

MURIE, OLAUS J., *A Field Guide to Animal Tracks,* Houghton, 1954. How to know what passed this way: not only animal tracks, but twig and limb clues.

POLGREEN, JOHN and CATHLEEN, *Backyard Safari,* Doubleday, 1971. Fine photographs illustrate the myriad forms of plant and animal life found in an ordinary suburban backyard.

PRINGLE, LAURENCE P., ed., *Discovering the Outdoors,* Natural History Press, 1969. A nature and science guide to investigating life in fields, forests and ponds.

STERLING, DOROTHY, *Fall Is Here!,* Natural History Press, 1966. How trees, plants, birds and animals prepare for winter. Good section: things to do in fall.

WENSBERG, KATHERINE, *Experiences with Living Things,* Beacon Press, 1966.

8

In the Beginning Is the Word:
Books and the Growing Child

I have never heard any parent question the value of reading. Quite the contrary. Though serious-minded adults sometimes ask, "Who needs art?" (or music, or shop, or physical education), they invariably assume that reading—like vitamins and fresh air—is essential for the growing child. Even the parent who never reads himself is concerned when his child shows no interest in books.

This universal passion would seem to guarantee a favorable home atmosphere for a child's first reading experiences. Unfortunately, many parents revere books for the wrong reasons. Having seen, perhaps, the results of studies showing a close correlation between reading habits and academic achievement, they conclude that the road to success is paved with books. So they want their children to read—"useful" nonfiction that will prepare them to become highly paid engineers, or fiction that will improve character, inspire. A very commonly held attitude is that of the mother who said to me, one school Visitors' Night, "I wish Steve would read more. He'll never get into college if he doesn't increase his vocabulary."

This notion—that children should read for a particular, practical purpose (improve their vocabulary, acquire meaningful goals, turn selfless and brave)—seems to me sad, and sadly mistaken. It's as if one were to give a child milk and cod-liver oil only so he might pass a physical fitness test. A child who reads will improve his vocabulary, no question. Almost certainly, too, he will develop—gradually, without conscious intent—a sympathetic understanding of others and values to live by. He may very well, through reading, discover a life interest and work. But he doesn't read for these reasons. He reads *to live.*

"It is only in childhood," says Graham Greene, "that books have any deep influence on our lives." I would go further and say that only in childhood can a book become a form of intensest life, more real than "reality." The adult reader, often, is impatient to finish, get what a book has to offer; a child, when he finds the right book, wants it never to end (and he'll read it again and again). Who can forget the excitement of mastering the simplest primer story, the moment when individual letters joined hands in a dance of words and ideas? Or the secret joy of reading under the bedclothes by flashlight after the lights had been turned out? "The magic words shall hold thee fast," Lewis Carroll writes in the prefatory verses to *Alice in Wonderland.* "Thou shalt not heed the winter blast." It is literally true, for many children, that real life pales before the intense vitality, the excitement and wonder of a really good book.

A child inhabits a world narrow, restricted, often frustrating. He feels himself small and defenseless; he is subject to authority that seems mysterious or unjust. So he reads for the deepest and most urgent reasons: to understand, to be reassured, to know and experience more, to escape, above all to *become—* more independent, more grown-up. That is why the two central themes of children's books involve on the one hand the vision of a secure, loving home (*Little Women, The Moffats*) and on the other, successful expressions of independence and rebellion (*Pippi Longstocking, Diana and the Rhinoceros*). Often the two elements unite in a way peculiarly satisfying to the young: Maurice Sendak's Max (*Where the Wild Things Are*) defies his mother, joins imaginary monsters for a jungle frolic, but comes home for supper; the supercompetent children of Arthur Ransome's *Swallows and Amazons* enjoy the wildest

adventures but are always back in time for tea. In books children find delights life has not yet offered—and, sometimes, consolation for sorrows already experienced. Dickens' account of
David Copperfield, escaping the Murdstone regime in the only
way possible, could stand for many children's salvation by
books. Bullied, punished and scorned, David comforts himself
with his dead father's library.

> From that blessed little room, Roderick Random, Peregrine
> Pickle, Humphrey Clinker, Tom Jones, the Vicar of Wake-
> field, Don Quixote, Gil Blas, and Robinson Crusoe, came
> out, a glorious host, to keep me company. They kept alive
> my fancy, and my hope of something beyond that place and
> time . . . It is curious to me how I could ever have consoled
> myself under my small troubles (which were great troubles
> to me), by impersonating my favorite characters in them—as
> I did—and by putting Mr. and Mrs. Murdstone into all the
> bad ones—which I did too. I have been Tom Jones (a child's
> Tom Jones, a harmless creature) for a week together.

In imagination, the defeated boy becomes "a captain and a
hero." "This was my only and my constant comfort," David
remembers. "When I think of it, the picture always rises in my
mind of a summer evening, the boys at play in the churchyard,
and I sitting on my bed, reading as if for life."

Reading for life. A phrase parents might remember when
choosing books for the young. In time, of course, the child will
turn to books to find out about things—the structure of crystals,
or the invention of the spinning jenny. But his first impulse is,
quite simply, to expand his universe. When I once asked a class
of high school students which early books had meant most to
them, I was interested (but not surprised) to find that all the
titles were fiction. In many cases, the fiction was decidedly second rate. Nancy Drew and the Bobbsey Twins were mentioned
more often than acknowledged "classics." What made these

books memorable, clearly, was their magical expansion of the child's world. "I gobbled up the tall adventure tales, reading every narrow escape": that's an overprotected only child recalling his passion for Tom Swift. A shy girl writes, "Nancy Drew had a most exciting life, and I wanted to share it."

"Black Beauty tore at my heart." "My mother used to say that while I was reading *Old Yeller* the house could have burned down and I wouldn't have known the difference." "My best friends were animals such as Reddy Fox and Bowser the Hound." The voices are different, but the tone is the same: discovery, excitement, pure delight. Sometimes the youthful reader loves at a distance; sometimes he moves through the looking glass, becoming one with his heroes. "For nearly two years I imitated Robin Hood, complete with bow and arrow, stealing from the rich and giving to the poor." An admirer of the Hardy boys recalls with unmistakable tenderness "when I was Frank and my friend was Joe, and we relieved the world of all crime. We were 'loved by the good and feared by the bad.' "

How can *The Romance of Wheat* or *The Miracle of Your Teeth* compare with that?

The vicarious experience children seek in their reading is not always of the captain-hero variety. Children identify with characters who suffer, boys and girls (and animals) who start out with several strikes against them. The Ugly Duckling, rejected by the other barnyard fowl because he looks queer; Cinderella, dressed in rags while her stepsisters cavort in silks; Mike Mulligan's old-fashioned steam shovel, outclassed by newer, smarter models; Sara Crewe, Heidi, Pollyanna, the orphans of Dickens—all these arouse a child's compassion and, in a curious subterranean fashion, reassure him. He is not the only person who has felt left out, misunderstood. For years, my older daughter's favorite reading was *Bad Little Hannah,* a book about one of the least appealing heroines in juvenile fiction. Plain and unloved, Hannah was despised for her freckles, her unruly hair, and most of all her rudeness. (Her brothers and sisters, mind you, were models of beauty and gentility.) Failure was the pattern of her life. And what made Hannah so attractive to *my* child? "I knew I was considered hopelessly bad-mannered," she says now, "though everyone thought my little sister charming. *Bad Little Hannah* made me feel less different, less alone. It comforted me to think that somewhere there might be a child far worse off than me."

Children look for themselves (and their friends) in books. They also look for illumination of their deepest problems and concerns. And what are those? By and large, the same concerns that trouble adults. Children are not (however much we might like to believe it) innocent spirits capering blithely in the Garden of Eden. They know fear and pain and confusion as adults do, though in varying degrees. They know that mothers and fathers are not always kind, not always reliable; that beloved persons may be taken from them forever; that they themselves are subject to nameless and dreadful desires. So serious (enduring) children's literature deals with the same emotions as does serious adult literature—loss (*Bambi*), grief (*Calico Bush*), violence (*Treasure Island*), pride (*The Wind in the Willows*), redemptive sacrifice (*The Little Mermaid*), love and the drive to achieve and death (*Charlotte's Web*). If you include the tales of Grimm and Andersen—and how can you not?—then you have to add that sexual passion is present too, a faint but haunting shadow. No wonder P. L. Travers, the creator of Mary Poppins, has said, "There's no such thing as a children's book. There are simply books of many kinds and some of them children read."

Actually, one can distinguish several classes of children's books. There are books written specially for children and really enjoyed only by them (or by adults for whom rereading stirs memories). Most picture books fall into this category. *In The Forest* (Marie Hall Ets), *The Saggy Baggy Elephant* (K. and B. Jackson), *Angus and the Ducks* (Marjorie Flack)—these an adult can read aloud happily to an eager listener, but his pleasure has a secondhand quality. Most series books are of this type. So are the good but essentially limited books by Robert McCloskey, James Daugherty, Eleanor Estes. These may have enormous value for a child who happens on them at the right moment, but few adults would choose to curl up with them on a rainy night. Then there are books intended for children but which can be thoroughly enjoyed by adults on another level: *Huckleberry Finn, Alice in Wonderland.* (Indeed, *only* adults can appreciate their brilliance and subtlety.) There are books intended for adults which can be read with pleasure, but imperfect understanding, by children: *Robinson Crusoe, Gulliver's Travels, Great Expectations.* And then there is that large class of books intended for adults but really, now, much better suited to older children. *Jane Eyre, The Last of the Mohicans, The Three Musketeers*: at an age when a reader can be enthralled by these, much of their content is incomprehensible. By the time he understands their background, the spell is broken: the novels are too empty, too psychologically crude. *Gone With the Wind* is another example here—irresistible to a fifteen-year-old girl, easy to resist ten years later.

Any of these books can be, for a child, what A. A. Milne's Pooh calls "a Sustaining Book." (Pooh, you may recall, finds himself stuck, honey-glutted, in Rabbit's doorway. So Christopher Robin reads him "a Sustaining Book, Such as would help and comfort a Wedged Bear in Great Tightness," and at the end of a week's reading, our bear comes free.) Every child has his "horrible Heffalump"—a problem, perhaps secret, that seems beyond his power to solve. Books lift him free—at least, give him hope. For surely one of the distinctive characteristics of children's literature is its deep incorrigible optimism. There is pain, yes, and violence and loss. But in the end *everything will come out all right*. Little in a world where bigness is freedom and power, the child turns to books for heartening stories about other little folk. Think of the titles: *Little Bear, Little Eddie,*

The Little Lame Prince, The Brave Little Tailor, The Little Engine That Could, The Little House, Little Tim and the Brave Sea Captain, Little Lord Fauntleroy . . . a whole host of littles who, by wisdom, wit, courage, simple goodness or perseverance, come shining through.

Books and the Baby: the Under-Twos

When does the love of books begin? Not long after the first rattle. Once a baby can sit up and really look at what he's holding (instead of grasping for grasping's sake), he's ready for his first book. With most children, this will be around nine months —which is also the moment for the first finger plays and games. "This little piggy" played on the toes and "Pat-a-cake" constitute, one might say, a kind of reading-readiness program, infant level: they introduce a baby to the pleasures of rhythmic language.

Beginning books should be chew-and-tear resistant—cloth or stiff heavy cardboard, so baby realizes from the start that a book is to *look* at. Avoid books with abstract, self-consciously arty pictures and those representing unfamiliar objects. A great many first books are full of elephants and giraffes and clowns, creatures adults associate with children but surely beyond the ken of the average nine-monther. The very best books are the simplest—clear, full color photographs of familiar things—ball, cup, spoon, chair, telephone, cat, blocks. No text. You provide that.

With baby snuggly nestled in your lap, turn the pages and talk about each picture. "Here's a kitty, The kitty says, MEE-OW! See, here's a telephone. Mummy talks on the telephone. Hello—hello! Oh, look, here's a cup of milk—*mmmmmmmmm* good!" And so on. Babies find this sort of thing endlessly fascinating. They love to stroke the kitty and listen to Mother—

wonderful Mother!—neighing like a horse or bleating like a lost lamb. By a year or so, they'll enjoy Dorothy Kunhardt's *Pat the Bunny*, a touchie-feelie that allows a small reader to rub Daddy's sandpaper beard, look into a real mirror, smell the flowers, put his finger through Mother's ring and, of course, pat the fluffy bunny.

As soon as baby begins to stammer his first honest-to-goodness words, he's ready for "real" books. These again should be close to daily life routines—the snug little world of his house, his toys, his family. A typical book of this sort has a rudimentary text of the This-is-baby's-room variety. You'll find that you begin to improvise and adapt, and that baby is overjoyed with your inventions—"Oh, here is Sarah's yellow duck. Nice duck. And here's Sarah's little bed, and Sarah's soft, warm blanket." Introduce little snatches of dialogue when possible. "See, here comes Daddy's car. Bzzzz, Zoom, says the car. Daddy says, 'Hello, Sarah!'" Strong rhymes are good for this age, and all sorts of imitative noises, from animal sounds to the whirring of the vacuum cleaner.

From these purely pictorial experiences, move on to first stories. Dick Bruna's little books are just right for this stage. Each time you turn a page of these sturdy volumes, a strong, vivid picture faces a few lines of well-water clear verse:

> In the grass of the farmyard
> So plain to see,
> Lay a snow-white egg.
> Whose could it be?

The answer to this thrilling question is pursued through ten pages of barnyard debate: there's a fine fat hen, a rooster (with appropriate sound effects), a mysterious black cat with green eyes and a red nose, a floppy puppy and finally a chipper duckling, newborn, in eggshell hat. The relationship between verse and pictures is so close that an eighteen-monther will soon be able to "read" the story himself; it's all there, in color and line. Margaret Wise Brown's *Goodnight Moon* is another ideal book

for toddlers: it offers the loved familiar home scenes and a
soothing pattern of repetition and rhyme:

> Goodnight bears
> Goodnight chairs . . .
> Goodnight mittens
> Goodnight kittens . . .
> Goodnight stars
> Goodnight air
> Goodnight noises everywhere.

Most children will want this read every night for the next year
and will make the book truly their own by adding private good-
nights (including, at our house, goodnight *book*). Another enchanting under-two volume is Ruth Krauss's *I Can Fly*, with its
short chiming rhymes and perfectly caught small-child tone,
modulating from semisense

> A bird can fly
> So can I.
>
> A cow can moooo
> I can too.

to delicious nonsense:

> Hubble, hubble, hubble,
> I'm a mubble in a pubble.

You'll want to invest early in a brightly illustrated children's
dictionary. My own experience has been that such books don't
interest the older children for whom, presumably, they're intended, as much as they do toddlers. Very young children feel
no need for continuity. They're interested in *things*, and they
just love to turn pages and look at the bright assortment
of familiar objects. Richard Scarry's many dictionary-type volumes are treasures (*Busy, Busy World*, *What Do People Do
All Day?*, *Best Word Book Ever*). And of course, there's
Mother Goose, as indispensable as vitamins and egg yolk. Don't

be troubled by the fact that baby can't possibly understand what goes on in "A dillar A dollar A ten o'clock scholar" or "Tom, Tom, the piper's son." Rhythm and sound are so magical that he responds instinctively. "I did not care . . . what happened to Jack and Jill & the Mother Goose rest of them," Dylan Thomas wrote of his early love affair with nursery rhymes. "I cared for the shapes of sound that their names, and the words describing their actions, made in my ears; I cared for the colours the words cast on my eyes. I realise that I may be, as I think back all that way, romanticising my reactions to the simple and beautiful words of those pure poems; but that is all I can honestly remember . . . I fell in love—that is the only expression I can think of—at once, and I am still at the mercy of words."

Reading, like singing, should be a part of baby's earliest experience. At its best, it's a family experience—something shared by the littlest along with mother, father, brothers and sisters if he has any. If you're reading *The Gingerbread Boy* to a five-year-old, baby won't follow the action, but he can still enjoy the pictures and bounce to the repeated, "Run, run, as fast as you can, You can't catch me, I'M THE GINGERBREAD MAN!"

Picture Books:
the Nursery School and Kindergarten Crowd

Between *Pat the Bunny* and *Black Beauty* lies, for many parents, an unchartered land. When they head for the six-years-and-up shelves, they know what to look for. *Grimm's Fairy Tales*, *Winnie-the-Pooh*, *The Wizard of Oz*, *Pinocchio*—these remembered titles are still current. But apart from Beatrix Potter's charming tales, there are few "classic" picture books. The great names here (Margaret Wise Brown, Maurice Sendak, Russell and Lillian Hoban, Dr. Seuss) are comparative newcomers, and every season brings a fresh crop, a deluge. Picture books are bigger than ever—and brighter, and more lavishly illustrated and more expensive. Twenty years ago, Wonder Books and Little Golden Books offered hundreds of titles; for 25 cents, you could make a three-year-old happy with a first-rate book. The Little Golden list (39 cents) has now shrunk to a very few titles, half of them rehashes of old cartoons and Disney movies. Some of the original 25-centers have been reissued, in larger format, at roughly twelve times the old price. Many of the best ones, like Kathryn and Byron Jackson's *Brave Cowboy Bill*, have disappeared altogether. So the book-buying parent now finds in the preschool department an array of unfamiliar titles at alarming prices. How is he to choose?

Nonbooks (Paper Toys)

The first thing to observe of many eye-catching newcomers is that they are not books at all. They are, in Jason Epstein's fine contemptuous phrase, "nursery fixtures made of paper." Consider, for example, *The Giant Comes to Town* by Michael Twinn, a Rand McNally Super-Giant book. Four feet high, weighing about five pounds (taller than most bookcases), it stands on the floor of juvenile book departments, a trap for indulgent uncles in search of a different gift. The child who crouches before this volume (no child could possibly *hold* it) can read all about the unkempt giant who's not allowed to play until he gets a haircut, takes a bath, dresses neatly and eats his dinner. "Now the giant looked so nice that he looked just like you." This mammoth novelty turns out, in short, to be a tame little lamb in wolf's clothing, an updated version of the moral tale in praise of cleanliness.

Also typical is *A Very Long Tail* by Eric Carle. This "book" is actually a strip of folded cardboard featuring a yard-long green snake within whose speckled coils a variety of animals disport themselves. The animals' names—kangaroo, peacock, mouse, seal—are helpfully printed on the back ("making this a book for learning as well as looking," says the publisher's note). Lest the parent imagine this wonder to be of limited usefulness, his attention is directed to its unusual versatility. It's "designed to grow with the child. For the very youngest, the book can be used as a decorative wall frieze. The slightly older child will set it up on floor or table where it becomes a circus, a jungle full of friendly creatures, or whatever his imagination creates." One would hope that an imaginative child could play circus even without a commercial backdrop.

Then there are the pop-ups, books designed to produce three-dimensional panoramas as a page is turned. Pop-ups are not new—they've been on the juvenile scene twenty years at least—though the most recent ones are perhaps unusually elaborate in what's called their "paper engineering." The case against pop-ups can be simply stated. They are expensive (all that cut-and-fold costs money); they tear easily, leaving the frustrated small owner with a tatter of cardboard bits; and, no doubt because so much thought goes into the book's mechanics, the text almost always seems an afterthought. Here, for example, is a selection from *The Pop-Up Book of Boats* by Albert G. Miller, illustrated by Akihito Shirakawa with Paper Engineering by Ib Penicki.

> Atomic subs are fantastic ships
> They sail for months on undersea trips.
> Manned by a hundred men in the crew,
> They're fast above and below the sea, too.

Or this, from *The Little One's Prayers Pop-Up Book* (Dean):

> Please teach us Lord, each girl and boy,
> To do our work with pride and joy,
> So that, when each one's task is done,
> We'll say: Dear God, it's been such fun!

The banality and the slickness of this verse is an insult to children.

Still another line of toys masquerading as books is the Random House Colorforms series, each volume offering a pocketful of "plastic shapes that stick to the pictures like magic—press on —lift off again and again. Educational, fascinating, fun." The Colorforms *Wizard of Oz* compresses Baum's entire story into six pages of heavy-handed drawings and verses that suggest a cartoon sound track:

> "Here?" gasped the Wizard.
> "Comin' here,
> Oh, jumpin' leapin' lizards!
> I can do *some* tricks—but Kansas?
> That trick's too hard for Wizards."

Voguish adult interest in sensitivity training and sensory awareness probably accounts for another fairly recent innovation: the touch and smell book. Pictures in the Downy Books (Rand McNally) are upholstered with a fuzzy furry stuff, the tactile equivalent of chalk squeaking on a blackboard. Grosset and Dunlap's Touch and Smell Books have even poorer text, a more ambitious range of textures. *Fun in the Country*, for example, by Oscar Weigle, features rayon chenille grass and a patch of real plywood on its barn. (It's very much in the spirit of this contrived experience that the reader can smell the apples and violets—but not the horse or the barn.)

Is there anything, anything at all, to be said for these "toy" books? The usual argument in their favor goes pretty much like this. *One*, it's generally agreed that increased sensory awareness is A Good Thing. Well, here are some prearranged sensory experiences: the child scratches the chemically treated paper and gets the real smell of lemons or chocolate. *Two*, reluctant readers may be seduced by these novelties into the reading of other books.

Let's consider these arguments. *One*, a child doesn't need a book to smell lemons or chocolate; he can go to the kitchen. *Two:* the text of these books, almost without exception, is so abominable that no child would be inspired to read if that's what reading is. Sample, from *Colors and Shapes* (Oscar Weigle), a book presumably intended for preschoolers: "The beans used to make chocolate and cocoa are found inside the seed pods of the cacao tree. The kernels of the beans or seeds are ground into a fine reddish-brown powder which can then be made into a delicious breakfast or bedtime drink."

Since the plot line is governed by a need to introduce as many smells as possible, stories range from boring to ridiculous. In *The Enchanted Island,* "a Young Reader's Scratch and Sniff Book including 14 fragrance pictures," Chips the cabin boy sets out on an adventure that will keep few young sniffers on the edge of their chairs: he's to gather food for the captain's dinner. Animals encountered along the way say interesting things like, "Here, take a sniff at this fruity spiced cake." How can volumes of this sort stimulate an appetite for anything except other gimmicky toys—or maybe for a snack? (I set aside the question, not altogether irrelevant, of how many good scratches are needed to deplete the fragrance supply.)

The Psychological Trap

A very different sort of specious appeal characterizes books aimed at superconscientious parents who are anxious to keep up with the latest in child development research. For many years, the magic parent-oriented signal was "vocabulary list"; publishers ground out dismal little volumes guaranteed not to strain the child's limited word power. This era produced the Children's Press *I Want to Be* . . . series. In *I Want to Be a Pilot,* by Carla Greene (Consultant: Dr. Paul Witty, Director, Psycho-Educational Clinic of Northwestern University), parents are assured that 116 of the 130 words used in this book

come from *The First Thousand Words for Children's Reading.*
Few readers will doubt that this limitation has been scrupulously observed:

> Joe is going to school.
> Mike is going to school, too.
> He goes to school at an airport.
> Mike goes to Flying School.

Though the controlled vocabulary list is still with us, a
stronger—or at least more fashionable—concern of the 1970's is
what might be called psychological engineering. Where once we
worried about unfamiliar words, now we worry about unfamiliar
concepts. Etienne Delessert's *How the Mouse Was Hit on the
Head by a Stone and So Discovered the World* is a bizarre construction based, we are told, on Piaget's research into the child
mind (how children forty years ago answered questions about
the origins of the sun, moon, clouds) and then tested on Swiss
five- and six-year-olds. The result, however impeccable from a
research standpoint, is a real sleep-inducer.

Then there are the Read Together Books for Children and
Parents, produced in association with the Children's Division
of the Menninger Clinic. On paper, the rationale of this series
sounds fine: who should understand more thoroughly than the
Menninger people a child's interests and problems? What better interpreter than Jane Werner Watson (author of *more than*
175 Golden Books)? The execution of the idea, alas, is uneasy-
making. For one thing, each book contains a prefatory essay
about the child development problem dealt with in the suc-
ceeding story. It's addressed to parents, of course. But a lot of
eight-year-olds would plow determinedly through that essay just
because it's not for them (as eight-year-olds I've known read and
commented acidly on the fine-print Explanation for Parents
that appears on some standard report cards). If I were giving
a child a book to help him cope with ambivalent feelings toward a new baby, I would not want the book to include a dis-

cussion of "overt resentment of the baby, regression, and infantile patterns." Furthermore, the book devoted to this very real problem is called *My Friend the Dentist*. Pretty tricky. Fully half the volume deals with a trip to the dentist, where the child-hero has a happy experience. (There's that wonderful chair that moves up and down, music coming from the wall, a special light. . . . No mention of a drill.) Having learned how to keep his teeth clean and strong, the child comes home and guess what? Mother phones: she's just had a baby. And father, sounding suspiciously like Dr. Haim Ginott, spells it all out. "Having this new baby in the family will be a change for us all. I know you are not sure how you feel about it right now. But we have enough love to give some to the new baby without any less for you."

Admirable and true, no doubt—but essentially didactic. Children—human beings generally—are affected, changed, not simply by intellectual argument but by stirrings of the heart and imagination. As Keats wrote, "Axioms in philosophy are not axioms until they have been proved upon our pulses." A child who reads *My Friend the Dentist* is not likely to feel one bit different about the little interloper in his house (though he's left with that unnerving association between dentists and new babies). A child who reads *Nobody Asked Me If I Wanted a Baby Sister* (Martha Alexander) or *A Baby Sister for Frances* (Russell and Lillian Hoban) will be most profoundly comforted. Because each of those books—written, as far as one can see, without benefit of clinic—constitutes an imaginative *experience*.

The Artistic Trap

Some of the most beautiful juvenile books on the market have minimal value for children. I have said earlier that children should be introduced to serious painting, that often they respond surprisingly well to abstract art. But what a child wants above all in a book is a good story and/or dramatic illustrations. Sometimes—very rarely—these demands are met in a book that happens also to be strikingly beautiful. I think of Leo Lionni's *The Biggest House in the World*. More often, the gorgeously illustrated children's book makes its principal appeal to artistically oriented parents. Look at *Colors*, every page a delight to the eye, but with few objects recognizable to a young child. The purple and blue cabbage looks like a giant dahlia, the gooseberries like peppermint drops or miniature beach balls. Look at *Hosie's Alphabet*, by painter Leonard Baskin—a set of bird and animal prints worth framing. But no child could learn his letters here. The quasi kiwi, the primordial protozoa, are too strange, and the italic lettering all but indecipherable. Or look at Celestino Piatti's *The Happy Owls*, a stunning collection of color woodcuts. The story's problem—why are the owls so happy when the barnyard fowl fight all the time?—is not one likely to engage a preschooler's interest. As for the solution— the owls are happy because they love Nature ("When everything is green and growing . . . we sit in a shady nook in the cool forest and are at peace with the world")—well, run *that* up a flagpole and see how many kids salute.

What Makes a Good Picture Book?

The ideal books for a very young child deal with the familiar, everyday world—animals, friends, vehicles of all sorts, games and toys and changing seasons, "community helpers" (policemen, firemen, storekeepers, doctors, etc.) and families. Talking animals and machines are fine—a three-year-old personalizes most inanimate objects—but the fiercer flights of fantasy are best left until kindergarten age at least. Wicked witches and parents who leave their children alone in the forest call for an emotional maturity not possessed by most nursery-schoolers.

At this age, children are fascinated by discoveries adults take for granted, the fact that *Everybody Eats* and *Everybody Has a House* (Mary Green). They will study the pages of a Richard Scarry dictionary, absorbed in details, thrilled by the profusion of *things*. They respond equally to stories about personalized vehicles (*Mike Mulligan and His Steam Shovel, Little Toot*) and to literal representations (*The Giant Nursery Book of Things That Go*, by George J. Zaffo). They want to know what happens in the great world beyond their house (*What Do People Do All Day?*). They also enjoy hearing about the experience of boys and girls just like themselves (Gunilla Wolde's charming *Tommy* books, in which a small boy cleans his room, goes to the doctor, takes a bath, plays dress-up . . .).

In addition to purely descriptive material, young readers like stories about recognizable problems. *Will I Have a Friend?*, the title of a first-school-experience book by Miriam Cohen, voices the concern of every child over three. It's reassuringly met here, and, on a more fanciful level, in Marie Hall Ets's *Play with Me*. *Bread and Jam for Frances* (Russell and Lillian Hoban), a deliciously warm, funny, human story, happens also—and not so incidentally—to deal with what parents call an eating problem. Going to the doctor or dentist; getting a new teacher— or a new baby in the family; confronting a strange dog, a dark room—all these fears grown-ups pooh-pooh are the stuff of books which vitally engage the preschooler. Above all, he responds to stories that satisfy his need for assurance in the most important area of all: *he is loved*. Elsa Minarik's Little Bear, setting bravely forth on adventures but wanting his mother's warm embrace at adventure's end, expresses perfectly the child heart.

And of course, children love picture books that are *fun*. A sense of the ludicrous develops early. So four-year-olds enter zestfully into the running joke of *Johnny Crow's Garden*, where

realistically drawn animals perform unlikely actions in verse that
emphasizes the pervasive lunacy:

> And the lion   [Turn the page]
> Had a green and yellow tie on.
>
> And the whale
> Told a very long tale.

They adore jaunty *Madeline* ("To the tiger in the zoo, Madeline
just said 'Pooh-pooh'") and Epaminondas, who is always one
step behind his mother's instructions. (Epaminondas ruins a
cake by scrunching it in his fist as he trots home. Patiently, his
mother explains that the right way to carry cake is to put it on
your head, under your hat. So when Epaminondas is given a
pound of sweet butter he carries it under his hat on a sunny
day. Instructed once more—"The way to carry butter is to cool
it first in the brook"—he brings home his next offering, a puppy,
half drowned. That produces another lecture—"The way to
carry a puppy is to tie a string around his neck and pull"—and
Epaminondas' final effort, a loaf of fresh bread pulled home,
puppy fashion, on the end of a rope.) Humor obvious or crude
to adults—like Babar's painting eyes on the rumps of his
elephant-soldiers to frighten the enemy—is greeted with ecstasy;
so is the pure zaniness of *The Cat in the Hat.*

Apart from humorous tales, where almost anything goes, a
preschool story should have a very simple plot line, one or at
most two central characters, a clear pattern and lots of repetition. The one-two-three rhythm of *Goldilocks* illustrates perfectly the sameness and variation young children enjoy. The
first bowl of porridge is too hot, the second bowl of porridge is
too cold, but the third one is *just right.* A similar pattern shapes
folk tales like *The Three Little Pigs* and *The Gingerbread Man*
—and stories like *Pelle's New Suit. Pelle's New Suit* begins
and ends with pictures of a boy and his lamb, only in the first

picture the lamb is superwoolly and the boy badly in need of a bigger jacket and trousers. Pelle shears his lamb and sets about a series of swaps. One grandmother cards the wool in return for his weeding the carrot patch; the other grandmother agrees to spin it if he'll tend the cows. And so it goes, as the wool is dyed, woven and finally tailored into a beautiful new suit, each episode combining satisfied anticipation and surprise.

If, along the way, a preschool story introduces interesting sounds and memorable phrases, that's an added delight. Look at Margaret Wise Brown's Noisy books, full of hissing radiators and growling stomachs, and Wanda Gag's infectious repetition: "hundreds of cats, thousands of cats, millions and billions and trillions of cats." Once familiar with a story, children love to join in, providing the bits they know. ("And he huffed, and he puffed, and he BLEW THE HOUSE DOWN!") Some books have a built-in provision for such participation: for example, the questions and answers of The Noisy Book.

> It began to snow.
> But could Muffin hear that?

or, when the little dog, blindfolded, hears a peculiar squeak:

Was it a policeman?	NO.
Was it a big horse?	NO.
Was it a garbage can?	NO.
Was it a big fierce lion?	NO.

In any case, a parent reading aloud can create occasions for the listening child to answer questions, join in. For though at ten, a child is content to enter imaginatively into the world of a book, at five he likes to be an active contributor.

A word about vocabulary. Children love language—as they love any new instrument for controlling their world. Long words, strange words, difficult words, all enchant when presented in the context of an appealing book. Read *The Duchess Bakes a Cake* to a preschooler and see if he doesn't soon join in on the chorused "A lovely light luscious delectable cake!" So there is surely no reason to seek out for the young books written in rudimentary English. Children take in, by ear, the often sophisticated language of the Babar books. And when they come to read for themselves, they will puzzle out really difficult words—if the story is good enough to make effort worthwhile.

The Young Reader: Age Six and Up

The variety of books available is staggering. There are yesterday's classics and today's shiny new offerings, biographies and histories and how-to-do-its, fairy tales and science fiction, collections of jokes and collections of poems, I Can Read primers and books that come equipped with cassette recordings (so a reluctant reader can literally plug in). Clearly, some distinctions are in order.

As a preliminary sorting-out step, one might divide this formidable array into two categories: books of information, and books that are—or aspire to be—imaginative literature. The first category can be simply dealt with: a book on solar energy or weaving is properly judged by such commonly accepted standards as clarity, intelligibility, correctness, comprehensiveness, usefulness, general attractiveness. The second category includes poetry (dealt with separately below) and fiction where, obviously, some of these standards have no relevance whatsoever. *Sue Barton, Student Nurse*, is "clearer" than *The Princess and the Goblin* and probably a good deal more "useful." On what grounds, then, does one judge *The Princess and the Goblin* a better book? Or, to put the question another way, what, in a child's terms, makes a good work of juvenile fiction?

Some Misconceptions

First, to dispose of three common myths:

1. Children don't like books told in the first person.
2. Children don't like "old-fashioned" books.
3. As far as possible, children should be protected from the violence and unrealism of fairy tales.

1. Many children *say* they dislike "I" books. (As one boy told me, "When somebody's writing the story himself, that spoils the suspense. Because then you know he's going to come through all the adventures safe.") But *Black Beauty, Robinson Crusoe, Treasure Island,* and *Gulliver's Travels* are perennial favorites.

"Old-Fashioned" Books

2. Children often reject—violently—as "old-fashioned" books pressed upon them by parents eager to share their own fondly remembered favorites. Almost certainly, when this occurs, the trouble is not the book's age but its expression of values subtly false even when the book was written and more glaringly false now. *Little Lord Fauntleroy,* said to have caused "a delirium of joy" when it first appeared, sentimentalizes its golden-haired, velvet-panted little hero in a way modern children find insufferable. But *The Secret Garden,* by the same author, remains readable and real because its unattractive hero and heroine are presented with truth and compassion. Some nineteenth-century works still vastly popular are loaded with morality and pietism. *Little Women* is a striking example. Most adults, returning to it with affectionate memories, will be astonished by the amount of preaching and heavy-handed goodness it contains. Young readers, absorbed by the heroines' personality and adventures,

simply pay no attention to the uplifting parts. Children have a built-in mechanism for filtering out everything that isn't interesting—the didactic, the sentimental, the incomprehensible—except as it casts a film of feeling over a passage.

Violence and Fairy Tales

3. Anthony Storr, a British psychiatrist, tells the story of a five-year-old girl listening rapt as her mother read from *The Brown Fairy Book:*

> All day long the boy stood at the window, looking over the sea by which the princess must travel; but there were no signs of her. And, as he stood, soldiers came and laid hands on him, and led him up to the cask, where a big fire was blazing, and the horrid black pitch boiling and bubbling over the sides. He looked and shuddered, but there was no escape . . . so he shut his eyes to avoid seeing.
>
> Suddenly, some men were seen running with all their might, crying as they went that a large ship with its sails spread was making straight for the city. No one knew what the ship was or whence it came; but the king declared he would not have the boy burned before its arrival. . . .

At this point the child burst into tears. "Don't cry," the mother comforted. "The boy will be saved. You'll see." The child sobbed harder. "But I *wanted* him to be thrown into the pitch!"

So much for children and their sensitivity to violence. Probably because they have known so little violence in real life, they react to its description with surprising coolness if not lively interest. I remember, years ago, my seven-year-old lamenting the death of Beth in *Little Women.* As I was about to commend her for her tender feeling, she said, "It's better when someone is left alive to suffer." A listening friend agreed warmly. "What

I like is people being run over by cars, or parents eaten up by dragons—no, a lion escaped from the zoo. There isn't enough of that."

The child who delights in violence and suffering is not a little monster. Nor is he in any danger of acting out his fantasies. As Dr. Storr observes, "a disturbed child who behaves in a delinquent way will sometimes say that he got the idea from a book, which is one way of disowning responsibility. But it is only the child who is already emotionally disturbed who will act out his fantasies. If this were not so we should all have strangled our brothers and sisters, slept with our mothers, castrated our fathers, and reduced to a pulp all those who in any way opposed us." When a child reads about Hansel and Gretel pushing the witch into the oven, or Jack sending the giant crashing to his death, he experiences a deep and satisfying release of his own buried aggressions. What child has never wished to polish off his witch-mother or giant-father? The realization that others feel this way is profoundly comforting.

And that leads to an associated question, the place of fairy tales in a child's life. Though some children remain cool, defiant or impatient when presented with anything contradicting their sense of literal truth, most, between the ages of seven and ten, embrace fairyland with a passion. *The Snow Queen, Beauty and the Beast,* become realler to them than *Let's Explore Electricity*—or than Mother's voice calling to dinner. Faced with this sort of total absorption, many parents become uneasy. Is the child perhaps losing contact with the real world? Is he in danger of being seduced away from practical responsibilities into a kind of Never Never Land? Is he simply wasting his time?

The answer to all those questions, I think, is NO. How can any activity be wasteful if it stirs the child's deepest emotions, fires his imagination? As for fairy tales presenting an unreal world—when I asked my grown daughter about that, she said, "I loved fairy tales because they were wildly, grotesquely funny, or because they were haunting and strange—but most of all, be-

cause *I saw them as true*. Though I could never have articulated
my feelings, I knew their impact lay in their closeness to life,
not in their apparent remoteness from reality."

Of course. Only consider. What girl has never felt like
Cinderella, tyrannized over and subjected to the whims of a
cruel mother? (In the fairy tale, the sisters are half-sisters and
the mother a stepmother. That softens the harsh picture of
family life.) What boy has never felt like the Beast in Perrault's
magical tale, imprisoned in a body that belies his true self?
What child has never met the Wolf, who tempts him from the
straight path through the woods—and, having succumbed to the
Wolf's blandishments, what child does not know the longing
for a rescuing woodcutter, a strong powerful figure to undo all
the damage and restore parental favor? The impossible task,
which runs like a scarlet thread through the world of Grimm
and Andersen, is a theme close to the hearts of the young. So
is the fatal bargain (*Rumpelstiltskin*), in which, for the sake
of a moment's safety or pleasure, a beleaguered spirit enters
into a devil's pact. Children know all about the mysterious prohibition, impossible to resist, which is law in Bluebeard's castle;
and they know that the transgressor emerges always fatally
marked. (Smile and deny as he will, the egg turns blue.) I remember once reading the story of Cupid and Psyche to an
eight-year-old and then explaining, helpfully, "Sometimes it's
dangerous to see too much." My small listener fixed me with a
withering glance. "Oh sure. I can hardly remember when I didn't
know *that*."

The world of fairy tales is not dreamland. On the contrary, as
Michael Hornyansky says in an essay on "The Truth of
Fables," these tales "do accurately reflect the child's picture of
himself and his family. The father *is* king, mother *is* queen in
this tiny world; and they ought to be wise, kind and strong. The
son, with light upon him from his parents' eyes, *is* a little
prince." But sometimes Daddy turns into a frightful giant whom
the little prince or princess loves and hates at once; Mummy,

getting bad news from her mirror, takes out her spite on blossom-
ing youth; and the royal children are cast out to wander through
menacing woods. Hornyansky's brilliant analysis of "Snow
White" as a story of mother-daughter rivalry, and of "Jack and
the Beanstalk" as a primitive father-son contest, will sober any
reader inclined to dismiss fairy tales as gossamer imaginings.
For the fairy tales and folk tales that haunt the mind are
genuine distillations of the human experience, representing
either what is true but cannot be openly uttered, or what the
heart feels *ought* to be true.

One charge sometimes leveled against fairy tales perhaps
deserves consideration: the notion that they encourage false
hopes. (Harry Overstreet, a popular psychologist of the fifties,
warned parents against "inflicting this primitivism, this pathetic
infantilism of the race on their children, forcing them to think
uncausally, magically, miraculously, forcing them to habituate
themselves to the technique of dreamy wish-fulfillment. . . .")
I can only say that I have never known a child who literally expected a magic wand to appear and solve his problems—though
I've known many who were cheered by the common folk belief
in a good heart's ultimate triumph. C. S. Lewis, himself an ad-
venturer into faerie, says something very wise on this point: that
supposedly "realistic" stories about school heroes and girl detectives can be far more deceiving than any fairy tale. "All stories
in which children have adventures and successes which are possible, in the sense that they do not break the laws of nature, but
almost infinitely improbable, are in more danger than the fairy
tales of raising false expectations."

Reading about "the lucky boy or girl who discovers the spy's
plot or rides the horse that none of the cowboys can manage,"
a ten-year-old may be consumed with longing that leaves him
unhappy, discontented with the real world. But fairyland, Lewis
insists, arouses a different and fundamentally healthy longing
"for he knows not what. It stirs and troubles him (to his lifelong

enrichment) with the dim sense of something beyond his reach and, far from dulling or emptying the actual world, gives it a new dimension of depth. He does not despise real woods because he has read of enchanted woods: the reading makes all real woods a little enchanted."

The Qualities of Good Juvenile Fiction

(Of course, no one book is likely to satisfy all these criteria. They're suggestive only.)

A Solid, Interesting, Intelligible World

A good book creates a rich and coherent world, one which is immensely interesting and believable. The Babar books, the tales of Oz, Lewis Carroll and Grimm and the *Arabian Nights*—all have this quality in common. Three pages, and you are there. Sometimes the distinctive quality of an imaginary world derives from its inhabitants—as in *The Borrowers*, say, where objects familiar in the real world (matchboxes, postage stamps, safety pins, buttons and blobs of sealing wax) are seen in a completely new way, their usefulness to the minute creatures who inhabit mantels and clockworks. A world may be created by the quality of action—fierce, glittering, treacherous as in the *Arabian Nights*, or gentle and hearth-centered as in *The Little House in the Big Woods*. Very often it's the product of style and tone. The world of Babar, for example, owes its curious serenity to a Gallic precision and irony of language and drawing. Babar's mother is shot and killed in one crisp sentence, but no little reader is ever discomfited by that; the cool prose insulates him. Nor does he worry when Babar and Celeste are marooned on an island. How could he? "Sitting on some large stones, they eat with relish an excellent rice broth well sweetened and cooked to perfection."

Real People

The good or great book introduces the child to a variety of characters, helps him understand why people behave as they do, develops his awareness of the infinite complexity of human nature. E. M. Forster has shrewdly observed that the difference between real and fictional people is not simply the difference between flesh and insubstantiality. It is that though you can see and touch real people, their lives and thoughts remain largely hidden. Fictional characters, on the other hand, you never see or touch—yet their real lives and true natures lie open before you.

Though the immature reader may label characters as "goodies" and "baddies," he comes to see—to sense, rather—that in most people good and evil are subtly intermingled. Long John Silver is wicked—but attractive too. Is Pinocchio good, bad, or, like most of us, torn by conflicting forces and achieving with great difficulty a triumph over darkness? Who is to be preferred, the Walrus or the Carpenter?

"I like the Walrus best," said Alice. "Because he was a *little* sorry for the poor oysters."

"He ate more than the Carpenter, though," said Tweedledee. "You see he held his handkerchief in front, so that the Carpenter couldn't count how many he took contrariwise."

"That was mean!" Alice said indignantly. "Then I like the Carpenter best—if he didn't eat so many as the Walrus."

"But he ate as many as he could get," said Tweedledum.

This was a puzzler. After a pause, Alice began, "Well! They were *both* very unpleasant characters—"

Through his books the child realizes, perhaps for the first time, how various and complicated and exciting is the world of men. Mr. Toad is insufferable—but pathetic and funny too; no

child will ever feel quite the same about vanity again after
The Wind in the Willows. Mary Poppins is an authoritarian
snob, yet she commands affectionate respect. Hypochondriacs
and perpetual complainers appear in a different light to children
who have read the account of Eeyore's birthday party in
Winnie-the-Pooh. From such books as *Strawberry Girl,* they
come to understand how behavior, a whole way of life, is affected by environment; from *The Secret Garden,* they glimpse
the relationship between maternal coldness and childish mean-
ness or spite. "Oh yes, if you please'm; my name is Mrs. Tiggy-
Winkle; oh yes, if you please'm, I'm an excellent clear-starcher!"
—how the voice here expresses the person! A child understands
(with the feelings, not the head) why Homily in *The Borrowers,*
arriving filthy and disheveled at Aunt Lupy's elegant house,
strikes so determinedly independent a note. " 'Poor dear
Lupy,' she was saying, glancing wearily about. 'What a lot of
furniture. Whoever helps you with the dusting?' " And though,
reading *Hop o' My Thumb,* he's primarily interested in story,
he doesn't miss the glancing impact of Perrault's sly observations on the human comedy: "This Peter was her eldest son
whom she loved above all the rest, because he was somewhat
carroty, as she herself was." "It is quite possible that the woodcutter was more vexed than his wife, but she kept teasing him
and he felt as many other people do who admire women who
say the right thing, but find extremely tiresome those who never
say anything *but* the right thing." Or, in "Toads and Diamonds,"
the unaccustomed sweetness of the cruel mother when she sees
jewels dropping from the lips of her oppressed younger daughter: " 'How is this, my daughter?' It was the first time she had
called her *daughter.*"

Exciting Action

A good book involves its reader in a problem, a dangerous

situation or a great adventure which challenges the imagination. *Treasure Island* is so full of risk and excitement and strange, thrilling characters that even a child "too young" for the story will push on, enthralled.

. . . for I had heard in the silent, frosty air, a sound that brought my heart into my mouth—the tap-tapping of the blind man's stick upon the frozen road. It drew nearer and nearer, while we sat holding our breath. Then it struck sharp on the inn door, and then we could hear the handle being turned. . . .

(It should be mentioned in passing that the sea exerts a special fascination as a setting of hazard and romantic possibility. Shipwrecked heroes, from Babar and Little Tim to Robinson Crusoe, are sure-fire drama.) Gluck's perilous journey to win back his inheritance (*The King of the Golden River*), Big Tiger and Christian, in the book of that name, surviving by energy and resourcefulness their encounters with Mongol tribesmen, the quests of King Arthur's knights and the escapades of Robin Hood—these are all examples of stories strong in sheer what-will-happen? power.

A Sense of Perspective

George Eliot has written of "the dim guesses, the strangely perspectiveless conception of life" in childhood. One important role of books in the early years is to provide perspective, to give the child a sense of time past and time future, of other countries and peoples. A child's feeling for history develops through familiarity with the Greek myths, the stories of Charlemagne and King Arthur, novels like *The Three Musketeers* or *The Last of the Mohicans*. Geography is humanized by fiction —though no child will ever think of the word "geography" as

he explores Berlin with *Emil and the Detectives.* Through
stories of America's past, a child gets something he is not likely
to get in school history periods, a feeling for *the way it was.* Indeed, the closer we get to colonizing the moon, the more important it seems to introduce the young, through books, to a
civilization less complicated, less mechanized, than our own.
The modern child takes special pleasure in a story which includes an old black iron stove, a well, a pond where men cut
blocks of ice in winter. What children remember best from
Laura Ingalls Wilder's stories about pioneer days in Wisconsin
is often not the meetings with Indians and bears, but the way
the family sugared-off in spring, or made cheese with rennet
from a calf's stomach.

Many juvenile books are written deliberately to illustrate a
particular foreign or historical background: *Caddie Woodlawn*
(American Civil War), *The Bronze Bow* (Biblical times), *The
Door in the Wall* (medieval England), *Hans Brinker* (Dutch history and customs). With few exceptions, such treatments are less
imaginatively compelling than books like *Pinocchio, Babar, The
Happy Lion, Madeline* in which, because they really are of a different place or period, there's no explanation of what's strange. A
child who reads his way through the *Babar* books will know a
good deal about the tone and style of French bourgeois life; a
reader of *Little Women* breathes in American home life of the
Civil War period (though the Civil War is never discussed or
even mentioned by name. It's just the war that has taken the girls'
father). Other things being equal, a child will get more from a
translation of a book written in Russia for Russian children than
from a book by an American called *How Russians Live.*

The Magic of Language

A good book develops a child's feeling for language—musical,
precise, inventive, humorous or richly suggestive. It is not plot

that makes a satisfying story—if that were so, who would ever re-read a book?—but the way a story is told. Most people, when they think of style at all, think of purple prose, and that's one kind of style that can make a child's book memorable. Kenneth Grahame's picture of the moon rising over the night river is, if not purple, at least a rich lavender:

> The line of the horizon was clear and hard against the sky, and in one particular quarter it showed black against a silvery climbing phosphorescence that grew and grew. At last, over the rim of the waiting earth the moon lifted with slow majesty till it swung clear of the horizon and rode off, free of moorings; and once more they began to see surfaces—meadows widespread, and quiet gardens, and the river itself from bank to bank, all softly disclosed, all washed clean of mystery and terror, all radiant again as by day, but with a difference that was tremendous.

But just as effective in language and rhythm is the radiantly simple description of the barn in *Charlotte's Web*:

> The barn was very large. It was very old. It smelled of hay and it smelled of manure. It smelled of the perspiration of tired horses and the wonderful sweet breath of patient cows. It often had a sort of peaceful smell—as though nothing bad could happen ever again in the world.

Children will persevere with even Malory's version of King Arthur and the Knights of the Round Table—not an easy book—moved by music as well as stirring action. I remember my children weeping—but softly, so as not to interrupt the story—at the terrible beauty of the moment when Sir Bedivere casts into the water the dying king's sword:

> Then Sir Bedivere departed, and went to the sword, and lightly took it up, and went to the water side; and there he

bound the girdle about the hilts, and then he threw the sword
as far into the water as he might; and there came an arm and
an hand above the water and met it, and caught it, and so
shook it thrice and brandished, and then vanished away the
hand with the sword in the water . . .

Then Sir Bedivere cried: "Ah, my lord Arthur, what shall
become of me, now ye go from me and leave me here alone
among mine enemies?

A child can be struck, pierced with delight by a single phrase:
Portia's boy cousin in *Gone-Away Lake* gaping at the braces on
her teeth and exclaiming, "When you smile it looks just like the
front of a Buick!" And, from the same book, a red cardinal
sounding "like a little bottle being filled up, up, up with some
clear liquid." Even in translation, Andersen's tales glow:

They drove on through the thick forest, but the coach
gleamed like a torch that dazzled the robbers' eyes, and they
could not bear it.

"That is gold! That is gold!" cried they, and rushed forward, and seized the horses, killed the postilions and the foot-
men, and then pulled little Gerda out of the carriage.

"She is fat—she is pretty—she is fed with nut-kernels!" said
the old robber woman, who had a very long matted beard and
shaggy eyebrows that hung down over her eyes. "She's as good
as a little pet lamb; how I shall relish her!"

And she drew out her shining knife, that gleamed in a horrible way.

Eleanor Estes' coinages in *The Witch Family* are a special delight to the young, who love word games: a *haunched* house (one
that sits up on its haunches waiting for ghosts); *witchiplication*,
a most important subject for witches in training; and *banquish*,
a nice blend of *vanquish* and *banish*. *Alice in Wonderland* is full
of word play:

"And how many hours a day did you do lessons?" said Alice, in a hurry to change the subject.

"Ten hours the first day," said the Mock Turtle: "nine the next, and so on."

"What a curious plan!" exclaimed Alice.

"That's the reason they're called lessons," the Gryphon remarked: "because they lessen from day to day."

In the same tradition is *The Phantom Tollbooth*, with its kingdom of Dictionopolis ruled over by King Azaz the Unabridged. At a royal banquet (where everyone must eat his own words, so guests are careful to mention in their speeches lots of hamburgers and chocolate pudding), the king describes his cabinet members' clever tricks: "The duke here can make mountains out of molehills. The minister splits hairs. The count makes hay while the sun shines. The earl leaves no stone unturned." Though this is sophisticated writing, it has affinities with the goofiest sort of playground humor. The same might be said of passages in *Charlie and the Chocolate Factory*: "They passed a yellow door on which it said: STOREROOM NUMBER 77—ALL THE BEANS, CACAO BEANS, COFFEE BEANS, JELLY BEANS, AND HAS BEANS."

Good books, in short, give a child a sense of the *possibilities* of language—for fun, for compression, for almost infinite reverberation. In any household where books matter, phrases from loved books become a kind of private shorthand, a family code: a Bear of Very Little Brain, an Expotition, a Useful Pot to put things in (for the utterly useless gift) from *Winnie-the-Pooh*; "Jam tomorrow and jam yesterday—but never jam *today*," "Curiouser and curiouser" to summon up the insane logic of Lewis Carroll; "O Best Beloved," "more-than-oriental splendour" and the "satiable curtiosity" which led the Elephant's Child to the banks of the great gray-green greasy Limpopo River, all set about with fever-trees (from Kipling's *Just-So Stories*).

Values and Standards

Good books develop in their readers, gradually and without moralizing, a sense of right and wrong and a faith to live by. Children do not learn the difference between good and bad by having labels pasted on characters, or by being *told*. In fact, most children actively resist books that set out to improve their characters. (Keats put this wonderfully well, talking about poetry: "We hate [writing] that has a palpable design upon us, and, if we do not agree, seems to put its hand into its breeches pocket. Poetry should be great and unobtrusive, a thing which enters into one's soul . . . How beautiful are the retired flowers! How would they lose their beauty were they to throng into the highway crying out, 'Admire me I am a violet!—Dote upon me I am a primrose!'") My children detested Munro Leaf's self-righteous little books, *Manners Can Be Fun* and *Grammar Can Be Fun*, with their goody-goody rules and their smug horror of badness; they learned about *real* manners, consideration for others, from Hans Christian Andersen, A. A. Milne, Eleanor Farjeon, and Kenneth Grahame—a curious but compatible company.

"The moral you put in," says C. S. Lewis, addressing himself to juvenile-book writers, "is likely to be a platitude, or even a falsehood, skimmed from the surface of your consciousness. . . . The only moral that is of any value is that which arises inevitably from the whole cast of the author's mind." And this, of course, is what children respond to. "The Snow Queen" is a magical story, an extravagant fantasy; very early in the tale, however, a child senses that this is not simply an entertainment, but something critically important—the struggle of good against evil. A demon makes an enchanted mirror

> which had this peculiarity, that everything good and beautiful
> that was reflected in it shrank together into almost nothing,
> but that whatever was worthless and looked ugly became

prominent and looked worse than ever. The most lovely landscapes seen in this mirror looked like boiled spinach, and the
best people became hideous, or stood on their heads and had
no bodies. . . .

When the mirror is shattered, a tiny fragment falls into the eye
of little Kay, whose vision of the world is suddenly transformed.
Everything he once admired and loved, even his friend Gerda,
seems monstrous and ugly. (" 'Why do you cry?' asked he; 'you
look so ugly when you cry . . . Fie! this rose has an insect in it,
and just look at this! after all they are ugly roses! and it is an
ugly box they grow in!' Then he kicked the box and tore off the
roses.") Soon the Snow Queen has him in her power; and it is
up to little Gerda to save him. The young reader who lives
through Gerda's long perilous journey and the final triumph,
when her hot tears of grief melt the ice splinter, has undergone
an experience that is in the fullest sense of the word *moral*.

Or consider *The Doll's House*. Rumer Godden doesn't talk
about good and evil, but those are the poles of her story: gay,
generous-hearted Birdie, the celluloid doll, and Marchpane,
beautiful but malevolent, a creation of stuffed kid and china.
Birdie seems trivial—the tinkling of a music box distracts her so
she can't remember anything, and her thinking processes are im-
paired by a head rattle. But when the baby-doll Apple is en-
dangered, she doesn't have to think: she throws herself over the
flames and dies. In passionate identification with fictional characters, a child develops his capacity to *feel* with others. He loves
selflessness in Birdie, courage and patience in Hans Brinker,
kindness in Dr. Dolittle, the grace of friendship in Ratty and
Mole. Robin Hood stirs the beginnings of social consciousness,
and King Arthur's betrayer Mordred arouses his hatred of
treachery.

Questions about what really matters spring up naturally as
flowers in *The Little Prince*. On a neighboring asteroid, the hero
meets a businessman so engrossed in counting he doesn't look up.

("Five-hundred-and-one million—I can't stop . . . I have so much to do. I am concerned with matters of consequence.") He's counting stars. What does he do with these stars, the little prince asks. "Nothing. I own them." And what's the good of owning them? It makes him rich. As for the good of being rich—"That makes it possible for me to buy more stars, if any are discovered." Surely no child ever came back from that encounter without food for thought.

And surely no child ever set down *The Velveteen Rabbit* without a sense of what ultimately makes human life worthwhile. The velveteen rabbit, an appealing but unspectacular Christmas gift, lies neglected a long time in a nursery full of smart, expensive mechanical toys who look down on the others and pretend *they* are real. The rabbit accepts his humble position. "He understood that sawdust was quite out-of-date and should never be mentioned in modern circles." Then he learns, from the old Skin Horse, that *realness* has nothing to do with internal machinery. "Real isn't how you are made. It's a thing that happens to you. When a child loves you for a long, long time, not just to play with, but really loves you, then you become real." Does it hurt? the rabbit wonders. Yes, he's told. Sometimes it does. But "when you are real, you don't mind being hurt." Of course the transformation doesn't occur all at once—or ever, to those who "break easily or have sharp edges or who have to be carefully kept. Generally, by the time you are real, most of your hair has been lugged off, and your eyes drop out, and you're getting loose in the joints and very shabby. But these things don't matter at all, because once you are real you can't be ugly, except to people who don't understand." Furthermore, "once you are real you can't become unreal again. It lasts for always."

The ultimate gift any child's book can confer is a feeling about the beauty and wonder and possibility of human life. This is what informs the violence of *King Arthur and the Knights of the Round Table* and the gentle domestic drama of Noel Streatfeild.

It is at the heart of some humorous books (*The Wind in the Willows*) and some deeply serious ones (*At the Back of the North Wind*). E. B. White, in a quiet comment, puts his finger on the quality that makes *Charlotte's Web* and other great children's books absolutely unforgettable: "All that I hope to say in books, all that I ever hope to say, is that I love the world. I guess you can find that in there, if you dig around."

Some Personal Notes on the Kind of Books I Wouldn't Buy

If your child brings home from the library—and loves—a book you think worthless, you should certainly not spoil his pleasure by supercilious comment. ("That's trash. Let me find you a *good* book, like *Tale of Two Cities*.") If, however, you are buying books for your child, making permanent additions to his collection, then surely you want the best. Though not all teachers and librarians would agree, here are some kinds of books I would avoid:

▪ *Rewritten or abridged children's classics*. Well-meaning attempts to simplify a "difficult" book almost always result in loss of quality and power. Remember the first appearance of Long John Silver in *Treasure Island?*

> I remember him as if it were yesterday, as he came plodding to the inn door with his sea chest following behind him in a hand-barrow; a tall, strong, heavy, nut-brown man; his tarry pigtail falling over the shoulders of his soiled blue coat, his hands ragged and scarred, with black, broken nails; and the saber cut across one cheek, a dirty livid white.

This is a Scott, Foresman modernization:

> I can see him as if it were yesterday, as he came to the inn door with his sea-chest following behind him in a hand-cart.

He was a tall, strong, heavy, nut-brown man. His pigtail fell
over the shoulders of his soiled blue coat. His hands were big,
with black, broken nails, and across one side of his face he
had an ugly white scar.

All the most vivid words have been conscientiously expunged
(plodding, tarry, ragged and scarred, saber, livid); the wonderfully balanced, suspenseful sentence has been chopped up into
tidy segments, its rhythm spoiled.

Presumably the three adaptors would justify these changes on
the grounds that they had brought a sophisticated work within
the range of slow readers. But what possible justification can be
offered for simplifying Beatrix Potter, master of one of the most
lucid prose styles in children's literature? Here is our old friend
Peter Rabbit:

> First he ate some lettuces and some
> French beans; and then he ate some
> radishes;
> and then, feeling rather sick, he went to
> look for some parsley.

And here he is in a version "specially edited in vocabulary and
style to meet the needs of the young child":

> In the garden he saw carrots and beans
>   and radishes.
> "Mmm," said Peter to himself, "Carrots,
> beans and radishes are what I like best.
> He began to eat.
> He ate some carrots.
> He ate some radishes.
> He ate and ate and ate.
> Peter ate so much he got sick.
> He went to look for some parsley.

The cadence is gone, the delicate variation, the sly humor and the character of the original protagonist. (The fellow who rubs his tummy and murmurs, "Mmm, carrots, beans and radishes are what I like best" is not Peter at all, but a Disney bunny.) This particular version takes further liberties. The fact that Peter's father was put into a pie by Mr. MacGregor (too gruesome?) is tactfully omitted. And above Pete Bunny's bed there now hangs a neatly lettered sign: "Good Bunnies Always Obey."

Children do their own editing as they read, skipping what's hard or dull. If a child is not old enough to read the original, he's not old enough to read the book. The only exceptions to that principle, I think, are retellings of truly archaic material by gifted writers (Malory by Roger Lancelyn Green, *The Merry Adventures of Robin Hood* by Howard Pyle).

▪ *Most easy-to-read books based on limited vocabulary lists.* Some writers survive this artificial restriction: Elsa Minarik in the Little Bear books, and Dr. Seuss (though the "real" Seusses seem to me vastly preferable to his I Can Read Books). If a child is being read to by his parents, if he knows *The Carrot Seed* and *Umbrella* and *Make Way for Ducklings*, how can he be satisfied with this sort of thing (from Ruth Jensen's *Come to the Farm*)?

> Bow-wow
> We want to play.
> Where are our friends?
> Will you come and play?

The argument for offering children predigested mental pabulum is that they can spoon it up for themselves and so experience the joy of mastery. But "what child-mind measurers call a feeling of mastery is often," as Clifton Fadiman observes, "only a feeling of boredom." It is perfectly possible to employ repetition (which speeds reading progress) without clobbering a child into stupefaction. Here, for example, in *Bedtime for Frances*, it's used

as a springboard for a fresh, funny family scene: Frances is making her umpteenth appearance in her parents' bedroom to confide
yet another night fear, the mysteriously moving curtains. Father
explains that's only the wind, going about his business. Everybody has a job:

"If the wind does not blow the curtains, he will be out of a
job. If I do not go to the office, I will be out of a job. And if you
do not go to sleep now, do you know what will happen to you?"
"I will be out of a job?" said Frances.
"No," said Father.
"I will get a spanking?"
"Right!" said Father.

(The Frances books are ideal for beginning readers because they
offer a nice alternation of easy bits—"It is bedtime for Frances.
Mother said, 'It is time for bed.' Father said, 'It is time for bed.'
Frances said, 'I want a glass of milk.'"—with hard bits that are
irresistible and so not hard after all; this is Frances in bed,
singing a little song about the alphabet, making it up as she goes
along:

A is for apple pie,
B is for bear,
C is for crocodile, combing his hair . . .
                    to
U is for underwear, down in the drier—

at which point she stops, stumped for a rhyme.)
    Parting thought on vocabulary lists: though the official figure
for first-grade comprehension is around 800 words, at least one
study claims a figure closer to 26,000. Split the difference, and
you've still got a lot of word leeway.

    ▪ *Works of fiction whose principal, overwhelming aim is to
instruct.* Instruction is the appropriate function of science books,

histories and biographies and how-to-do-its; it is not the story-teller's business. That's not to say information, correct and use-ful, may not enter into a good story. But when it does, it must do so naturally, as integral to plot or character. Consider, for in-stance, the scene in *Charlotte's Web* in which Charlotte the spider and Wilbur the pig discuss legs:

> "You have awfully hairy legs, Charlotte," said Wilbur, as the spider busily worked at her task.
>
> "My legs are hairy for a good reason," replied Charlotte. "Furthermore, each leg of mine has seven sections—the coxa, the trochantur, the femur, the patella, the tibia, the meta-tarsus, and the tarsus."
>
> Wilbur sat bolt upright. "You're kidding," he said.
>
> "No, I'm not, either."
>
> "Say those names again, I didn't catch them the first time."
>
> "Coxa, trochantur, femur, patella, tibia, metatarsus, and tarsus."
>
> "Goodness," said Wilbur, looking down at his own chubby legs, "I don't think *my* legs have seven sections."
>
> "Well," said Charlotte, "you and I lead different lives. You don't have to spin a web. That takes real leg work."
>
> "I could spin a web if I tried," said Wilbur, boasting. "I've just never tried."

This is not only exact; it's funny, and it's deeply, wonder-fully characteristic of the two friends—Charlotte brisk and prac-tical, Wilbur foolish and vain but chubby-lovable. Compare the way the "science" here is introduced with this passage of *A Wrinkle in Time*:

> "Who have our fighters been?" Calvin asked.
>
> "Jesus!" Charles Wallace said. "Why, of course, Jesus!"
>
> "Of course!" Mrs. Whatsit said. "Go on, Charles, love. There were others. All your great artists. They've been lights for us to see by."

"Leonardo da Vinci?" Calvin suggested tentatively. "And Michaelangelo?"

"And Shakespeare," Charles Wallace called out, "and Bach! And Pasteur and Madame Curie and Einstein!"

Now Calvin's voice rang with confidence. "And Schweitzer and Gandhi and Buddha and Beethoven and Rembrandt and St. Francis!"

I have never read all of Madeleine L'Engle's prize-winning novel. Having come upon this passage, I know I never shall. For the hands are the hands of Charles and Mrs. Whatsit, but the voice is the voice of my grade-school teacher.

Some depressing books are written for good reasons. This is notably true of many books inspired by the Women's Movement (designed to promote a more active, achieving female image) and those intended to provide a wholesome self-image for blacks. Stories like *Mommies at Work* and *Martin's Father* may aid in the disintegration of sex-role stereotypes, but they are not likely to take the place of *Katy and the Big Snow* (about a heroic tractor who just happens to be female) and *Pippi Longstocking*, with its liberated heroine who has never heard of Women's Lib. And some of the books most likely to promote a black child's self-esteem don't talk about blackness at all. They simply feature a black protagonist.

▪ *Sentimental Aren't-Kiddies-Cute books*, which present the young bathed in a pale pink light that never was on land or sea (and which no honest-to-goodness child would recognize). Much children's poetry is of this sort—a wistful, nostalgic sighing by adults who would like to turn back the clock. Some popular writer-illustrators belong to the same school. Tasha Tudor's books for Little Ones seem to me aimed straight at their mothers. This is the opening of *First Delights*, a preschool story—with an epigraph from Tennyson, no less, "Alone and warming his five wits, The white owl in the belfry sits": "Sally lives on a farm. As the seasons change from winter to spring, from summer to fall, she uses her five senses to see, hear, smell, touch and taste the things that happen in the year's turning . . ." What child, after such delights, would cry, "Read it again!"?

Another minority opinion. The many little volumes by Joan Walsh Anglund—*A Friend Is Someone Who Likes You, Love Is a Special Way of Feeling, Spring Is a New Beginning*—all express a romantic-sentimental view of childhood (adorable, innocent, charming, sweet, cute) and all attempt a vague philosophizing utterly unlike the way children think. Though some readers bracket Ruth Krauss and Joan Walsh Anglund together as diviners of the child mind, there's a world of difference between the clarity and vividness of Krauss's "mud is to jump in and slide in and yell doodleedoodleedoo" (*A Hole Is to Dig*) and Anglund's verse.

Help for the Reluctant Reader

Parents who themselves read passionately as children are naturally distressed when their child never, of his own accord, curls up with a book and an apple; they know what he's missing. And parents who grew up largely without books feel, vaguely, that they lost out on something pretty important; they want to do better by *their* offspring. Either way, then, the reluctant reader becomes a cause of concern (and often, the object of misguided pressures).

What can parents do to foster a child's interest in reading?

▪ *Try to understand.* The forces competing for a child's attention today are infinitely more various and tempting than they were a generation ago. What could a ten-year-old do on Sunday thirty years back? He could play—provided his family didn't object to play on the Sabbath; he could go to church; he could read. (When I was a child, I had friends who were not even allowed to read, Sundays, unless they turned to devotional literature—Jeremy Taylor's sermons, Pascal's *Pensées*.) Many chose to read. Sundays, now, a child can ski or swim, attend concerts, go to club meetings, see a movie, read (magazines and popular novels as well as children's books) and, above all, watch television. Television has revolutionized the whole pattern of youthful recreation. This is not just a matter of time spent (an average of twenty to twenty-two hours weekly for preschool and elementary school children); it's also a matter of expectations created. If a ten-year-old isn't interested within five minutes after a situation comedy begins, he switches channels. Is it any wonder that he puts down *Bleak House*, his father's favorite book? A whole chapter, and nothing *happens*. (In that amount of time, a Western would have had a stampede or a shoot-out.)

▪ *If adults in a household never read anything but the newspaper and TV Guide, how is a child to get the idea that reading is pleasurable?* As a teacher of high school students, I've often heard parents complain bitterly, "He never picks up a book unless it's assigned." Tactful inquiries frequently disclose the fact that the parent doesn't read either—can't recall the name of a single book read during the previous year.

If you haven't, all your life, been a reader, you probably can't start now just to set a good example. But this much you can do: you can show an active interest in your child's reading. Most parents read aloud to preschoolers; many drop the practice altogether as soon as the child starts school. That seems to me a great pity; sharing books promotes not only a love of reading but also close parent-child relationships. The best children's books can be enjoyed at *any* age. Read books together, taking parts or turns. Read favorite books on special occasions—and not just the obvious ones, like *'Twas the Night Before Christmas* on December 24. Make your own traditions with *Many Moons* (James Thurber), the doughnut episode from *Homer Price* (Robert McCloskey), Tom Sawyer's meeting Becky Thatcher for the first time, Christina Rossetti's *Goblin Market* (wonderful for Halloween). Talk with the child about stories he's read and liked; let him know that you're interested too. But don't quiz him to see if he's read carefully, or make him look words up in the dictionary.

■ *Start the library habit early.* A three-year-old, entering a good children's room, senses immediately that this is A Very Special Place—furniture just the right size, bright pictures and interesting things to look at and touch, a friendly person in charge and, best of all, lots of other children busy with books. Many children's book departments have story hours, excursions and special interest clubs; most eagerly solicit—and post—dictated or hand written "reviews" of books children enjoyed. A child who can read will feel very important using the card catalog and then locating books on his own. Many a reluctant reader has been dazzled, won over, by the discovery that the book room isn't all *stories.* "They have books on magic tricks!" a nine-year-old told me, eyes shining. "And one about how to build a tree house!" Encourage your child to keep lists of books read—children love making lists—either in an attractive notebook or on a wall poster. Get a box of colored stars so he can establish a rating system—one star for "not so good" and four stars for "I'm going to read it again."

For a young child, the weekly library trip can be made even more special by a regular ceremony like going for ice cream afterwards or coming home, popping corn, and then settling in to read a new book together.

■ *Though a library provides the foundation for a lifetime's reading pleasure, it's important to help a child build his own collection.* Good books are expensive, true—but so are good toys and sports equipment. A child rapidly outgrows his ten-dollar skates; he never outgrows *Alice in Wonderland.* An adult is not likely to know the whereabouts of that super-duper dump truck he got for his fifth birthday—but many, many parents still possess their childhood copy of Andersen's *Fairy Tales.* Certain books every child should own in sturdy and beautiful editions—

and with the original illustrations, where that matters, as with
Tenniel's drawings for *Alice,* Shepard's for the Christopher
Robin books. Stay away from matched sets, "children's classics"
bound in imitation leather. They're forbidding. I think it's a
good idea to give a child a book allowance, separate from any
regular allowance he receives, so he can save up for books he
particularly wants. Get him a good supply of book plates—his
own choice of design—to stimulate a healthy pride in his library.

In addition to a core collection of fine books, a child should
have lots and lots of inexpensive editions. For the under-sixes,
there are still some under-a-dollar books available (Golden
Books, Wonder Books). For readers, the best paperback bargain
is the very extensive Scholastic library, over a thousand items
ranging from 50 cents to $1.00. From Scholastic you can get such
classic picture books as *Goodnight Moon* and *Georgie,* and for
older children, the most popular series books (Beverly Cleary's
Henry Huggins, Robert McCloskey's *Homer Price,* Donald Sobol's *Encyclopaedia Brown*). Scholastic also offers editions of
standard classics, but in most cases you'll want those in well-
bound editions that are a pleasure to hold; paperbacks are for
ephemeral reading.

Since a great many schools participate in Scholastic's book
club program, your child may be able to order books through his
classroom teacher. If not, you can get a complete (free) catalog
from Scholastic Book Services, 904 Sylvan Ave., Englewood Cliffs,
N.J. 07632.

▪ *Never, never push a child to read.* ("Why don't you put
away that baseball mitt and read a good book for a change?")
An approach of this sort suggests that reading is a chore. Even
worse—and by no means uncommon in academically ambitious
families—is the insistence that a child do some "serious" reading
before he goes out to play. How much better to offer reading as
what it is, a special treat: "If you finish tidying up your room,
I'll sit down with you and read *Curious George.*" Maybe your

child isn't (yet) all that eager for a story; but few children can resist the offer of a parent's undivided attention. Nonreaders often turn into readers because they associate books with the presence and interest of a loved person.

■ *Don't criticize the child's taste in books.* It's possible for a young reader to have a really great experience with a third-rate book. (See the adolescent recollections, earlier in this chapter, of Nancy Drew and the Hardy Boys.) What to an adult is trite or sentimental may to the innocent heart be deeply moving. As for "junk" reading in general: perhaps no book that makes a child want to read another book is bad.

This whole question, of whether children ought to keep their noses to the good book only, is controversial. Lillian Smith, a distinguished librarian and children's book specialist, takes a firm line. "We should put into [children's] hands only the books worthy of them, the books of honesty, integrity and vision—the books on which they can grow." Childhood, she feels, "is so receptive and brief that a child has less need of and less time for the mediocre than an adult." But anyone who remembers the long, often aimless summers of childhood knows very well that children have plenty of time. The early years are, as Miss Smith says, a period of discovery—but we are surely romanticizing children if we expect them to show obvious signs of growth at every moment. A youngster who appears to be wasting his childhood on Tom Swift and the Bobbsey twins *may* be growing; he may be enlarging his perceptions or developing his own standards. And how, indeed, can a child learn to distinguish good from bad, the false from the true, unless he has experienced both? Why not let *him* discover that *Huckleberry Finn* is more interesting than the Rover Boys? Perhaps he can't tell the difference between fine writing and what is churned out by industrious hacks, but he does recognize real excitement and humor and pathos. When he finds these qualities, he'll keep reading. All the parent can do—or should do, for that matter—is encourage the child's own search for the books he can wholeheartedly enjoy.

Don't worry, incidentally, if some of the books a child is reading seem too babyish. (At times an old book, like an old toy, is a great comfort.) Still less if they seem too hard. If a book really is too hard, he'll drop it. But when a child is genuinely interested, he will persevere through what seems impossibly dense material.

■ *Don't overlook magazines as a temptation to read.* Children love getting mail; any child would enjoy a subscription in *his* name. A year's worth of *Humpty Dumpty* (for preschoolers), *Highlights for Children, Boy's Life, Calling All Girls* for older children, makes a nice birthday-present-in-installments.

Juvenile Magazines

Child Life (1100 Waterway Blvd., Indianapolis, Ind. 46202). Articles on science, nature and general information; short stories, plays suitable for living room production and craft projects. Ages 4–12.

Children's Digest (52 Vanderbilt Ave., New York, N.Y. 10017). Published by the Parents' Magazine Press, a reprint magazine for children ages 7 to 12.

The Golden Magazine (850 Third Ave., New York, N.Y. 10022). For boys and girls 8–12. General articles, fiction, poetry and crafts.

Highlights for Children (803 Church St., Honesdale, Pa. 18431). The widest age range of the juvenile magazines (2 to 12). A well-edited, high-quality collection of articles (science, history, animals, famous persons, life in other countries) and stories— both those a preschooler will enjoy hearing and those an older child will eagerly read for himself. Also finger plays, puzzles, party ideas, arts and crafts.

Humpty Dumpty's Magazine (52 Vanderbilt Ave., New York, N.Y. 10017). Read-aloud stories, both realistic and fanciful, and stories for beginning readers; poetry. For ages 3 to 8.

Jack and Jill (Independence Square, Philadelphia, Pa. 19105). Articles about science and nature; things to make and do, realistic adventure and animal stories; puzzles, riddles, jokes and songs and games. Ages 4 to 10.

Some children are temperamentally not disposed to any activity that involves sitting still. They want to be up and doing with friends. *If your child seems not to have the patience for books, wait for the moment when his activities can be enriched or facilitated by reading.* Is he a baseball enthusiast? There are books about famous players, books about the history of the game and books with practical pointers for the young. Is he a collector? Whether it's stamps, rocks, butterflies, coins . . . the library has books that will help.

And some children read—comics only. If your child seems permanently stuck at the *Batman* level, take a look at Daniel N. Fader's *Hooked on Books,* the report of an experiment with determined nonreaders and comic-book addicts. The best course, Dr. Fader found, was to offer youngsters a wide choice of books that appeared both accessible and relevant. His subjects—adolescent boys in a reform school—discovered *Dennis the Menace* and *Peanuts* with joy. (Mostly pictures. What a relief.) From picture humor, they moved on to James Bond, tales of horror and suspense, science fiction, hot-rod stories, nonfiction about sex and dating. . . . *Real things.* The approach here is suggestive: not "What *should* a child read?" but "What will this child read?" Once a child finds that reading is a source of pleasure, he's on his way.

If your child resists even trips to the library, try giving him money to choose his own paperback at a book store.

Poetry for Children

A child who never encounters poetry until schoolteachers introduce a *poetry unit* is very likely to resist. "I hate that stuff." But if poetry has been part of his life from the very beginning, he need never *learn* to like it, he just *does*. The feeling for cadenced, rhythmical speech is as natural as breathing.

That babies tend to babble rhythmically has often been noted. "Endlessly he jabbers rhymed nonsense," Chukovsky cites a mother's report. "For hours he 'talks' to himself in rhymed syllables: *alia, valia, dalia, malia.*'" A baby's chatter is not, of course, poetry. Neither is "Rub a dub dub, three men in a tub." Yet it is with these very basic patterns of rhythm and rhyme that response to poetry begins. To the young, almost any activity is made more pleasurable by an accompanying chant. "Ride a cock horse, to Banbury Cross, To see a fine lady ride on a white horse. . . ." How that adds to the delight of a jouncing ride on Father's knee! Skipping rope, playing jacks, bouncing a ball and counting out—all these inspire verse, some of it genuinely haunting-rich, like "Sea shells, cockle bells, Eevy, ivy, o-ver!" and

> Intry, mintry, country corn,
> Apple seed and apple thorn.
> Wire, brier, limber, lock,
> Twelve geese in a flock.
> One flew east, one flew west,
> One flew over the cuckoo's nest.

Children too young to understand what's going on in "Hickory, dickory dock" and "A frog he would a-wooing go" want to hear the verses over and over. "With a rowley, powley, gammon and spinach, Heigho says Anthony Rowley": the only word there likely to mean anything to a three-year-old is *spinach*, but who cares? The lilt, the sprightliness, the sheer *sound* is enough.

This essentially musical pleasure is a permanent source of poetic appeal. At five, a child loves, "Sing a song of sixpence," with its arresting images floating on a stream of sound. At ten, he may like the obvious stirring beat of "The Highwayman" who comes "riding, riding, Up to the old inn door" or the sub-tler jazz rhythms of Vachel Lindsay:

> Darius the Mede was a king and a wonder.
> His eye was proud, and his voice like thunder.
> He kept bad lions in a monstrous den.
> He fed up the lions on Christian men.

Sound and sense are inseparable in poetry. Often, indeed, the sound *is* the sense. So poems must be read aloud, as songs must be sung. Read poetry to a tired child, an unhappy child, an ex-cited one who needs to calm down. One of the pleasantest pos-sible goodnight rituals is reading favorite poems as a child snuggles down for the night. Blake's "Little lamb, who made thee?" De la Mare's "Silver" ("Slowly and silently now the moon Walks the night in her silver shoon"), Tennyson's "Bugle Song" ("The splendor falls on castle walls And snowy summits old in story; The long light shakes across the lakes . . .")—these have just the right kind of radiant quiet.

In addition to sheer sensuous pleasure, good poetry offers the excitement of language that may be sharply precise or thrillingly suggestive-vague. What child would not shiver with delight at this description of Queen Nefertiti?

> Spin a coin, spin a coin,
> > All fall down;
> Queen Nefertiti
> > Stalks through the town.

Over the pavements
> Her feet go clack
Her legs are as tall
> As a chimney stack;

Her fingers flicker
> Like snakes in the air,
The walls split open
> At her green-eyed stare. . . .

The young are not surprised by Dylan Thomas's "fire green as grass," Edward Lear's "runcible spoon" or E. E. Cumming's salute to spring "when the world is puddle-wonderful." The right poem may help a child see in a new way. It may articulate his own formless feelings so that he experiences a delicious shock of recognition. (Of poets who wrote specially, devotedly for children, A. A. Milne and R. L. Stevenson notably possess this power. "The Swing" and "The Land of Counterpane" from *A Child's Garden of Verses*, "Halfway Down" from *When We Were Very Young*, are experiences that seem almost to have come from inside a child's head, but more perfectly articulated than any child could make them.)

Reading poetry to a child is not just diversion (though most children find it diverting to be read to—and much poetry is simply and purely fun). It is educating the child's feelings, stocking his mind with images, ideas, sensations, dim premonitions of experiences that lie ahead. Whether children fully understand the poetry they read or hear does not greatly matter. When Yeats writes of Innisfree, where he longs to build a cabin of clay and wattles made, it's not necessary to know where Innisfree is, whether wattles are brick, stone or paper. The very name is evocative, suggesting a magical place removed from the everyday world. A good poem may linger in the consciousness for years, like a tune half remembered, before life makes its meaning clear. (Children soon grow out of "There are fairies at the bottom of our garden"; they grow *into* "Tyger, tyger, burning bright In the forests of the night. . . .")

Edward Blishen, editor of one of the best collections of poetry for children, observes truly that a poem may be an important experience even if the reader can't exactly say what it was "about." "Words, lines, whole poems may come to us as mysteries. They may be mysteries that please us, that give us a strange deep feeling of this or that. That feeling may be our way of understanding a poem . . . Understanding, in the usual meaning of the word, may come to us later, or it may never come. . . . A poem does not need to have [a] clear, definite meaning, any more than a magic spell does, or any more than does the feeling we have when we smell, say, autumn leaves, or lavender, or the salt on our skins when we come out of the sea." The peculiar pleasure of poetry, in short, is that it satisfies not only our minds but also "our hearts and the whole *feeling* part of us."

How should one go about choosing for the young poems of permanent value? Parents who are themselves poetry readers will have their own favorites. Others would do well to invest in a few really first-rate collections. *Mother Goose*, of course; there are at least a dozen attractive modern editions. An illustrated anthology, for young children. (*The Oxford Book of Verse*, illustrated by Brian Wildsmith, and *The Golden Journey*, edited by Louise Bogan and William Jay Smith, are good choices.) And, for a somewhat older child, a collection offering a real range of styles, subjects and voices. (Look at Geoffrey Grigson's *The Cherry Tree*, Walter de la Mare's *Come Hither*.) Stay clear of anthologies that are too literary, the kind that presents all the English poets in chronological order with biographies and explanatory footnotes. Similarly, any book that consists exclusively of "children's poets" like Rose Fyleman and Dorothy Aldis is not really worth buying. Such a collection gives children a mistaken notion of what poetry is (fairies and flowers and assorted prettinesses). Furthermore, whatever appeal it has quickly evaporates. There is a time for David McCord, but not a very long time. Far better to select a book that will grow with the child, one that includes Herrick and Shakespeare and Coleridge, Emily Dickinson and Robert Frost. "In Xanadu did Kubla Khan a stately pleasure dome decree" has a resonance that lingers in the mind for years. The same can be said of English and Scottish ballads like "Lord Randal":

> "O where ha you been, Lord Randal my son?
> And where ha you been, my handsome young man?"
> "I ha been at the greenwood; mother, mak my bed soon,
> For I'm wearied wi hunting, and fain wad lie down."

A good collection should suggest the variety of poetry, from lyrics and epigrams to full-scale narratives like "The Pied Piper of Hamlin" and "Goblin Market." For children, the best arrangement of poems is by subject—not, for example, by historical period or literary genre. Look at *The Looking Glass Book of Verse*, with its immediately enticing divisions: Poetry, Music and Dancing; Night and Day, Seasons and Weathers; Beasts and Birds; Children; Victuals and Drink—and so on. Or consider one of the many good anthologies unified by a single theme or subject: *A Book of Nature Poems* and *The Sea, Ships and Sailors*, both edited by William Cole, or Gwendolyn Reed's *Bird Songs*. And don't overlook the many marvelous anthologies of humorous verse (a good beginning for a child who thinks poetry is solemn stuff). *Oh, What Nonsense!* (William Cole) is a specially good one.

An anthology-browsing child coming upon Matilda "who told such Dreadful Lies It made one Gasp and Stretch one's Eyes," may then romp through all Hilaire Belloc's *Cautionary Verses*. Richard Cory may send him to the dramatic verse portraits of Edward Arlington Robinson, and Macavity the Mystery Cat to T. S. Eliot's early verse. From a single good anthology, a child can move out into the whole world of poetry.

In the Beginning Is the Word:
Books and the Growing Child

GUIDES FOR PARENTS: BOOKS ABOUT BOOKS AND READING

ARBUTHNOT, MAY HILL, *Children and Books*, Scott, Foresman, 1964. An absolutely basic book for both parents and teachers, covering all aspects of children's reading from poetry to encyclopedias, from fantasy to history (and with a special chapter on mass media). The bibliographies at the end of each section are invaluable.

—— and others, *Children's Books Too Good to Miss*, Western Reserve University Press, 1971. A judicious selected list, regularly revised.

ARNSTEIN, FLORA J., *Adventures in Poetry*, Stanford University Press, 1951. An imaginative teacher's account of an experiment in creative writing with elementary school children.

BECHTEL, LOUISE SEAMAN, *Books in Search of Children*, Macmillan, 1969. Mrs. Bechtel's style is pleasantly readable, and her vigorous emphasis on the need for intelligent criticism of children's literature is refreshing, yet the book's emphasis seems out of date (extensive discussion, for example, of Rachel Field and Elizabeth Coatsworth, writers no longer widely read).

BETZNER, JEAN, and ANNIE F. MOOR, *Every Child and Books*, Bobbs, 1940.

CAMERON, ELEANOR, *The Green and Burning Tree*, Little, 1962. Eleanor Cameron understands the secret and very special bond between a child and a loved book; her concern throughout is with finding memorable books for children, books that are experiences rather than passing diversions. Highly personal essays on general matters like style and characterization and on individual writers—Beatrix Potter, Eleanor Farjeon, Wanda Gág.

DUFF, ANNIS, *"Bequest of Winds"; a Family's Pleasures with Books*, Viking, 1954. An enthusiastic personal account of reading experiences with two children.

EAKIN, MARY K., ed., *Good Books for Children*, University of Chicago Press, 1962. Annotated selection of children's books reviewed in the *Bulletin of the Center for Children's Books, 1948–1961*.

EATON, ANNE THAXTER, *Treasure for the Taking*, Viking, 1957. An experienced Teachers College librarian comments succinctly and with insight on a considerable list of "best books."

EGOFF, SHEILA, ed., G. T. STUBBS, and L. F. ASHLEY, *Only Connect*, Oxford University Press, 1969. A superlative collection of essays by distinguished children's book writers and critics: P. L. Travers, Roger Lancelyn Green, C. S. Lewis, Rumer Godden, J. R. Tolkien. Everything here is of interest: Michael Hornyansky on fairy tales, Edward W. Rosenheim on values in children's books, Sheila Egoff on changing emphases in children's literature. . . . The most provocative book of its kind I know—and one of the best books of essays by various hands on *any* subject.

EGOFF, SHEILA, *The Republic of Childhood*, Oxford, 1967. A critical guide to Canadian children's literature in English, with lucid and thoughtful introductions to chapters on the various genres.

FENNER, PHYLLIS, *The Proof of the Pudding: What Children Read*, Day, 1957. Lively and readable, a book "for the fathers and mothers and grandparents who want to, and should, buy and borrow books for their children." Unlike most such guides, it starts from what *is* rather than what *ought* to be: the books children really enjoy, the nature of their appeal, and the approximate age at which a child will read them with pleasure.

FENWICK, SARA I., *A Critical Approach to Children's Literature*, University of Chicago Press, 1967. A collection of essays on such topics as "Machine Animism in Modern Children's Literature," "Social Values in Children's Literature." Most are not of great interest to parents, and some look like required reading for an education course.

FISHER, MARGERY, *Intent upon Reading: A Critical Appraisal of Modern Fiction for Children*, Brockhampton, 1965. A deeply literate overview written with taste and style. Mrs. Fisher's standard of value is enjoyment: she looks for fiction that meets the child's need for energy, sincerity and imagination—and when she recommends a book, I believe her.

FRANK, JOSETTE, *Your Child's Reading Today*, Doubleday, 1954. A practical and common-sense treatment which relates reading not only to the child's emotional and intellectual development but also to its chief competitors—movies, comics, and TV.

FRANKEL, BERNICE, *How to Give Your Child a Love of Books*, Birk, 1964.

GREEN, ROGER LANCELYN, *Teller of Tales. Children's Books and Their Authors from 1800 to 1964*, Edmund Ward, 1965. A guide to British juvenile literature, prepared by a writer distinguished for his own retellings of myths and legends.

GUILFOILE, ELIZABETH, *Books for Beginning Readers*, National Council of Teachers of English, 1963. Over 300 books for children who have just learned to read.

———, *Adventures with Books*, Signet, 1966. Prepared in consultation with the NCTE Committee on the Elementary School Book List: a comprehensive guide to 1,250 books for children ages 3 to 14, organized by subject categories and reading interest level.

HAVILAND, VIRGINIA, ed., *Children's Literature: A Guide to Reference Sources*, Library of Congress, 1966. An extensive and fully annotated listing of books, articles and pamphlets relating to children's literature. Handsomely produced and illustrated.

HAZARD, PAUL, *Books, Children and Men*, The Horn Book, Inc., 1944. An official "classic" in the field, somewhat romantic-sentimental in its view of children. (Hazard seems to have in mind only one type of child—happy and carefree, eager for delightful fantasies to enrich his imaginative life.)

HURLIMANN, BETTINA, *Picture-Book World*, trans., and ed. B. W. ALDERSON, Oxford, 1968. Worldwide in scope and abundantly illustrated, a survey of modern picture books.

LARRICK, NANCY, A *Parent's Guide to Children's Reading*, Doubleday, 1964. Prosaic but useful.

ROBINSON, EVELYN R., ed., *Readings About Children's Literature*, McKay, 1966. A mixed bag of essays, ranging from dreary to helpful-lively. Sections on choosing and evaluating children's books, juvenile book illustration, special types of fiction (regional, ethnic, etc.) and nonfiction.

SMITH, JAMES STEEL, A *Critical Approach to Children's Literature*, McGraw, 1967. The organization of this book is better suited to a college course in children's literature than to a guidance-seeking parent, but the book lists are full and helpful.

SMITH, LILLIAN H., *The Unreluctant Years*, American Library Association, 1953. Well written and perceptive, though distinctly on the conservative side. (Of A. A. Milne: "will anyone maintain that it is poetry?") The book ranges from general matters (What constitutes good reading for the young?) to very specific ones (What are the finest collections of fairy tales? the best retellings of Greek myth?).

VIGUERS, RUTH H., *Margin for Surprise: About Books, Children, and Librarians*, Little, 1964.

WHITE, DOROTHY, *Books Before Five*, Oxford, 1954. Based on a mother's journal record of books read to a little girl between the ages of 2 and 5.

BOOKS FOR BABIES

ADAMS, GEORGE, *First Things*, Platt, n.d. Large clear pictures of familiar objects in natural color.

BROWN, MARGARET WISE, *Goodnight Moon*, Harper, 1947. A bunny drifts off to sleep in a green room (that grows dark as you turn the pages), murmuring affectionate good-byes to all the beloved objects around him.

BRUNA, DICK, *The Egg*, Follett, 1968. Also *The Apple, The Circus, The Fish, The King* and many others, all simple, cheerful, bright-colored and strongly-bound.

FREEMAN, ALICE, *Baby's Lullabies*, Grosset, 1965.

FUJIKAWA, GYO, *Babies*, Grosset, 1963. Just lots of other babies to touch and talk to.

HOGSTROM, DAPHNE D., *The Real Book of First Pictures*, Rand McNally, 1972. Kitchens, stores, animals, toys, all bright and cheerful.

KUNHARDT, DOROTHY, *Pat the Bunny*, Golden Press, 1962. A book of interesting textures and pictures.

MATTHIESEN, THOMAS, *Things to See*, Platt, n.d. Clear color photographs, one to a page.

SCHLESINGER, ALICE, *Baby's Mother Goose*, Grosset, 1959. Tearproof.

———, *Here We Go Round the Mulberry Bush*, Grosset, 1964.

SEIDEN, ART, *Counting Rhymes*, Grosset, 1959. Hard board pages for the youngest.

———, *Book of Toys*, Grosset, 1965.

———, *Kittens*, Grosset, 1962.

WILLIAMS, GARTH, *Baby Animals*, Golden Press, 1959. Also: *Baby Farm Animals*.

READING FOR LIFE

What are the "best" books? To some extent, that depends on the child. Books listed as "indispensable" represent a kind of informal consensus: they are the works librarians and teachers most frequently cite as "best loved"—plus a few that I personally couldn't bear to omit. The second list contains, to the round number of one hundred, other good books to grow on. Your child, once started reading, will add many others.

I have not attempted to categorize books precisely by age or grade: children differ so greatly. Some five-year-olds love Winnie-the-Pooh, some ten-year-olds love Frances the badger —thereby confounding the usual classifications. Even the rough division into picture books and books for readers troubles me. *Diana and the Rhinoceros* is a picture book, and preschoolers adore it—but I'm fond of it myself, and have reread it with pleasure.

INDISPENSABLE PICTURE BOOKS

BANNERMAN, HELEN, *The Story of Little Black Sambo*, Lippincott, 1923. Tigers who play dress-up only to become butter for a family's pancakes, a gullible little boy, and luck all blend.

BEMELMANS, LUDWIG, *Madeline*, Viking, 1939. Twelve little girls (in two straight lines) live in a Paris boarding school. The smallest one is our heroine, and a braver and more indomitable little stalwart would be hard to find. Even through appendicitis.

BESKOW, ELSA, *Pelle's New Suit*, Harper, 1929. Families—round, cheerful, and loving—form the background of this simple story about an enterprising little boy who trades his way to a fine new Sunday suit. Pictured details of indoor and outdoor activities will entrance the young.

BISHOP, CLAIRE HUCHET, *Five Chinese Brothers,* Coward-McCann, 1938. Because of a small boy's stubbornness, one of the five brothers is to be put to death. But because of the five brothers' unusual abilities and their identical faces, they save the doomed brother from burning, drowning, suffocating and beheading.

BROOKE, LESLIE, *Johnny Crowe's Garden,* Warne, 1903. Whimsical pictures bring to life all the inhabitants of Johnny Crowe's garden—an elegant crane prancing through the rain with a pale blue umbrella, a bored hippopotamus, an elephant (who "said something quite irrelevant"), a smartly cravated lion and others. Two rhyming lines to a page. Also, *Johnny Crowe's New Garden.*

BURTON, VIRGINIA LEE, *The Little House,* Houghton, 1942. A cozy cottage experiences alarming urban growth all around, and the reassuring cycles of the seasons—budding trees, swimming children, brilliantly colored leaves and gently falling snow.

————, *Mike Mulligan and His Steam Shovel,* Houghton, 1939. Mike and his working partner, steam shovel Mary Anne, have pursued a long and successful career together, digging their holes swiftly and well. Their record is unchallenged —until they agree to accept a bet from the town of Poppersville.

DAUGHERTY, JAMES, *Andy and the Lion,* Viking, 1938. Andy is a resourceful boy who always keeps pliers handy in his back pocket—just in case he might happen upon a lion who needs a thorn taken out of his paw. A sprightly modern retelling of an old tale.

DE BRUNHOFF, JEAN, *The Story of Babar,* Random House, 1933. Babar the elephant begins life tragically, as a hunter kills his mother. He soon finds consolation, however, in the dear little old lady, Parisian elevators, green suits with spats, photographs of himself, and Celeste, his beautiful elephant bride. Wish-fulfillment for humans, in an elephant world. Also *The Travels of Babar, Babar and Father Christmas*.

ETS, MARIE HALL, *In the Forest*, Viking, 1944. When the little boy and his trumpet started the day, he was merely in the forest. But by day's end, he could look back on an animal parade, a picnic, and a final game of hide-and-seek.

FLACK, MARJORIE, *The Story About Ping*, Viking, 1933. Ping is a duck who lives with his mother, his father, two sisters, three brothers, eleven aunts, seven uncles and forty-two cousins on a boat in the Yangtze River. Slap! the spank descends on Ping's back—but he's finally home, back from a series of alarming happenings.

GÁG, WANDA, *ABC Bunny*, Coward-McCann, 1933. ABC bunny hops briskly from red juicy apples through a big fat zero, leaving lettuce and half-chewed flowers trailing behind him.

———, *Millions of Cats*, Coward-McCann, 1928. Cats here! Cats there! Millions of cats! How will the elderly couple feed them all—or choose just one? Fortunately, the cats themselves solve the problem and leave only one (he crawled away in fright when the hissing and clawing began) who curls up by the fire.

GRAMATKY, HARDIE, *Little Toot*, Putnam, 1939. Little Toot is a tugboat, scorned and ridiculed by the other ships because of his size and happy-go-lucky temperament. Through an SOS made of his own smoke balls, he manages to rescue a distressed ocean liner and wins their respect. Also, *Little Toot on the Thames*.

KRAUSS, RUTH, *A Hole Is to Dig*, Harper, 1952. Toes are to dance on, dishes are to do, noses are to rub, principals are to take out splinters, dogs are to kiss people—and this is a little book of first definitions.

LEAF, MUNRO, *The Story of Ferdinand*, Viking, 1936. Ferdinand is a pacific bull whose one desire is to sit quietly beneath a cork tree and smell the flowers. When, however, he settles his rump atop a bumblebee, he becomes (briefly) as fierce and terrible a bull as any matador could desire. He is chosen for the bull ring. *Then* . . .

MC CLOSKEY, ROBERT, *Make Way for Ducklings*, Viking, 1941. A story of birth and dwelling places, and of a family of mallard ducks who live on the Charles River. We accompany the ducks through their search for a site to raise the ducklings, across crowded city streets with a police escort—to the swan-boat pond in the Boston Public Gardens.

MINARIK, ELSE, *Little Bear*, illustrated by Maurice Sendak. Harper, 1957. A book of love and confidence between a small bear and his mother. Little Bear journeys to the moon (by jumping out of a tree), where he finds a Mother Bear amazingly like his own. Another day he is cold in the snow and goes through a coat, hat and trousers before he discovers that his own fur coat is warmest. Also *Little Bear's Friend, Little Bear's Visit, Father Bear Comes Home*.

MUNARI, BRUNO, *Bruno Munari's ABC*, World, 1960. Brilliantly yellow-red apples, drippingly pink ice-cream cones and enticing packages. A hospitable fly will direct you through the pages.

POTTER, BEATRIX, *The Tale of Peter Rabbit*, Warne, 1903. Peter is a naughty little rabbit with a passion for Mr. MacGregor's lettuce. Unfortunately, Mr. MacGregor catches sight of him munching away, and it is only by hiding in a watering can that he manages to escape. Arriving home, he gets his just deserts—a stomachache, a cold, and a dose of camomile tea. Also *The Tale of Benjamin Bunny, The Tale of Squirrel Nutkin, The Tale of Jemima Puddle-Duck, The Tale of Mrs. Tiggy-Winkle, The Tale of Tom Kitten.*

REY, H. A., *Curious George*, Houghton, 1941. Curious George is a mischievous little monkey with good intentions but an infallible knack for getting into uncomfortable situations and often disastrous adventures. The Man With the Yellow Hat rescues him, however, and inevitably everything works out. Also *Curious George Takes a Job*, *Curious George Rides a Bike*, *Curious George Gets a Medal*.

SENDAK, MAURICE, *Where the Wild Things Are*, Harper, 1963. A ferocious book, in which are heard the terrible roars and teeth-gnashing of the horrible monsters Max sails away to visit. But he tames them all with a wave of his hand and comes home to find his dinner still hot.

SEUSS, DR. (Theodor Geisel), *A Cat in the Hat*, Random House, 1957. A strange, mad, wildly wacky story of a dreary rainy day that turns into a joyful disaster area when the Cat arrives. (But what will happen when Mother comes home?) Also *The Cat in the Hat Comes Back!*

AND SEVENTY-SEVEN MORE PICTURE BOOKS TO GROW ON

ALEXANDER, MARTHA, *Blackboard Bear*, Dial, 1969. Told almost entirely through pictures, a whimsical-sad fantasy about a boy who's thought too little to play with the big kids.

ARDIZZONE, EDWARD, *Little Tim and the Brave Sea Captain*, Walck, 1936. A small boy goes to sea, copes with a shipwreck and returns casually triumphant.

——, *Diana and Her Rhinoceros*, Walck, 1964. A brave, sensible, supercompetent child takes over when a stray rhinoceros terrifies her parents at teatime.

BALET, JAN, *The King and the Broom Maker*, Delacorte, 1967. A sage little fable about the king who envies a broommaker (*he* can hang a sign on his door, "Back in 10 minutes," and go fishing). And of course the broommaker envies the king, who seems to have nothing to do but peer out the window and eat delicious meals. Changing places briefly leaves both wiser—and content.

BOND, MICHAEL, *A Bear Called Paddington*, Houghton, 1958. A beguiling Peruvian bear with a talent for getting into trouble adopts an English household and turns their lives upside down. Also *Paddington Helps Out, More About Paddington, Paddington Abroad, Paddington At Large.*

BROWN, MARGARET WISE, *The Dead Bird*, W. R. Scott, 1948. A serene and delicate tale of children confronting death with tenderness, real sorrow, a feeling for poetic ritual—and a child's capacity to forget, move on.

———, *The Noisy Book*, Harper, 1939. Muffin's blindfolded, but he can hear. A book alive with all the fascinating noises of the daily world. Also *The City Noisy Book, The Country Noisy Book, The Summer Noisy Book, The Winter Noisy Book.*

BROWN, MYRA BERRY, *Benjy's Blanket*, F. Watts, 1962. Benjy can't go anywhere without his old ragged security blanket until, discovering an important practical use for it, he makes a very grown-up gesture.

BURTON, VIRGINIA LEE, *Katy and the Big Snow*, Houghton, 1943. A female bulldozer scores a smashing triumph.

CAUDILL, REBECCA, *Did You Carry the Flag Today, Charley?* Holt, 1966. A curious, lively Appalachian mountain child gets the coveted honor at last.

COHEN, MIRIAM, *Will I Have a Friend?*, Macmillan, 1967. A warm, reassuring answer to first-day-at-school tremors.

CONGER, LESLIE, adapter, *Tops and Bottoms*, Scholastic, 1970. Lively, funny adaptation of the old folk tale about an ingenious farmer who outwits a goblin on a crop-sharing scheme. (He gets tops in a corn year, bottoms when the crop is carrots.)

CRETAN, GLADYS, *Me, Myself and I*, Morrow, 1969. Text a bit stiff and self-conscious, but Don Bolognese's illustrations project vividly a six-year-old's imagined identities. He's a lion tamer, a knight, a baseball champ, a horse, a color, a leaf, a musical march. . . . "I am whatever I want to be. But especially, particularly, positively . . . ME."

DOMANSKA, JANINA, *If All the Seas Were One Sea*, Macmillan, 1971. An old nursery rhyme stunningly elaborated and illustrated, leading up to a knockout *splish splash* at the end.

ETS, MARIE HALL, *Play with Me*, Viking, 1955. The animals won't join in, until the little girl sets about amusing herself. Then "I was happy, as happy as could be, All of them, ALL OF THEM were playing with me!" Free, scratchy, homely pictures and a delicate story create the feeling of a world full of possibilities.

FATIO, LOUISE, *The Happy Lion*, illustrated by Roger Duvoisin, McGraw, 1954. A gentle and very happy lion is surprised by the townspeople's reaction when he strolls out of his cage one day to take in the sights. A friendly little boy sets things right. Also *The Happy Lion in Africa, The Happy Lion Roars, The Three Happy Lions, The Happy Lion's Quest.*

FENTON, EDWARD, *Penny Candy*, Holt, 1970. A nice blend of realism and fantasy in this tale, set in the hungry 1920's, of a six-year-old who unexpectedly acquires a nickel to spend. Edward Gorey's illustrations add dash and fascinating detail.

FLACK, MARJORIE, *Angus and the Ducks*, Doubleday, 1930. A curious, feisty little Scotch terrier explores the world beyond his favorite sofa—and is awfully glad to get back. Also *Angus and the Cat, Angus Lost.*

——, *Ask Mr. Bear*, Macmillan, 1932. Mr. Bear tells a small boy the perfect birthday present for his mother.

GREEN, MARY M., *Everybody Eats* and *Everybody Has a House*, W. R. Scott, 1961. The world of animals engagingly described.

HALEY, GAIL E., *Noah's Ark*, Atheneum, 1971. The Biblical story reinterpreted from an ecological point of view. (Man threatening the animals through pollution, deprivation of living space and outright destruction.)

HOBAN, RUSSELL, *Bread and Jam for Frances*, illustrated by Lillian Hoban, Harper, 1964. An absolutely enchanting little-girl badger, devoted to bread and jam, is persuasively converted to a more varied and sophisticated diet. Fresh, funny, lovable. Also *A Baby Sister for Frances*, *A Birthday for Frances*, *Best Friends for Frances*, *A Bargain for Frances*, *Egg Thoughts and Other Frances Songs* (the collected poems of Frances)—all wonderful.

HOFF, SYD, *Danny and the Dinosaur*, Harper, 1958. The adventures of a boy and a museum dinosaur who takes the day off.

HOGROGIAN, NONNY, *One Fine Day*, Macmillan, 1971. All about the fox who finally got the grain to give to the hen to get the egg to pay the peddler to get the bead to give the maiden to get the jug . . . well, you get the idea. A gay Armenian folk tale constructed according to a familiar cumulative pattern.

HUTCHINS, PAT, *The Surprise Party*, Macmillan, 1969. A rabbit issues a party invitation with instruction to "pass it on." The distortions of various messengers end in a real surprise.

JOSLIN, SESLYE, *Brave Baby Elephant*, illustrated by Leonard Weisgard, Harcourt, 1960. A very human little-boy elephant makes ambitious plans, assembles gear for a great adventure . . . and succumbs to the familiar comforts of his bed. Also, *Baby Elephant and the Secret Wishes*, *Baby*

Elephant Goes to China, Baby Elephant's Baby Book, Baby Elephant's Trunk.

KAHL, VIRGINIA, *The Duchess Bakes a Cake*, Scribner, 1955. A lovely, lively jouncing verse narrative about the Duchess who adds extra yeast to her batter and is lifted skywards as the cake rises.

KEATS, EZRA JACK, *Apt 3*, Macmillan, 1971. A tenement setting not romanticized but warmed by friendly feelings and a sense of rich possibility as two boys trace the source of the harmonica music that floats mysteriously into their apartment.

——, *Peter's Chair*, Harper & Row, 1967. A slight but beautiful book. Peter watches his father painting his old high chair pink for baby sister; the cradle's pink already—and his old blue chair is clearly next in line. So he prepares to run away—until he finds the old chair's too small for him, and anyway Mother has made something special for lunch.

——, *The Snowy Day*, Viking, 1962. A small black boy has a happy, snowy experience. Continued in *Whistle for Willie.*

KENT, JACK, *Clotilda*, Random House, 1969. The cheerful, foolish-wise tale of a little boy who doesn't believe in fairy godmothers and a rather schoolmarmish fairy, unemployed, looking for a child to godmother.

KRASILOVSKY, PHYLLIS, *The Shy Little Girl*, Houghton, 1970. A sensitive and gentle story about a little girl many readers will recognize: she hates her freckles, thinks her clothes are ugly, is afraid to speak up in school and most of all afraid to invite anyone home or ask to play. But a friend finds her.

KRAUS, ROBERT, *Leo the Late Bloomer*, Windmill Books, 1971. Young children may be initially puzzled by the basic metaphor here (the little tiger whose parents are waiting for him to bloom). But the story line is comforting (in his own good time, the backward tiger learns to read, write, draw, eat neatly and speak) and the pictures are a delight.

KUMIN, MAXINE, and ANNE SEXTON, *Joey and the Birthday Present*, McGraw, 1971. An appealing story of two mice who surmount their cultural differences. (Joey is a brown and white field mouse, Prince a purebred white with a pet-shop background.)

LATTIMORE, ELEANORE, *Little Pear*, Harcourt, 1931. A mischievous Chinese boy turns out to be, after all, not very different from mischievous children anywhere. Also *Little Pear and His Friends*, *Little Pear and the Rabbits*.

LEAF, MUNRO, *Noodle*, Four Winds Press, 1969. A dachshund, "very long from front to back, and very short from top to bottom," is offered (by the dog fairy) a chance to change his shape. After consulting friends at the zoo (giraffe, zebra, hippo) about ideal proportions, he comes to the inevitable satisfying conclusion and curls up on the sofa, completely happy.

LENSKI, LOIS, *The Little Auto*, Walck, 1934. The cheerful ordinariness of this (and books about other vehicles driven by Mr. Small) is comforting for the very young. Also *The Little Train*, *The Little Airplane*, *The Little Sailboat*, *The Little Fire Engine*, and the chronicles of the Small family: *Policeman Small*, *Cowboy Small*, *Papa Small*.

LEVARIE, NORMA, *I had a little . . .* , Random House, 1961. A series of amusing guess-the-ending rhymes that children will want to hear (and say) over and over. ("I had a little minnow and I put it in a pail, I had a little luck and it turned into . . . a whale.")

LEXAU, JOAN M., *Emily and the Klunky Baby and the Next-Door Dog*, Dial, 1972. A book that deals tenderly, compassionately and subtly with the feelings of children after a divorce. Emily's mother is always busy now, the baby a nuisance and a bore. So Emily runs away to find Daddy.

Lost (with baby, sled and dog), she makes some important discoveries. Lovely pictures by Martha Alexander.

LIONNI, LEO, *The Biggest House in the World*, Pantheon, 1968. A little snail learns from his father, the wisest snail on the cabbage, the folly of aiming at the biggest house in the world—and turns Thoreauvian. "I shall keep [my house] small, and when I grow up I shall go wherever I please." A rare combination, a real story and exquisite illustrations to delight any adult, intrigue any child.

——, *Fish Is Fish*, Pantheon, 1970. An engaging fable with an unobtrusive moral ("frogs are frogs and fish is fish"—all things have their proper place) and a charming hero. A list-free vocabulary that takes for granted children's ability to understand (or willingness to puzzle out) richly reverberating words like "luminous" and "triumphantly."

MC CLOSKEY, ROBERT, *Blueberries for Sal*, Viking, 1948. Sal loses sight of her own mother on a berry-picking expedition . . . and follows somebody else's mother by mistake. Meantime, a little bear has lost sight of *his* mother and . . .

MC GINLEY, PHYLLIS, *All Around the Town*, Lippincott, 1948. A handsome, funny, bouncing alphabet book.

MERRIAM, EVE, *What Can You Do with a Pocket?* Knopf, 1964. No story or logical sequence, just smashing pictures and some liberated imagining.

MILES, BETTY, and JOAN BLOS, *Just Think!*, Knopf, 1971. A simple, gay but provocative introduction to important ideas. "Just think . . . Things are how you see them: with a magnifying glass—big. In a mirror—backward. Through sunglasses—dark. When you love them, lovely."

MIZUMURA, KAZUE, *Way of An Ant*, Crowell, 1970. An ambitious ant tries to climb to the sky. A blade of grass, a dandelion, a sunflower, an apple tree—all prove not tall enough. Wisdom—and mellowness—comes with age: "As long as he kept on climbing, the blue sky grew higher and higher."

Still, he doesn't dream of discouraging the young ant he sees setting out on the same mission. Lovely watercolor illustrations.

———, *If I Were a Mother*, Crowell, 1968. A little girl dreams of some day having her own children. Reflecting on the example of bird and animal parents ("Like Mother Cat with loving care, I would keep them clean . . . Like Mother Lion I would train my children not to cry over a scratch or a hurt"), she concludes that most of all, she'd like to be a mother just like the mother she has.

PARKER, BERTHA M., *The New Golden Dictionary*, Golden Press, 1972. Lots and lots and lots of pictures to look at and talk about.

PÈNE DU BOIS, WILLIAM, *Bear Party*, Viking, 1963. A logical and diverting fantasy about belligerent bears who turn peaceful and good in the course of a fancy dress party.

PIERCE, ROBERT, *The Grin and Giggle Book*, Golden Press, 1972. Just right for a smart-aleck five-year-old who will drive his family crazy with these jokes and riddles.

SANDBURG, CARL, *The Wedding Procession of the Rag Doll and the Broom Handle and Who Was in It*, Harcourt, 1967. One of the *Rootabaga Stories* illustrated with brilliant originality by Harriet Pincus. A carnival of sights and sounds, with language wonderfully alive. There are the Spoon Lickers, some with gravy spoons, some with marshmallow fudge and butterscotch ("Everyone had something slickery sweet or fat to eat on the spoon"). And there are the Musical Soup Eaters, whistling, chuzzling and snozzling. The Chubby Chubs, roly-poly, round-faced snackers and snoozers. . . . A truly grand procession.

SCARRY, RICHARD, *Busy, Busy World*, Golden Press, 1972. Like other Scarry books—*Funniest Storybook Ever, What Do People Do All Day?, Nicky Goes to the Doctor, Best Word*

Book Ever—this is full of marvelously rich, detailed, vivid pictures.

SCHENK DE REGNIERS, BEATRICE, *May I Bring a Friend?* Atheneum, 1964. A small boy takes his animal friends to tea with the King and Queen.

——, *What Can You Do with a Shoe?*, ill. by Maurice Sendak, Harper, 1955. A delicious alternation of sober sense and wild nonsense. What can you do with a shoe? "You can put it on your ear, On your beery-leery ear, You can put it on your ear, tra-la

> Or wear it on your head
> Or butter it like bread
> Or use apple jam instead, ha ha.

A book that will inspire young readers to invent loony rhymes and see familiar objects in new ways.

SEGAL, LORE, *Tell Me a Mitzi*, Farrar, Straus, 1970. A city family, portrayed without cuteness or sentimentality, has some typical experiences (everybody coming down with a cold at the same time) and some thrillingly untypical ones.

SENDAK, MAURICE, *Higglety Pigglety Pop! or There Must Be More to Life*, Harper, 1967. An enchanting, witty, poignant tale about Jennie, the dog who had everything she needed, including two windows to look out of and a loving master, but who nevertheless set off into the wide world in search of adventure.

——, *In the Night Kitchen*, Harper, 1970. A wild, joyous fantasy about a boy who falls out of bed into . . . well . . .

SEUSS, DR. (Theodor Geisel), *The 500 Hats of Bartholomew Cubbins*, Vanguard, 1938. Every time the hero takes off his hat to the king, another takes its place, and another. Even in the shadow of the royal executioner, the hats continue to appear.

SKORPEN, LIESEL M., *Elizabeth*, Harper, 1970. Kate's Christmas doll can't walk or talk or turn somersaults. " 'It's an ugly doll,' she said to herself inside. 'It's an ugly doll, and I hate it very much.' " But long after fancy Charlotte Louise, her friend's doll, has hit the ash can, the Christmas doll goes on sharing Kate's life. An old pattern made new.

SLOBODKINA, ESPHYR, *Caps For Sale*, W. R. Scott, 1947. A treeful of monkeys gets individually capped when the peddler takes a nap under their perch.

SPIER, PETER, *Fast-Slow, High-Low*, Doubleday, 1972. A book of opposites, introducing the child, through sharp, cheerful pictures, to the visible differences between long and short, old and new, dark and light, empty and full and so on. A useful preschool introduction to basic concepts.

STEWART, ROBERT, *The Daddy Book*, American Heritage, 1972. Not inspired—but it gives the child a closer look at the world of those mysterious figures who generally leave early and return late. Scrupulously rejects sex-role stereotypes and respects all races.

STOLZ, MARY, *Belling the Tiger*, Harper, 1961. Two mice, delegated to bell the house cat, end up with bigger game.

TISON, ANNETTE, and TALUS TAYLOR, *The Adventures of the Three Colors*, World, 1971. A novelty item that works: transparencies and overlays dramatically illustrate the combining of primary colors to produce magic rainbows. Also *Inside and Outside*, a handsomely designed volume full of surprises, satisfying a child's desire to see *inside*—boats, houses, castles, tree trunks.

TRESSELT, ALVIN, *White Snow, Bright Snow*, Lothrop, 1947. A small child learns about winter and the seasons. A gentle, reassuring, hopeful book.

UNGERER, TOMI, *Crictor*, Harper, 1958. Simple and deliciously comic, the tale of a little old lady and her pet boa constrictor,

an amiable fellow willing on occasion to serve as slide or
skipping rope for the young.

WABER, BERNARD, *Ira Sleeps Over*, Houghton, 1972. Can a big
boy take to a friend's house, for an overnight visit, his special
teddy bear—particularly one called Tah Tah? Funny, touching, real.

WARD, LYND, *The Biggest Bear*, Houghton, 1952. A small boy
goes hunting for a bearskin—and brings home a baby bear.

WILDSMITH, BRIAN, *Birds*, Oxford, 1967. Glorious, colorful illustrations are the book's chief distinction. Text is extremely
simple, and glancingly playful.

WOLDE, GUNILLA, *Tommy Cleans His Room*, Houghton, 1971.
Tommy starts cleaning his room to find Bear, but everything
he finds tempts him to play. He tosses fat Jumbo, bounces
his ball, pulls his train, goes to try on his floppy red hat—
and *there's* Bear. A joyful, daily quality. Also *Tommy Goes
to the Doctor, Tommy Builds a House, Tommy Takes a
Bath, Tommy and Sarah Dress Up*, all gay and funny and
charmingly illustrated (also sensibly priced).

YASHIMA, TARO, *Crow Boy*, Viking, 1955. A lonely child wins
recognition from his classmates at last.

———, *Umbrella*, Viking, 1958. A little girl longs for a rainy day
so she can sport her new blue umbrella and her shiny red
boots.

ZAFFO, GEORGE, *The Giant Nursery Book of Things That Go*,
Doubleday, 1959. A smashing collection of fire engines, lo-
comotives, sailboats, planes—every conceivable variety of
each—drawn with meticulous attention to detail and accompanied by bold, simple text.

ZION, GENE, *All Falling Down*, Harper, 1951. Everything falls
down—leaves, snow, nuts, flower petals, building blocks, rain.
But when Daddy throws his little boy into the air, he
doesn't fall. What joy: *Daddy catches him.*

ZION, GENE, *Dear Garbage Man*, Harper, 1957. A poetic and generous-natured garbage collector can't bear to junk any of the treasures he finds—until he learns some hard, amusing truths about human nature.

ZOLOTOW, CHARLOTTE, *Big Sister and Little Sister*, Harper, 1966. A book about warm human family feeling—loving, caring, sharing and helping.

——, *Hold My Hand*, Harper, 1972. A physically beautiful little book about friendship on a cold, cold day. As bright, clean and sharply delineated as snowflakes on a blue mitten.

INDISPENSABLE BOOKS FOR READERS

ALCOTT, LOUISA, *Little Women*, Crowell, 1955. Meg holds the gloves, Jo the pen, Beth the music and Amy the paintbrush. Marmee is the mother, and she guides them through disastrous dinner parties, unhappy love affairs, excess vanity and marriage, to their own Celestial City. New England family togetherness during the Civil War.

ANDERSEN, HANS CHRISTIAN, *Fairy Tales*, World (Rainbow Classics), 1946. The shivering match girl, standing on an empty street corner; the gullible emperor who strides between hordes of his subjects wearing nothing but his vanity, the mermaid who, for love of a prince, allows her tongue to be cut out—all are waiting in Andersen's fairy tales. Sadly-smiling, poignant, deeply human.

ARABIAN NIGHTS, ed. Andrew Lang, McKay, 1946. Harems, curled-toe slippers, magic lanterns, robbers, veiled princesses, handsome servant boys, wicked uncles and a wife-killing sultan alternately intermarry and kill one another in these two hundred tales.

ATWATER, RICHARD and FLORENCE, *Mr. Popper's Penguins*, Little, 1938. Mr. Popper is a retired zoo-keeper who is also a penguin lover. When a large package arrives containing two penguins, he allows them to move into his refrigerator—and there begins a wildly funny tale.

BROWN, MARCIA, editor and illustrator, *Cinderella*, Scribner, 1954. An unusually vivid modern retelling: two dog-faced stepsisters, a glass slipper, a handsome prince and a fairy godmother combine, as always, to give Cinderella a happily-ever-after.

BURNETT, FRANCES HODGSON, *A Little Princess*, Platt, 1967. The eternally fascinating theme of the underdog (in this case a much-abused girl at boarding school who comes out on top).

——, *The Secret Garden*, Lippincott, 1962. Mary, a spoiled rudeness of a child; Colin, wheelchair-ridden; and Dickon, a robin-taming country boy, mingle with the result that a mysterious garden blooms again. A moral tale, from which all emerge purged.

CARROLL, LEWIS, *Alice's Adventures in Wonderland* and *Alice Through the Looking Glass*, illustrated by John Tenniel. Macmillan, 1923. If Alice isn't growing, shrinking, chasing white rabbits or drinking tea with the Mad Hatter, she will undoubtedly be playing croquet with the Queen. Look for her there. On the way you'll find a book as funny and sad as the Mock Turtle, as savage as the pepper-sniffing Duchess, as philosophically dreamy as the Red King and as logical as Alice herself.

CHUTE, MARCHETTE, *The Innocent Wayfaring*, Dutton, 1955. Anne is a strong-minded young miss that even Fem. Libbers might be proud of. Rebelling against the constant embroidery and housekeeping at the convent, she runs away to London to become a vaudeville artist. All is well until she meets Nick, a handsome young poet who decides to protect and guard her for *at least* the remainder of her journey.

COLLODI, C., *The Adventures of Pinocchio*, Macmillan, 1951. Pinocchio, a wooden puppet, is a long-nosed liar who wants to be a boy. The Blue Fairy tells him that he must first prove himself honest and courageous. Pinocchio sets out, though not without error, to do just that.

DAHL, ROALD, *Charlie and the Chocolate Factory*, Knopf, 1964. "Slurp" go the jaws of the incessant gum-chewer who stands beside the marathon TV-watcher, the Eater, and the Brat. And there is Charlie, OUR HERO, right between them. In a few moments they will enter Willie Wonka's Chocolate Factory, from which none of them emerge quite the same.

ESTES, ELEANOR, *The Moffats*, Harcourt, 1941. Dig into your pocket! For ten pins you can see the Moffats' latest production. It may be an organ recital, a circus, a play or a turtle race, but you can be sure it will be no ordinary presentation. Four children and one ringmaster parent direct the action. Also *The Middle Moffat* and *Rufus M.*

FARJEON, ELEANOR, *The Silver Curlew*, Viking, 1954. Doll, a golden-haired dumpling, is rescued from a room full of flax waiting to be spun by a small black imp. Being a thrifty (though soulless) little devil, he demands payment in the form of her first child—unless she can guess his name. A modern treatment of the *Rumpelstiltskin* story.

FITZHUGH, LOUISE, *Harriet the Spy*, Harper, 1964. She strides purposefully along, her flashlight, water canteen and penknife rattling comfortably. This is Harriet, on her way to the first stop on her spying route. With her is her notebook, in which she records all the intimate details of her life and personal comments about her friends. When her class finds and reads her notebook, events leap into dreadful focus.

FORBES, ESTHER, *Johnny Tremain*, Houghton, 1943. Johnny Tremain is an apprentice silversmith during the Revolutionary War. Through the treachery of a fellow worker, he maims his hand and loses his job. Crippled and helpless, he discovers that no one else wants him either. The only available employment seems to be as partner to the intrigues of war.

GODDEN, RUMER, *The Doll's House*, Viking, 1962. There are four members of the doll family—Tottie, a wooden Dutch doll who supports them all through the terrible happenings; Birdie, his sprightly wife; Mr. Plantaganet, whose gloomy eyes still recall past days in the toy cupboard; and Apple, the mischievous thumb-sized boy doll. And then Marchpane arrives—vain, beautiful, exquisitely dressed—to take over their house and make life temporarily miserable.

GRAHAME, KENNETH, *The Wind in the Willows*, illustrated by Ernest Shepard, Scribner, 1954. Toad, a bold, vain entrepreneur; Badger, an easygoing bachelor; Mole, an industrious fellow; and Rat, a strong-minded reformer, live their lives along the riverbank in moderate tranquillity—barring a few rollicking episodes.

GREEN, ROGER LANCELYN, *King Arthur*, Penguin, 1962. Knights in glistening armor, unrequited love, the clash and clang of battle, the waving pennants and brightly colored shields, the tournaments—all are contained in the histories of the knights of the Round Table.

GRIMM, JACOB, *Favorite Fairy Tales*, Little, 1959. Meet Rapunzel the long-haired, Little Red Riding Hood the wolf-tempter, Hansel and Gretel, inhabitors of a gingerbread house complete with witch; these are among the fascinating, sometimes horrifying tales of Grimm.

KIPLING, RUDYARD, *Just So Stories*, Doubleday, 1972. (A bold, beautiful, imaginative new edition with illustrations by Etienne Delessert.) Butterflies, leopards, kangaroos, camels, armadillos, zebras and cavemen create the alphabet, develop spots, originate and acquire a hump within these pages. Here you will find folklore with a personal touch, as you become the author's "Best Beloved."

LAWSON, ROBERT, *Rabbit Hill*, Viking, 1944. There are new folks on Rabbit Hill, and the good times have come back at last. Unfortunately, an endless procession of animal munchings and gobblings distorts the focus of this book; everyone seems to be incessantly eating.

LEWIS, C. S., *The Lion, the Witch, and the Wardrobe*, Macmillan, 1950. The Lion is Aslan, a golden-maned wonder; the White Witch is a pusher-of-Turkish-Delight; and the Wardrobe lets Lucy, Peter and Susan and boy-villain Edmund into the strange and terrifying land of Narnia.

LINDGREN, ASTRID, *Pippi Longstocking*, Viking, 1950. A wonderfully free nine-year-old lives alone with her monkey, her horse, and her treasure chest. Mad adventures.

LOFTING, HUGH, *The Story of Dr. Dolittle*, Lippincott, 1920. Doctor Dolittle, originally a frustrated M.D., turns veterinarian and begins to travel. Along the way (thanks to his knowledge of the meaning of animal grunts, growls and quacks) he and his menagerie of house pets meet unique and unusual animals such as the Pushmi-pullyu and the monkeys in need of vaccination.

MC CLOSKEY, ROBERT, *Homer Price*, Viking, 1943. Homer Price is an enterprising boy who seems determined never to let a day go by in which he doesn't jump, yell, bite, scream or kick his way into a disaster—and then, slick as a greased doughnut (which he incidentally produces) slides out of it into heroism.

MILNE, A. A., *Winnie-the-Pooh*, illustrated by E. H. Shepard, Dutton, 1954. Pooh is a rotund little bear who bumps along through the pages humming his hums (between licks from the Hunny Pot beside him), hunting for Heffalumps and pretending—with some help from Christopher Robin's balloon —to be a little black cloud. Piglet, a frail pink beast; Eeyore, a gloomy donkey; Kanga and Roo, strong-minded hippety-hoppers, and Owl, a would-be intellectual, are Pooh's companions.

MUHLENWEG, FRITZ, *Big Tiger and Christian*, Pantheon, 1952. Big Tiger and Christian begin their journey in Peking, their final destination Urumchi. When they at last arrive, they have left behind them a trail of stabbings, secret meetings, battles and robber-strewn mountain paths.

NESBIT, E., *Five Children and It*, Random House, 1959. Irrepressible, dirty children find a Psammead (a now extinct type of genie) in an abandoned sand pit. Since they have dug him out, he supposes that he might as well grant them a wish or two—angel wings, money, an old castle under attack . . . all to last until sunset. Also *The Enchanted Castle, The Phoenix and the Carpet, The Story of the Amulet,* other adventures of the Bastable children.

NORTON, MARY, *The Borrowers*, Harcourt, 1953. Their walls are papered with "borrowed" stamps, and their sink is a thimble. The Clock family lives beneath the floorboards and suffers all the difficulties and adventures that come of being six inches tall. Also *The Borrowers Afield, The Borrowers Afloat, The Borrowers Aloft.*

PÈNE DU BOIS, WILLIAM, *Twenty-One Balloons*, Viking, 1947. Perhaps you might want to begin your day on Krakatoa by sunbathing on the rolling sands. Later on, you could visit the diamond mines, tour the houses and marvel at their inventions, or perhaps take a ride on the flying merry-go-round. Tonight, you might find it enjoyable to join us at dinner in one of our fifteen restaurants. But Professor Sherman never did get to sit down to a comfortable dinner; the island began to rumble dangerously just as he took his first bite.

SPYRI, JOHANNA, *Heidi*, Grosset, 1963. Heidi's affectionate, happy nature wins over her taciturn old grandfather. Home and homesickness are made very real in this story of a child taken from her beloved mountains to a town post as companion to a sick girl.

STEVENSON, ROBERT LOUIS, *Treasure Island*, Scribner, 1911. Long John Silver is a properly evil, though occasionally benevolent, pirate, and the boy Jim loses some of his innocence as he and Long John battle over buried treasure.

TRAVERS, P. L., *Mary Poppins*, Harcourt, 1934. A mistress of umbrella travel, laughing gas and tutti-frutti medicine, Mary Poppins is the sharp-nosed and impeccably dressed nanny of Jane and Michael Banks. Although a stern and no-nonsense person generally, she may, if you flatter her in the right direction, let some of her magic glimmer through.

TWAIN, MARK (Samuel L. Clemens), *Tom Sawyer*, Heritage, 1952. Told in a comradely fashion, this book relates the adventures of the spirited, naughty and engaging Tom. Hear him tell of his love affairs, his wart cures, his involvement in murders, haunted houses, uninhabited islands—and running away.

WHITE, E. B., *Charlotte's Web*, Harper, 1952. Wilbur is a pig, more humble and terrific than most. Charlotte is a spider, and as sincere a friend as a pig could wish to have. Together they save Wilbur from the ax, and the humans lose again.

——, *Stuart Little*, Harper, 1945. Stuart Little is an aristocratic mouse who owns and drives his own car, is an expert sailor, and dresses in perky suits made by his own tailor. Life is perfect—until he falls in love with a nomadic pigeon.

WILDER, LAURA INGALLS, *The Little House in the Big Woods*, illustrated by Garth Williams, Harper, 1953. Pa's fiddle playing will comfort you through all the worst moments as a small pioneer family fights Indians, nearly starves in a snowstorm, and slaughters pigs in Wisconsin. Also *Little House on the Prairie, Farmer Boy, On the Banks of Plum Creek, By the Shores of Silver Lake*.

AND SIXTY-SIX MORE TO GROW ON

AESOP'S FABLES, selected and adapted by Louis Untermeyer with illustrations by A. and M. Provensen, Golden Press, 1971. A stylish and original edition with tales crisply told.

ANNO, MITSUMASA, *Topsy-Turvies, Pictures to Stretch the Imagination*, Weatherhill, 1970. A fascinating book for the off-beat child (or one who needs to be a little less on-beat than he is). No text, just strange, mind-troubling pictures of little people engaged in impossible activities—climbing *up* stairways that take them *down* to a lower level; casting shadows that have a life of their own. The author hopes his book will "keep all of us younger a little longer, will stretch our imaginations enough to keep us magically human." Also *Upside Downers.*

BARRIE, SIR JAMES, *Peter Pan*, Scribner, 1950. The Never-Never Land adventures of Peter Pan, the boy who will not grow up, Tinker Bell the fairy who loses her shadow and the three children who join them in battles with pirates, redskins and a ticking crocodile.

BAUM, FRANK L., *The Wizard of Oz*, Grosset, 1958. Swept away in a cyclone, Dorothy meets the Tin Woodman, who needs a brain, the Cowardly Lion, who wants a heart, and travels with them to the Emerald City.

BENNETT, ANNA ELIZABETH, *Little Witch*, Lippincott, 1953. This one rides to school on a broomstick. (What else?)

BIANCO, MARGERY W., *The Velveteen Rabbit*, Doubleday, 1926. A genuinely affecting story about a boy and his rabbit—and the meaning of two large words, *real* and *love.*

BLUE, ROSE, *A Quiet Place*, F. Watts, 1969. The gentle, compassionate story of a nine-year-old black foster child, constantly moved about in the big city, who is faced with the loss of his only refuge, the library. Sensitive and reassuring.

BOSTON, LUCY M., *The Children of Green Knowe*, Harcourt, 1955. When Tolly comes to his great-grandmother's house at Green Knowe, he finds the children who lived there three centuries before. The mystery and magic of the past are delicately suggested. Also *Treasure at Green Knowe, An Enemy at*

Green Knowe, The River at Green Knowe, A Stranger at Green Knowe.

BOYCE, BURKE, *The Emperor's Arrow*, Lippincott, 1967. Based on a medieval legend, this tale of the peasant lad who finds a cure for the Black Death offers young readers a historical perspective as well as an exciting story.

BRINK, CAROL, *Caddie Woodlawn*, Macmillan, 1935. An appealing tomboy and her two brothers in an exciting story of the Wisconsin frontier.

BROWN, MARCIA, *Stone Soup*, Scribner, 1947. A wise old tale retold: three hungry soldiers offer to make greedy villagers a soup out of stones. Of course they'll need a few other ingredients . . .

CARLSON, NATALIE SAVAGE, *The Family Under the Bridge*, Harper, 1958. A warmhearted old Paris tramp gives up his freedom to provide for three homeless children who move into his shelter under the bridge.

——, *The Happy Orpheline*, Harper, 1957. Twenty merry little French girls in a dilapidated orphanage fear nothing but adoption—and take ingenious pains to prevent it. Also *A Pet for the Orphelines, A Brother for the Orphelines, The Orphelines in the Enchanted Castle.*

CLEARY, BEVERLY, *Henry Huggins*, Morrow, 1950. How can Henry keep and support the marvelous mongrel who strays into his life? Where will he keep his rapidly multiplying guppies come canning season, when Mother needs the jars? Henry's problems are always agonizing, always hilarious. Also *Henry and Beezus, Henry and Ribsy, Henry and the Clubhouse, Henry and the Paper Route, Beezus and Ramona*, all purest Americana.

COLUM, PADRAIC, *Children of Odin*, Macmillan, 1962. Thor, Odin and Baldur the Beautiful—Norse tales to touch a child's heart and imagination.

DEFOE, DANIEL, *Robinson Crusoe,* illustrated N. C. Wyeth, Scribner, 1920. Shipwrecked on a desert island, Crusoe exhibits a daring and ingenuity that fascinates children.

DICKENS, CHARLES, *The Magic Fishbone,* illustrated Louis Slobodkin, Vanguard, 1953. A comic fairy tale that is both witty and fantastic. The good fairy is a crotchety old lady (with wings at the back of her lavender gown), the king and queen are the poverty-stricken parents of nineteen children (all under seven) and Princess Alicia is a resourceful child who saves the whole family.

EAGER, EDWARD, *Half Magic,* Harcourt, 1954. This story of four children who discover a magic charm is an ingenious twist of E. Nesbit's fantasy, *Five Children and It.* The charm belonging to Eager's children is only *half* magic. Thus, when they idly wish they were on a desert island, they end up stranded on a desert with no water in sight. Playful and funny.

ENRIGHT, ELIZABETH, *Gone-Away Lake,* Harcourt, 1957. Portia and her cousin Julian explore a swamp that was once a lake, meet two old people who have known the area years before, and are tempted into adventures.

ESTES, ELEANOR, *The Hundred Dresses,* Harcourt, 1944. A little Polish girl who wears the same faded blue dress every day is teased and tormented by her classmates until . . .

———, *The Witch Family,* Harcourt, 1960. A charming comic fantasy enlivened by a rare feeling for wordplay (one of the magic characters is Malachi, the Spelling Bee) and for the private dream worlds of small children. The heroines bring their fantasies to life when they decide to "banquish" Old Witch to the dismal glass hill, then create a family for her (Little Witch and Weeny Witchie).

FARJEON, ELEANOR, *Martin Pippin in the Apple Orchard,* Oxford, 1952. Apparently a simple but resourceful countryman, Martin is really a magical-romantic figure.

FIELD, RACHEL, *Hitty, Her First Hundred Years*, Macmillan, 1945. Hitty, a wooden doll carved from mountain ash by a Maine peddler, tells her own story. Adventures include abduction by a crow, a sea voyage and shipwreck, worship by a tribe of savages, a winter with field mice. The last chapter finds her in an antique shop—looking forward to many more excitements.

GARNER, ALAN, *Elidor*, Walck, 1967. An enthralling fantasy: four children exploring an English church about to be razed are drawn into the strange world of Elidor to combat the evil which threatens it.

GATES, DORIS, *Blue Willow*, Viking, 1940. The daughter of a family of migrant workers longs for roots and a home.

GEORGE, JEAN, *My Side of the Mountain*, Dutton, 1959. A fourteen-year-old city boy leaves his family and subsists entirely on his own in a mountain wilderness. With fascinating Crusoe-like details—flour from acorns, clothes from deerskins, a lamp from deer fat burned in a turtle's shell.

GODDEN, RUMER, *The Story of Holly and Ivy*, Macmillan, 1964. It is Christmas Eve. Ivy, an orphan, has nowhere to go; Holly, a Christmas doll, has not been sold; lonely Mrs. Jones has a tree, but no children. All three make wishes that come true. An appealing story told with great warmth.

GRAHAME, KENNETH, illustrated by Ernest Shepard, *The Reluctant Dragon*, Holiday, 1938. A boy befriends a very peaceable dragon with a taste for poetry and absolutely no interest in fighting or fire-breathing.

GREEN, ROGER LANCELYN, *Heroes of Greece and Troy*, Walck, 1961. A splendid collection of Greek myths imaginatively ordered and retold.

HALE, LUCRETIA P., *Peterkin Papers*, Houghton, 1924. A lovable upside-down family is periodically put to rights by "the lady from Philadelphia."

HARRIS, JOEL CHANDLER, *Uncle Remus Stories*, retold by Jane Shaw, Collins, 1972. A folklore legacy from the Old South, the tales of Brer Rabbit, whose wit and agility enable him to triumph over bear, wolf and fox.

HAYWOOD, CAROLYN, *"B" Is for Betsy*, Harcourt, 1939. Betsy's problems and experiences are thoroughly familiar to her readers: that's the source of their appeal. The ordinary activities —at school, home, camp—of a pleasant, ordinary American girl. Also *Back to School, Betsy and Billy, Betsy and the Boys, Betsy's Busy Summer.*

——, *Little Eddie*, Morrow, 1947. Eddie's quick eye for "valuables" (like an antiquated fire engine, full size, and a goat with a good appetite) leads to trouble at home and elsewhere. Also *Eddie's Pay Dirt, Eddie and His Big Deals, Eddie and Luella, Eddie Makes Music.*

JANSSON, TOVE, *Who Will Comfort Toffle?*, Walck, 1969. A frightened, lonely child finds a friend.

KANTROWITZ, MILDRED, *Maxie*, Parents Magazine Press, 1970. A little old lady feels unneeded until she learns of her importance to the whole neighborhood.

KASTNER, ERICK, *Emil and the Detectives*, Doubleday, 1930. A young boy, with friends' assistance, tracks down the thieves who robbed him on his way to Berlin.

KLINK, J. L., reteller. *Bible for Children: Vol. I, The Old Testament, with Songs and Plays*, translated by Patricia Crampton, Westminster, 1968. The most dramatic incidents of the Old Testament vividly retold, with spirited illustrations. A very handsome book.

KRUMGOLD, JOSEPH, *. . . and now Miguel*, Crowell, 1953. A growing-up story, set in New Mexico, about a young sheepherder who, after many difficulties, proves himself. A story imbued with strong, dignified family feeling.

LANGTON, JANE, *The Diamond in the Window*, Harper, 1962.

Two children are magically, thrillingly, transported to the Concord of Thoreau and Louisa May Alcott.

LEAR, EDWARD, *The Four Little Children Who Went Around the World*, Macmillan, 1968. A zany fantasy utterly unique—not perhaps for the superlogical child, but pure delight to one who enjoys playing with language and ideas, who would be delighted rather than puzzled by the prospect of "pellucid pale periwinkle soup."

L'ENGLE, MADELEINE, *A Wrinkle in Time*, Farrar, Straus, 1962. A science fiction fantasy takes a brave girl on a dangerous space mission with serious moral implications.

LENSKI, LOIS, *Strawberry Girl*, Lippincott, 1945. A sturdily determined girl helps her father on their backwoods Florida farm —and reforms the shiftless neighbors. One of a series of realistic protrayals of regional U. S. groups (*Blue Ridge Billy, Judy's Journey, Boom Town Boy, Cotton in My Sack*), all emphasizing the cohesive force of family love and loyalty.

LINDGREN, ASTRID, *The Tomten*, Constable, 1962. Poetry in prose about a little tomten-elf who takes care of the barn animals. Peacefully serene.

LOBE, MIRA, *The Grandma in the Apple Tree*, McGraw, 1970. A Viennese boy who has no grandmother to talk to solves his problem in an amusing, fantastic way.

MACDONALD, GEORGE, *At the Back of the North Wind*, Macmillan, 1950. A strange, confusing but tantalizing story about a boy swept into adventures by the North Wind.

MAC GREGOR, ELLEN, *Miss Pickerell Goes to Mars*, McGraw, 1957. Science fiction crossed with nonsense as a brisk, normally cautious old lady is whisked off to mad adventures (retaining, always, her old-lady cool). Also *Miss Pickerell and the Weather Satellite, Miss Pickerell Goes Undersea, Miss Pickerell Goes to the Arctic, Miss Pickerell and the Geiger Counter, Miss Pickerell Harvests the Sea*.

MC NEILL, JANET, *Tom's Tower*, Little, 1967. "The castle is there," says the note, in Tom's handwriting. Tom swears he didn't write it. His teacher makes him copy out, four hundred times, "Impossible things don't happen, not very often"— and then, of course, they begin to happen. Full of wit and free-wheeling adventure.

MUEHL, LOIS, *The Hidden Year of Devlin Bates*, Holiday, 1967. Devlin feels strange because he likes to be alone and can't seem to do his homework. Absorbing plot and a persuasive solution to the hero's difficulties.

NESS, EVALINE, *Sam, Bangs and Moonshine*, Holt, 1966. An incorrigible fantasizer, Sam(antha) gives up her "moonshine" after it almost brings disaster.

O'BRIEN, JACK, *Silver Chief: Dog of the North*, Holt, 1933. The classic story of a magnificent dog—part husky, part wolf.

PERRAULT, CHARLES, *All the French Fairy Tales*, retold by Louis Untermeyer, illustrated by Gustave Doré, Didier, 1946. Stories to enchant a child and haunt an adult with their wit, drama and delicate-ironic observation of the human comedy: "Cinderella," "Sleeping Beauty," "Puss in Boots," "Hop o' My Thumb," the darkly strange "Beauty and the Beast."

PICARD, BARBARA L., *The Mermaid and the Simpleton*, Criterion, 1970. Fifteen original fairy tales that use traditional motifs in distinctively modern ways. Haunting and strange. (A sad princess stitches herself into a tapestry, a tree takes on human shape.)

PYLE, HOWARD, *The Merry Adventures of Robin Hood*, Scribner, 1946. The bold outlaw—with Friar Tuck, Little John and Maid Marian—manages to do good and outwit his enemies while leading a happy greenwood existence.

RANSOME, ARTHUR, *The Fool of the World and the Flying Ship*, Farrar, Straus, 1968. A retelling of a folk tale which preserves not only the simplicity of the original, but also the special flavor of its Russian setting and characters.

RANSOME, ARTHUR, *Swallows and Amazons*, Cape, 1938. English children camp out on an island and lead an adventurous life independent of adults.

RUSKIN, JOHN, *The King of the Golden River*, World, 1946. A thrilling, chilling story about a scorned youngest son whose kindness brings a strange adventure—and happiness.

SAINT-EXUPÉRY, ANTOINE DE, *The Little Prince*, trans. Katherine Woods, Harcourt, 1943. A sophisticated fantasy with multiple reverberations.

SEREDY, KATE, *The Good Master*, Viking, 1935. A tempestuous motherless girl learns love and respect when she goes from Budapest to live on her uncle's ranch. Children love the vividly depicted brattishness of the unregenerate Kate and the appealing vision of Hungarian country life.

SINGER, ISAAC BASHEVIS, *Alone in the Wild Forest*, Farrar, Straus, 1971. A magical fairy tale full of real-life reverberations. The boy Joseph meets an angel; she gives him an amulet with which to satisfy all his wishes. But to win the hand of the princess, he must personally vanquish the forces of evil.

STREATFEILD, NOEL, *Ballet Shoes*, Dent, 1936. Combines the fascinating details of the theater and dance world with real, likable characters.

TAYLOR, SIDNEY, *All-of-a-Kind Family*, Follett, 1951. The five children of this Jewish family, living in New York's lower East Side at the turn of the century, are all of a kind, all girls—and all full of *joie de vivre*. A lost library book precipitates a crisis, happily solved, like all the other teapot tempests that disturb their warm family-centered world. Also *More All-of-a-Kind Family* and *All-of-a-Kind Family Uptown*.

THURBER, JAMES, *Many Moons*, illustrated by Louis Slobodkin, Harcourt, 1943. A charming, fanciful story of the little princess who wanted the moon and got it—much to the astonishment of the lord chamberlain, the royal wizard, and the court mathematician, reasonable fellows all.

TOLKIEN, J. R., *The Hobbit*, Houghton, 1938. A literary fairy tale with overtones of Malory, Spenser and *Beowulf*. Bilbo Baggins, the reluctant hero ("I have absolutely no use for dragon-guarded treasures"), is a furry little creature, neither fairy nor human, persuaded by a wizard to destroy the terrible dragon Smaug. A singularly rich and exciting world very fully realized.

UCHIDA, YOSHIKO, *In-Between Miya*, Scribner, 1967. This story of a Japanese middle child who has always longed for responsibility—and then muffs her first chance at it—has universal appeal. Miya learns, after trials, to see herself and her family in a new way.

WHITE, ANNE TERRY, *The Golden Treasury of Myths and Legends*, Golden Press, 1959. Handsomely illustrated by Alice and Martin Provenson, this collection includes vigorous retellings of central Greek, Norse, German and Celtic myths.

WHITE, E. B., *The Trumpet of the Swan*, Harper, 1970. White's unique blend of realism, fantasy and generous humanity in a story about Louis, the trumpeter swan who has no voice.

Poetry for Children

ANTHOLOGIES

ADSHEAD, GLADYS L., and ANNIS DUFF, *An Inheritance of Poetry*, Houghton, 1948. A plum pudding, a fruit cake, a whole feast. The fullness of this collection (almost 400 pages) and the free arrangement makes this principally suitable for parents to read aloud from.

ARBUTHNOT, MAY HILL, *Time for Poetry*, Scott, Foresman, 1952. Not a book for children to hold and browse in (it carries a heavy freight of editorial material) but a treasure-house for parents and teachers.

BLISHEN, EDWARD, *Oxford Book of Poetry for Children*, F. Watts, 1963. Beautifully illustrated by Brian Wildsmith, a book for all seasons of the heart. These are poems chosen with taste, joy and love.

BOGAN, LOUISE, and WILLIAM JAY SMITH, *The Golden Journey*, Reilly & Lee, 1965. Handsome format and a tempting, highly individual collection. Poems whimsically grouped: "Slight Things," "What Is Pink?," "All That's Past."

BONTEMPS, ARNA, *Hold Fast to Dreams*, Follett, 1969. A stirring collection made by a man who believes "all people need poetry and must have it in order to stay *alive*." Many poems here will speak especially to blacks.

CLARK, LEONARD, *Flutes and Cymbals*, Crowell, 1969. This book looks and feels right. Off-beat selections (many, unfortunately, excerpts from longer poems); the total effect is rich and various.

COFFEY, DAIRINE, *The Dark Tower*, Atheneum, 1967. Nineteenth-century narrative poems—dramatic, exciting, romantic. Among the best here: Christina Rossetti's "Goblin Market," Keats's "La Belle Dame Sans Merci," Tennyson's "Morte d'Arthur."

COLE, WILLIAM, *A Book of Nature Poems*, Viking, 1969. An eye- and sense-opening collection of poems about the green world —seasons and growth and rivers and skies. Sensitively chosen by a poet who prefers, to large vistas, "small majesties . . . the tiny perfect wild-flowers on the forest floor, the surprise of mushrooms, the way a tree announces rain."

———, *Oh, That's Ridiculous*, Viking, 1972. Daft illustrations by Tomi Ungerer catch the spirit of the pervasive nonsense. Here you will find the Spangled Pandemonium, Winkelman Von Winkel (the wisest man alive) and the Ichthyosaurus who fainted with shame when he first heard his name and departed a long time before us.

COLE, WILLIAM, *Oh, What Nonsense!*, Viking, 1966. Full of shenanigans, twiddle-twaddle, monkeyshines and poppy-cock—with appropriate line drawings by Tomi Ungerer.

———, *The Sea, Ships and Sailors*, Viking, 1967. A collection of poems, songs and shanties that suggest the fantastic variety of the sea—"hurricanes and lullabies, gaiety and doom, crashing surf and quiet depths."

DE LA MARE, WALTER, *Come Hither*, Knopf, 1966. A poet's collection of favorites, accompanied by notes and commentary illuminating and utterly unpedantic.

DICKINSON, PATRIC, and SHEILA SHANNON, *Poems to Remember*, Harvill, 1970. Runs the full gamut, in difficulty, from "Star light, star bright, First star I see tonight . . ." to Wordsworth and Milton.

EVANS, PATRICIA, *Rimbles: A Book of Children's Classic Games, Rhymes, Songs, and Sayings*, Doubleday, 1961. Rhymes for skipping rope, bouncing balls, counting out, playing jacks and other street games.

GREGORY, HORACE, and MARYA ZATURENSKA, *The Silver Swan*, Holt, 1966. A highly sophisticated and literary collection—poems of romance, mystery, magic—for older children already serious about poetry.

GRIGSON, GEOFFREY, *The Cherry Tree*, Vanguard, 1949. Over 500 poems, an imaginative and wide-ranging collection for older children.

HANNUM, SARA, and GWENDOLYN REED, *Lean Out of the Window: an Anthology of Modern Poetry*, Atheneum, 1965. A very fine collection that includes Wallace Stevens, Robert Frost, e. e. cummings, W. B. Yeats, and many others. Some of the poems (like cummings' "little tree") are suitable for even the youngest child, and all will maintain their appeal over the years.

MC DONALD, GERALD D., A *Way of Knowing*, Crowell, 1959. Subtitled "a collection of poems for boys," this book will interest girls too. Here are ballads, folk songs and anonymous rhymes for the youngest child, plus Shakespeare, Frost and Blake for his older brothers and sisters. An anthology that will grow with the child.

MC GINLEY, PHYLLIS, *Wonders and Surprises*, Lippincott, 1968. Some of the wonders here are richly romantic—and some concern the everyday depthless wonder of dogs, bats, seals and snails. Swinging ballads, lively nonsense—and some marvelous curses.

REED, GWENDOLYN, *Bird Songs*, Atheneum, 1971. Robins, wrens, crows, cardinals and owls, all caught and held for a moment in poetry and line drawings. Selections span four centuries, many countries.

SMITH, JANET ADAM, *The Looking Glass Book of Verse*, Random House, 1959. "There is no poem in the book that has not been liked by children," the editor says. I believe it.

SMITH, JOHN, *My Kind of Verse*, Macmillan, 1968. Very personal and off-beat, full of happy surprises.

WITHERS, CARL, A *Rocket in My Pocket: the Rhymes and Chants of Young Americans*, Holt, 1948. Over 400 traditional rhymes, chants, game songs and tongue twisters.

EDITIONS OF INDIVIDUAL POETS

BLAKE, WILLIAM, *Songs of Innocence*, Doubleday, 1966. Blake's luminous poems of childhood accompanied by bold, colorful woodcuts.

BELLOC, HILAIRE, *Cautionary Verses*, Knopf, 1959. Wicked, funny, elegant—a joy for the sophisticated young reader. With eloquent illustrations.

DE LA MARE, WALTER, *Peacock Pie*, Holt, 1941. An enchanting illustrated collection by one of the great children's poets.

DE LA MARE, WALTER, *Rhymes and Verses: Collected Poems for Children*, Holt, 1942.

FARJEON, ELEANOR, *Poems for Children*, Lippincott, 1951. The author herself says that though she once dreamed of being a "real" poet, the dream died, and she settled for writing children's verse. Not immortal, these lyrics, but pleasing.

POEMS OF W. S. GILBERT, ed. William Cole, Crowell, 1967. Here are the Duke of Plaza-Toro, who "led his regiment from behind (He found it less exciting)," the true-born Englishman, the humane Mikado and other unforgettable characters from the operettas. Witty, graceful, acrobatic verse.

GODDEN, RUMER, *St. Jerome and the Lion*, Viking, 1961. Verse narrative tells of the Bethlehem monastery where even the hens were trained to lay eggs clean enough for angels and of the gold-eyed lion who served the saint.

GRAVES, ROBERT, *Ann at Highwood Hall*, ill. by Edward Ardizzone, Doubleday, 1964. A handful of charming lyrics and two full-blown verse narratives. Nice.

THE KATE GREENAWAY TREASURY, ed. Ruth Hill Viguers, World, 1967. An extraordinarily beautiful book, this collection of poems, songs, stories and games contains all of those illustrations through which Kate Greenaway projected her tender and graceful vision of childhood. The poems themselves are not remarkable; the harmony of poem and picture is ravishing.

POEMS OF THOMAS HOOD, ed. William Cole, Crowell, 1968. Divided into Light, Twilight and Dark, these poems cover a wide emotional range. The "dark" poems have not weathered too well, because of their sentimentality, but the comic verse (like "Faithless Nellie Gray") has life in it.

LEAR, EDWARD, *The Complete Nonsense Book*, Dodd, 1946. In its illustrations, language, fantasticality, a wonderful and totally original book.

MILNE, A. A., *The World of Christopher Robin: The Complete When We Were Very Young and Now We Are Six*, ill. by E. H. Shepard, Dutton, 1958. The feelings, fantasies, delights and wonderings of childhood have seldom been rendered with such absoluteness—and charm. If I were to buy only one poetry book for a child under ten, this would be it.

RIEU, E. V., *The Flattered Flying Fish*, Dutton, 1962. Witty, literate nonsense in the tradition of Lear, Lewis Carroll, Hilaire Belloc.

ROSSETTI, CHRISTINA G., *Sing Song and Other Poems for Children*, Macmillan, 1924. Fanciful, funny, tender—the work of a genuine poet.

STEVENSON, ROBERT LOUIS, *A Child's Garden of Verses*, Scribner, 1905. The things that most matter to the young have not greatly changed since Stevenson set down these winning verses. The friendly cow all red and white, the little shadow that goes in and out with me, the swing that flies up in the air so blue. . . . Unforgettable.

TENNYSON, ALFRED, *The Charge of the Light Brigade*, ill. by Alice and Martin Provensen, Golden Press, 1964. Stunningly illustrated and printed, a famous verse account of a dramatic, disastrous battle during the Crimean War.

EDITIONS OF MOTHER GOOSE

CHWAST, SEYMOUR, *The Flip-Flap Mother Goooooose*, Random House, 1972. A handsome exception to the principle that most "paper engineering" is for the birds. The pages of this volume fold in and out in such a way that the book's practical life will not be affected—and there's a surprise in every fold.

DE ANGELI, MARGUERITE, *Nursery and Mother Goose Rhymes*, Doubleday, 1954. A Caldecott Honor book with rather more sweetness than distinction in the illustrations. Majority are black and white drawings (disappointing to children) and the color pictures have a vague, misty quality.

GROVER, EULALIE OSGOOD, *Mother Goose, The Classic Volland Edition,* Hubbard, 1971. A period piece reprint, attractive but probably more so to parents than to children.

PIPER, WATTY, *Mother Goose,* ill. by Tim and Greg Hildebrandt, Platt, 1972. The special attraction of this edition—a quite sizable collection—is the multiracial character of the children who cavort through its pages.

ROJANKOVSKY, FEODOR, *The Tall Book of Mother Goose,* Harper, 1942. Pleasing shape and bright modern pictures.

SCARRY, RICHARD, *Mother Goose,* Golden Press, 1972. A very small group—23 verses.

WILDSMITH, BRIAN, *Mother Goose,* F. Watts, 1965. Good basic addition to a child's library, stunningly illustrated in glowing color.

WRIGHT, BLANCHE FISHER, *The Real Mother Goose,* Rand McNally, 1971. First printed in 1916, this collection has a charming period quality in pictures and typography. Rich color and lots of good detail.

9

Breaking Through

"There is at bottom only one problem in the world," Thomas Mann writes in Dr. *Faustus*, "and this is its name: how does one break through? How does one get into the open? How does one burst the cocoon and become a butterfly?" Every child is at birth a bundle of potentialities. If these are nourished and brought to fulfillment, he goes forth into life confident of his powers, eager to use them. If his potentialities are frustrated, he languishes like Blake's sick rose, gnawed by an invisible worm. Every child has something he can do well. But to find his best gift, he must explore all the options. Unless he has a chance to paint and dance and sing and build and read and do puzzles and sculpt and look through a microscope or use a hammer, how can a child possibly know what kind of activity is most quintessentially him? "That ye may have life and have it more abundantly": the New Testament phrase defines precisely a goal which I see as the natural consequence of creative growth.

A word of caution. There is always a danger, in viewing child development from one particular angle, of losing perspective. The writer whose concern is physical fitness may forget that children sometimes need to loll and be lazy; the writer interested in intellectual development may slight emotional health. I know that my own passion for the creative life has at times burdened my children with the feeling that *everything* they did had to be distinctly, obviously creative.

I think, for example, of the time my seven-year-old daughter spent a week in the hospital. Every day, before visiting, I would hunt up for her some small surprise—a box of pastels, a magnet, Japanese origami paper—taking, yes, particular care to see that the surprise contained an element of challenge. One afternoon, when I couldn't seem to find anything just right, I settled on a pack of cards (telling myself that cards lent themselves to creative uses). The fact that the cards were decorated with characters from Disney movies bothered me—I would have preferred good abstract designs—but I was in a hurry. At the hospital, my child, pale on the pillows, listlessly unwrapped the package. She looked—stared—then exploded, all delighted surprise. "Mummy! *I didn't know it was all right to like Mickey Mouse!*"

Well. There's a moral here, and I pass it on. It *is* all right for children to like Mickey Mouse—as it's all right for them to idle, to fool around with coloring books or wind-up cars, to glut themselves, occasionally, with a full morning of TV cartoons. Being creative twenty-four hours a day would be a strain for anyone. It is quite enough if, in general, a child discovers that active pleasures are superior to passive ones, and that the world is full of infinite possibility for those who remain curious, observant, alive and free.

Directory of Book Publishers

ABELARD-SCHUMAN LIMITED, 257 Park Ave. S., New York, N.Y. 10010.

ABINGDON PRESS, 201 Eighth Ave. S., Nashville, Tenn. 37203.

ALLYN & BACON, INC., 470 Atlantic Ave., Boston, Mass. 02210.

AMERICAN BOOK COMPANY, 450 W. 33 St., New York, N.Y. 10001.

AMERICAN HERITAGE PUBLISHING CO., INC., 551 Fifth Ave., New York, N.Y. 10017.

AMERICAN LIBRARY ASSOCIATION, 50 E. Huron St., Chicago, Ill. 60611.

AMPHOTO, 915 Broadway, New York, N.Y. 10010.

APPLETON-CENTURY-CROFTS, 440 Park Ave. S., New York, N.Y. 10016.

ASSOCIATION FOR CHILDHOOD EDUCATION INTERNATIONAL, 3615 Wisconsin Ave., N.W., Washington, D.C. 20016.

ASSOCIATION PRESS, 291 Broadway, New York, N.Y. 10007.

ATHENEUM, 122 East 42 St., New York, N.Y. 10017.

ATHERTON PRESS, 70 Fifth Ave., New York, N.Y. 10011.

BALLANTINE BOOKS, INC., 101 Fifth Ave., New York, N.Y. 10003.

BANTAM BOOKS, INC., 666 Fifth Ave., New York, N.Y. 10019.

A. S. BARNES & CO., INC., Forsgate Drive, Cranbury, N.J. 08512.

BARNES & NOBLE, INC., 10 E. 53 St., New York, N.Y. 10022.

BASIC BOOKS, INC., 10 E. 53 St., New York, N.Y. 10022.

BEACON PRESS, 25 Beacon St., Boston, Mass. 02108.

BEGINNER BOOKS, 201 E. 50 St., New York, N.Y. 10022.

BELWIN-MILLS PUBLISHING CORPORATION, 250 Maple Ave., Rockville Centre, N.Y. 11570.

CHARLES A. BENNETT, 809 Detweiller Drive, Peoria, Ill. 61614.

BIRK & CO., 3 W. 57 St., New York, N.Y. 10019.

BASIL BLACKWELL, 108 Cowley Road, Oxford, England.

BLAISDELL PUBLISHING CO., 51 Weymouth St., London, England.

THE BOBBS-MERRILL CO., INC., 4300 W. 62 St., Indianapolis, Ind. 46268.

BOOSEY & HAWKES, MUSIC PUBLISHERS LTD., 295 Regent St., London, England.

BOSTON MUSIC CO., 116 Boylston St., Boston, Mass. 02167.

CHARLES T. BRANFORD, 28 Union St., Newton Center, Mass. 02159.

BRIGHAM YOUNG UNIVERSITY PRESS, 209 University Press Building, Provo, Utah 84601.

BRITISH BROADCASTING CORPORATION, 35 Marylebone High St., London, England.

BROCKHAMPTON PRESS, LTD., Salisbury Road, Leicester, England.

WILLIAM C. BROWN, 135 S. Locust St., Dubuque, Iowa 52001.

BRUCE BOOKS, 8701 Wilshire Blvd., Beverly Hills, Calif. 90211.

BURGESS PUBLISHING CO., 426 S. Sixth St., Minneapolis, Minn. 55415.

CAMBRIDGE UNIVERSITY PRESS, Bentley House, P.O. Box 92, 200 Euston Rd., London, England.

JONATHAN CAPE LTD., 30 Bedford Sq., London, England.

CHARTWELL PRESS, 84–86 Chancery Lane, London, England.

CHILDREN'S PRESS, 1224 W. Van Buren St., Chicago, Ill. 60607.

CLARENDON PRESS, Oxford, England.

COHEN & WEST (ROUTLEDGE & KEGAN PAUL, LTD.), 68–74 Carter Lane, London, England.

WILLIAM COLLINS & CO., LTD., 215 Park Ave. S., New York, N.Y. 10003.

COLUMBIA UNIVERSITY PRESS, 562 W. 113 St., New York, N.Y. 10025.

CONSTABLE & CO., LTD., 10 Orange St., Leicester Square, London, England.

COWARD, MC CANN & GEOGHEGAN, INC., 200 Madison Ave., New York, N.Y. 10016.

THOMAS Y. CROWELL CO., 666 Fifth Ave., New York, N.Y. 10019.

CROWELL COLLIER & MACMILLAN, INC., 866 Third Ave., New York, 10022.

DAVIS PUBLICATIONS, 229 Park Ave. S., New York, N.Y. 10003.

DELL PUBLICATIONS, 245 E. 47 St., New York, N.Y. 10017.

T. S. DENISON & CO., INC., 5100 W. 82 St., Minneapolis, Minn. 55431.

J. M. DENT & SONS, LTD., Aldine House, 10–13 Bedford St., London, England.

DIAL PRESS, 245 E. 47 St., New York, N.Y. 10017.

DIDIER, 182–184 High Holborn, London, England.

DODD, MEAD & CO., 79 Madison Ave., New York, N.Y. 10016.

DOUBLEDAY & CO., INC., 277 Park Ave., New York, N.Y. 10017.

DOVER PUBLICATIONS, 180 Varick St., New York, N.Y. 10014.

DRAKE PUBLISHERS, INC., 381 Park Ave. S., New York, N.Y. 10016.

DUELL, SLOAN & PEARCE, 250 Park Ave., New York, N.Y. 10017.

E. P. DUTTON, 201 Park Ave. S., New York, N.Y. 10003.

EMERSON BOOKS, INC., 251 W. 19 St., New York, N.Y. 10011.

ESSANDESS SPECIAL EDITIONS, 630 Fifth Ave., New York, N.Y. 10020.

EVANS BROTHERS, Montague House, Russell Square, London, England.

EXPOSITION PRESS, Warner House, Folkestone, Kent, England.

FABER & FABER, LTD., 3 Queen St., London, England.

FARRAR, STRAUS & GIROUX, 19 Union Sq., W., New York, N.Y. 10003.

FEARON PUBLISHERS, 6 Davis Dr., Belmont, Calif. 94002.

FOLLETT PUBLISHING CO., 1010 W. Washington Blvd., Chicago, Ill. 60607.

THE FREE PRESS, 866 Third Ave., New York, N.Y. 10022.

FUNK & WAGNALLS, INC., 53 E. 77 St., New York, N.Y. 10021.

GINN & CO., 191 Spring St., Lexington, Mass. 02173.

GOLDEN PRESS, 850 Third Ave., New York, N.Y. 10022.

GROSSET & DUNLAP, 51 Madison Ave., New York, N.Y. 10010.

E. M. HALE & CO., PUBLISHERS, 1201 S. Hasting Way, Eau Claire, Wisc. 54701.

HARCOURT BRACE JOVANOVICH, INC., 757 Third Ave., New York, N.Y. 10017.

HARPER & ROW, PUBLISHERS, 10 E. 53 St., New York, N.Y. 10022.

HARVILL PRESS, 23 Lower Belgrave St., London, England.

HASTINGS HOUSE, PUBLISHERS, INC., 10 E. 40 St., New York, N.Y. 10016.

HAWTHORN BOOKS, INC., 70 Fifth Ave., New York, N.Y. 10011.

HEARTHSIDE PRESS, 445 Northern Blvd., Great Neck, N.Y. 11021.

WILLIAM HEINEMANN, LTD., 15–16 Queen St., London, England.

HERITAGE PRESS, 1221 Ave. of the Americas, New York, N.Y. 10020.

HER MAJESTY'S STATIONERY OFFICE, 49 High Holborn, London, England.

HOLIDAY HOUSE, INC., 18 E. 56 St., New York, N.Y. 10022.

HOLT, RINEHART AND WINSTON, INC., 383 Madison Ave., New York, N.Y. 10017.

THE HORN BOOK, INC., 585 Boylston St., Boston, Mass. 02116.

HOUGHTON MIFFLIN CO., 2 Park St., Boston, Mass. 02107.

HUBBARD PRESS, 2855 Sherman Rd., Northbrook, Ill. 60062.

HUMANITIES PRESS, INC., 303 Park Ave. S., New York, N.Y. 10010.

INTERNATIONAL TEXT BOOK, Scranton, Penna. 18515.

INTEXT, 257 Park Ave. S., New York, N.Y. 10010.

JAPAN PUBLICATIONS TRADING CO., 1255 Howard St., San Francisco, Calif. 94103.

JOHN DAY CO., INC., 257 Park Ave. S., New York, N.Y. 10010.

ALFRED A. KNOPF, INC., 201 E. 50 St., New York, N.Y. 10022.

LAWRENCE PUBLISHING CO., 617 S. Olive St., Los Angeles, Calif. 90014.

LIBRARY OF CONGRESS, Washington, D.C., 20540.

J. B. LIPPINCOTT CO., E. Washington Sq., Philadelphia, Pa. 19105.

LITTLE, BROWN & CO., 34 Beacon St., Boston, Mass. 02106.

LOTHROP, LEE & SHEPARD CO., 105 Madison Ave., New York, N.Y. 10016.

MACDONALD & EVANS, 3 John St., London, England.

MC GRAW-HILL BOOK CO., 1221 Ave. of the Americas, New York, N.Y. 10020.

DAVID MC KAY CO., INC., 750 Third Ave., New York, N.Y. 10017.

THE MACMILLAN CO., 866 Third Ave., New York, N.Y. 10022.

THE MASSACHUSETTS INSTITUTE OF TECHNOLOGY PRESS, Kendall Square Bldg., 77 Massachusetts Ave., Cambridge, Mass. 02142.

MARKS MUSIC, 136 W. 52 St., New York, N.Y. 10019.

MAZEL (BRUNNER/MAZEL), 80 E. 11 St., New York, N.Y. 10003.

CHARLES E. MERRILL PUBLISHING CO., 1300 Alum Creek Dr., Columbus, Ohio 43216.

MERRILL-PALMER INSTITUTE, 71 Ferry St., Detroit, Mich. 48202.

METHUEN & CO., LTD., 11 New Fetter Lane, London, England.

MILLS MUSIC LTD., 20 Denmark St., London, England.

WILLIAM MORROW & CO., INC., 105 Madison Ave., New York, N.Y. 10016.

MUSEUM OF MODERN ART, 11 W. 53 St., New York, N.Y. 10019.

NATIONAL ART EDUCATION ASSOCIATION, 1201 16 St. N.W., Washington, D.C. 20036.

NATIONAL ASSOCIATION FOR THE EDUCATION OF YOUNG CHILDREN, 1834 Connecticut Ave., N.W., Washington, D.C. 20009.

NATIONAL COUNCIL OF TEACHERS OF ENGLISH, 1111 Kenyon Rd., Urbana, Ill. 61801.

NATIONAL KINDERGARTEN ASSOCIATION, 8 West 40 St., New York, N.Y. 10018.

NATIONAL PRESS BOOKS, 850 Hansen Way, Palo Alto, Calif. 94304.

NATURAL HISTORY PRESS, 277 Park Ave., New York, N.Y. 10017.

THOMAS NELSON INC., Copewood and Davis Sts., Camden, N.J. 08103.

NEW AMERICAN LIBRARY, 1301 Ave. of the Americas, New York, N.Y. 10019.

W. W. NORTON & CO., INC., 55 Fifth Ave., New York, N.Y. 10003.

ONTARIO DEPARTMENT OF EDUCATION, 44 Eglinton Ave., West, Toronto, Canada.

OXFORD UNIVERSITY PRESS, 200 Madison Ave., New York, N.Y. 10016.

PANTHEON BOOKS, INC., 201 E. 50 St., New York, N.Y. 10022.

PARENTS' MAGAZINE PRESS, 52 Vanderbilt Ave., New York, N.Y. 10017.

PARKER PUBLISHING CO., Englewood Cliffs, N.J. 07632.

W. PAXTON & CO., LTD., 36–38 Dean St., London, England.

PEGASUS PUBLISHING, 4300 W. 62 St., Indianapolis, Ind. 46268.

PELICAN PUBLISHING CO., INC., 630 Burmaster St., Gretna, La. 70053.

PENGUIN BOOKS INC., 7110 Ambassador Rd., Baltimore, Md. 21207.

PERGAMON PRESS, INC., 4 and 5 Fitzroy Sq., London, England.

PHILOSOPHICAL LIBRARY, INC., 15 E. 40 St., New York, N.Y. 10016.

PLATT & MUNK, 1055 Bronx River Ave., Bronx, N.Y. 10472.

PLAYS, INC., 8 Arlington St., Boston, Mass. 02116.

POCKET BOOKS, 630 Fifth Ave., New York, N.Y. 10020.

PRAEGER PUBLISHERS, INC., 111 Fourth Ave., New York, N.Y. 10003.

PRENTICE HALL, Englewood Cliffs, N.J. 07632.

PRUETT PRESS, Boulder, Colo. 80302.

PUBLIC AFFAIRS PAMPHLETS, 381 Park Ave. S., New York, N.Y. 10017.

G. P. PUTNAM'S SONS, 200 Madison Ave., New York, N.Y. 10016.

QUADRANGLE BOOKS, INC., 330 Madison Ave., New York, N.Y. 10017.

RAND CORPORATION, 405 Lexington Ave., New York, N.Y. 10017.

RAND MC NALLY & CO., Box 7600, Chicago, Ill. 60680.

RANDOM HOUSE, 201 E. 50 St., New York, N.Y. 10022.

REINHOLD, 450 W. 33 St., New York, N.Y. 10001.

RONALD PRESS CO., 79 Madison Ave., New York, N.Y. 10016.

RYERSON PRESS, 299 Queen St., W., Toronto, Canada.

G. SCHIRMER, INC., 609 Fifth Ave., New York, N.Y. 10017.

SCHOCKEN BOOKS INC., 200 Madison Ave., New York, N.Y. 10016.

SCIENCE AND BEHAVIOR BOOKS, INC., 599 College Ave., Palo Alto, Calif. 94306.

W. R. SCOTT INC., 333 Ave. of the Americas, New York, N.Y. 10014.

SCOTT, FORESMAN & CO., 1900 E. Lake Ave., Glenview, Ill. 60025.

CHARLES SCRIBNER'S SONS, 597 Fifth Ave., New York, N.Y. 10017.

SILVER BURDETT, 250 James St., Morristown, N.J. 07960.

SIMON & SCHUSTER, INC., 630 Fifth Ave., New York, N.Y. 10020.

STANFORD UNIVERSITY PRESS, Stanford, Calif. 94305.

STERLING PUBLISHING CO., INC., 419 Park Ave. S., New York, N.Y. 10016.

ST. MARTIN'S PRESS, 175 Fifth Ave., New York, N.Y. 10010.

SUMMY-BIRCHARD CO., 1834 Ridge Ave., Evanston, Ill. 60204.

SYRACUSE UNIVERSITY PRESS, Box 8, University Sta., Syracuse, N.Y. 13210.

TAPLINGER PUBLISHING CO., INC., 200 Park Ave. S., New York, N.Y. 10003.

CHARLES C. THOMAS, PUBLISHER, 301–27 E. Lawrence Ave., Springfield, Ill. 62703.

TRIDENT PRESS, 630 Fifth Ave., New York, N.Y. 10020.

UNIVERSITY OF CALIFORNIA PRESS, 2223 Fulton St., Berkeley, Calif. 94720.

UNIVERSITY OF CHICAGO PRESS, 5801 Ellis Ave., Chicago, Ill. 60637.

UNIVERSITY OF LONDON PRESS, St. Paul's House, Warwick Lane, London, England.

UNIVERSITY OF WASHINGTON PRESS, Seattle, Wash. 98105.

UNIVERSITY OF WISCONSIN PRESS, Box 1379, Madison, Wis. 53701.

VANGUARD PRESS, INC., 424 Madison Ave., New York, N.Y. 10017.

VAN NOSTRAND REINHOLD CO., 450 W. 33 St., New York, N.Y. 10001.

THE VIKING PRESS, INC., 625 Madison Ave., New York, N.Y. 10022.

WADSWORTH PUBLISHING CO., INC., Belmont, Calif. 94002.

HENRY Z. WALCK, INC., 19 Union Sq., W., New York, N.Y. 10003.

WALKER & CO., 720 Fifth Ave., New York, N.Y. 10019.

EDMUND WARD PUBLISHERS (KAYE & WARD, LTD.), 21 New St., London, England.

FREDERICK WARNE & CO., INC., 101 Fifth Ave., New York, N.Y. 10003.

WATSON-GUPTILL PUBLICATIONS, 165 W. 46 St., New York, N.Y. 10036.

FRANKLIN WATTS, INC., 845 Third Ave., New York, N.Y. 10022.

JOHN WEATHERHILL, INC., 149 Madison Ave., New York, N.Y. 10016.

WESTERN PUBLISHING CO., INC., 1220 Mound Ave., Racine, Wisc. 53404.

THE WESTMINSTER PRESS, Witherspoon Bldg., Philadelphia, Pa. 19107.

ALBERT WHITMAN & CO., 560 W. Lake St., Chicago, Ill. 60606.

JOHN WILEY & SONS, 605 Third Ave., New York, N.Y. 10016.

WORLD PUBLISHING CO., 110 E. 59 St., New York, N.Y. 10022.

Note: British books can be ordered by mail from Blackwell's, Broad St., Oxford, England. The firm will either advise customers of costs in advance, or send books and bill simultaneously. Charge for postage, insurance and packing runs approximately 7 percent of a book's cost. Books sent by sea arrive in six to eight weeks.